PHILOSOPHY AND SIMULATION

By the same author:

Intensive Science and Virtual Philosophy
A New Philosophy of Society

Also available from Continuum:

PHILOSOPHY AND SIMULATION

The Emergence of Synthetic Reason

Manuel DeLanda

continuum

Continuum International Publishing Group

The Tower Building   80 Maiden Lane
11 York Road   Suite 704
London SE1 7NX   New York, NY 10038

www.continuumbooks.com

British Library Cataloguing-in-Publication Data
A catalogue record for this book is available from the British Library.

ISBN: HB: 978-1-4411-7028-6

Library of Congress Cataloging-in-Publication Data
De Landa, Manuel.
Philosophy and simulation: the emergence of synthetic reason /
Manuel Delanda.
    p. cm.
ISBN: 978-1-4411-7028-6
1. Emergence (Philosophy) 2. Science–Philosophy. I. Title.

Q175.32.E44D4 2010
003–dc22

                                        2010020325

Typeset by Newgen Imaging Systems Pvt Ltd, Chennai, India
Printed and bound in India by Replika Press Pvt Ltd

Contents

CONTENTS

INTRODUCTION
Emergence in History

The origin of the modern concept of emergence can be traced to the middle of the nineteenth century when realist philosophers first began pondering the deep dissimilarities between causality in the fields of physics and chemistry. The classical example of causality in physics is a collision between two molecules or other rigid objects. Even in the case of several colliding molecules the overall effect is a simple addition. If, for example, one molecule is hit by a second one in one direction and by a third one in a different direction the composite effect will be the same as the sum of the two separate effects: the first molecule will end up in the same final position if the other two hit it simultaneously or if one collision happens before the other. In short, in these causal interactions there are no surprises, nothing is produced over and above what is already there. But when two molecules interact chemically an entirely new entity may emerge, as when hydrogen and oxygen interact to form water. Water has properties that are not possessed by its component parts: oxygen and hydrogen are gases at room temperature while water is liquid. And water has capacities distinct from those of its parts: adding oxygen or hydrogen to a fire fuels it while adding water extinguishes it.[1]

The fact that novel properties and capacities emerge from a causal interaction was believed to have important philosophical implications for the nature of scientific explanation. In particular, the absence of novelty in physical interactions meant that explaining their effects could be reduced to deduction from general principles or laws. Because deductive logic simply transfers truth from general sentences to particular ones without adding anything new it seemed like an ideal way of modeling the explanation of situations like those involving rigid collisions. But the synthesis of water does produce something new, not new in the absolute sense of something that has never existed before but only in the relative sense that something emerges that was not in the interacting entities acting as causes. This led some philosophers to the erroneous conclusion that *emergent effects could not be explained*, or what amounts to the same thing, that an effect is emergent only for as long as a law from which it can be deduced has not yet been found.[2] This line of thought went on to become a full fledged philosophy in the early twentieth century, a philosophy based on the idea that emergence was intrinsically unexplainable. This first wave of "emergentist" philosophers were not mystical thinkers but quite the opposite: they wanted to use the concept of emergence to eliminate from biology mystifying entities like a "life force" or the "élan vital." But their position toward explanation gave their views an inevitable mystical tone: emergent properties, they said, must be accepted with an attitude of intellectual resignation, that is, they must be treated as brute facts toward which the only honest stance is one of natural piety.[3]

Expressions like these were bound to make the concept of emergence suspect to future generations of philosophers. It was only the passage of time and the fact that mathematical laws like those of classical physics were not found in chemistry or biology—or for that matter, in the more historical fields of physics, like geology or climatology—that would rescue the concept from intellectual oblivion. Without simple laws acting as self-evident truths (axioms) from which all causal effects could be deduced as theorems the axiomatic dream eventually withered away. Today a scientific explanation is identified not with some logical operation but with the more creative endeavor of elucidating the mechanisms that produce a given effect. The early emergentists dismissed this idea because they could not imagine anything more complex than a linear clockwork mechanism. But there are many other physical mechanisms that are nonlinear. Even in the realm of human technology we have a plurality of exemplars to guide our imagination: steam engines, thermostats, transistors. And outside technology the diversity is even greater as illustrated by all the different mechanisms that have been discovered in chemistry and biology.

Armed with a richer concept of mechanism the emergent properties of a whole can now be explained as an effect of the causal interactions between its component parts. A large portion of this book will be dedicated to describe the wide variety of *mechanisms of emergence* that have been elucidated in the decades since the original emergentists first wrote.

Thus, what is different today from the early twentieth century views is the *epistemological* status of emergence: it does not have to be accepted as a brute fact but can be explained without fearing that it will be explained away. What has remained the same is the *ontological* status of emergence: it still refers to something that is objectively irreducible. But what kinds of entities display this ontological irreducibility? The original examples of irreducible wholes were entities like "Life," "Mind," or even "Deity." But these entities cannot be considered legitimate inhabitants of objective reality because they are nothing but reified generalities. And even if one does not have a problem with an ontological commitment to entities like these it is hard to see how we could specify mechanisms of emergence for life or mind in general, as opposed to accounting for the emergent properties and capacities of concrete wholes like a metabolic circuit or an assembly of neurons. The only problem with focusing on concrete wholes is that this would seem to make philosophers redundant since they do not play any role in the elucidation of the series of events that produce emergent effects. This fear of redundancy may explain the attachment of philosophers to vague entities as a way of carving out a niche for themselves in this enterprise. But realist philosophers need not fear irrelevance because they have plenty of work creating an ontology free of reified generalities within which the concept of emergence can be correctly deployed.

What kinds of concrete emergent wholes can we legitimately believe in? Wholes the identity of which is determined historically by the processes that initiated and sustain the interactions between their parts. The historically contingent identity of these wholes is defined by their emergent properties, capacities, and tendencies. Let's illustrate the distinction between properties and capacities with a simple example. A kitchen knife may be either sharp or not, sharpness being an actual property of the knife. We can identify this property with the shape of the cross section of the knife's blade: if this cross section has a triangular shape then the knife is sharp else it is blunt. This shape is emergent because the metallic atoms making up the knife must be arranged in a very particular way for it to be triangular. There is, on the other hand, the capacity of the knife to cut things. This is a very different thing because unlike the property of sharpness which is always actual the capacity to cut may never be actual if the knife is never used. In other words, a capacity may remain only potential if it is never actually exercised. This already points to a very different ontological status between properties and capacities. In addition, when the capacity does become actual it is not as a state, like the state of being sharp, but as an event, an event that is always double: *to cut-to be cut*. The reason for this is that the knife's capacity to affect is contingent on the existence of other things, cuttable things, that have the capacity to be affected by it. Thus, while properties can be specified without reference to anything else capacities to affect must always be thought in relation to capacities to be affected. Finally, the ontological relation between properties and capacities displays a complex symmetry. On one hand, capacities depend on properties: a knife must be sharp to be able to cut. On the other, the properties of a whole emerge from interactions between its component parts, interactions in which the parts must exercise their own capacities: without metallic atoms exercising their capacity to bond with one another the knife's sharpness would not exist.

A similar distinction can be made between emergent properties and tendencies. To stick to the same example: a knife has the property of solidity, a property that is stable within a wide range of temperatures. Nevertheless, there are always environments that exceed that range, environments in which the temperature becomes so intense that the knife is forced to manifest the tendency to liquify. At even greater intensities the molten metal may gasify. These tendencies are as emergent as the shape of a knife's blade: a single metallic atom cannot be said to be solid, liquid, or gas; we need a large enough population of interacting atoms for the tendency to be in any of these states to emerge. Tendencies are similar to capacities in their ontological status, that is, they need not be actual to be real, and when they do become actual is as events: to melt or to solidify. The main difference between tendencies and capacities is that while the former are typically finite the latter need not be. We can enumerate, for example, the possible states in which a material entity will tend to be (solid, liquid, gas, plasma) or the possible ways in which it may tend to flow (uniformly, periodically, turbulently). But capacities to affect need not be finite because they depend on the capacities to be affected of innumerable other entities: a knife has the capacity to cut when it interacts with something that has the capacity to be cut; but it also has the capacity to kill if it interacts with large organisms with differentiated organs, that is, with entities that have the capacity to be killed.

Since neither tendencies nor capacities must be actual to be real it would be tempting to give them the status of possibilities. But the concept of a possible event is philosophically suspect because it is almost indistinguishable from that of a real event, the only difference being the former's lack of reality. Rather, what is needed is a way of specifying the *structure of the space of possibilities* that is defined by an entity's tendencies and capacities. A philosopher's ontological commitment should be to the objective existence of this structure and not to the possibilities themselves since the latter exist only when entertained by a mind. Some possibility spaces are continuous having a well-defined spatial structure that can be investigated mathematically, while others are discrete, possessing no inherent spatial order but being nevertheless capable of being studied through the imposition of a certain arrangement. The space of possible regimes of flow (uniform, periodic, turbulent) is an example of a continuous possibility space in which the only discontinuities are the critical points separating the different tendencies. The space of possible genes, on the other hand, is an example of a discrete space that must be studied by imposing an order on it, such as an arrangement in which every gene has as neighbors other genes differing from it by a single mutation. As we will see in the different chapters of this book the structure of possibility spaces plays as great a role in the explanation of emergence as do mechanisms.

The chapters are deliberately arranged in a way that departs from the ideas of the original emergentists. These philosophers believed that entities like "Space-Time," "Life," "Mind," and "Deity" (not "god" but the sense of the sacred that emerges in some minds) formed a pyramid of progressively ascending grades. Although the levels of this pyramid were not supposed to imply any teleology it is hard not to view each level as leading to the next following a necessary sequence.

To eliminate this possible interpretation an entirely different image is used here, that of a contingent accumulation of layers or strata that may differ in complexity but that coexist and interact with each other in no particular order: a biological entity may interact with a sub-atomic one, as when neurons manipulate concentrations of metallic ions, or a psychological entity interact with a chemical one, as when subjective experience is modified by a drug. The book begins with purely physical entities, thunderstorms, that are already complex enough to avoid the idea that their behavior can be deduced from a general law. It then moves on to explore the prebiotic soup, bacterial ecosystems, insect intelligence, mammalian memory, primate social strategies, and the emergence of trade, language, and institutional organizations in human communities. Each of these layers will be discussed in terms of the mechanisms of emergence involved, drawing ideas and insights from the relevant fields of science, as well as in terms of the structure of their possibility spaces, using the results of both mathematical analysis and the outcomes of computer simulations.

Simulations are partly responsible for the restoration of the legitimacy of the concept of emergence because they can stage interactions between virtual entities from which properties, tendencies, and capacities actually emerge. Since this emergence is reproducible in many computers it can be probed and studied by different scientists as if it were a laboratory phenomenon. In other words, simulations can play the role of laboratory experiments in the study of emergence complementing the role of mathematics in deciphering the structure of possibility spaces. And philosophy can be the mechanism through which these insights can be synthesized into an emergent materialist world view that finally does justice to the creative powers of matter and energy.

CHAPTER ONE
The Storm in the Computer

Let's begin with the simplest emergent properties, properties like temperature or pressure characterizing wholes made out of a large number of identical parts, such as a body of water in a container. Being composed of billions of molecules that are qualitatively the same makes a body of water much simpler than, say, an ecosystem in which hundreds of different species constantly interact. But this simplicity is what makes the mechanism of emergence behind temperature or pressure a promising starting point for philosophical thought. To begin with, in what sense are these properties emergent? Temperature is defined as the average energy that a molecular population has by virtue of the motion of its parts, the more violent the motion the more intense the temperature. Pressure is defined as the average degree to which the population pushes against the walls of the container by virtue of the momentum of its parts, the faster and more massive the molecules the more intense the pressure exerted. These definitions have tempted philosophers in the past to think that temperature and pressure can be reduced to kinetic energy and momentum, that is, that they are not emergent. But temperature and pressure are in fact irreducible because they are the result of an *objective averaging process* that takes place spontaneously in molecular populations.

To understand how this works let's imagine two bodies of water at different temperatures. The moment we place these bodies in contact with each other energy will flow from the body with higher temperature to the one with lower temperature, the flow continuing until the temperature difference disappears. In other words, the difference in temperature will display a tendency to average itself out. Thus, saying that a body of water possess a certain temperature, and that possession of that property defines an enduring state, implies that departures from that state are constantly being counteracted by an objective tendency. For the same reason defining "sameness of temperature" can be done by placing two bodies of water into contact and verifying that no flow of energy is taking place between them. Thus, in this simple case the irreducible status of a property like temperature is established by elucidating a mechanism through which the property emerges, a mechanism involving the manifestation of tendency. Accounting for this tendency, in turn, demands switching scales and focusing on the interactions between the parts of the whole, interactions in which the parts exercise their capacities to affect and be affected. In particular, for a temperature difference to cancel itself the component molecules must exercise their capacity to collide and redistribute energy in those collisions.

We can visualize the series of events leading to the emergence of an average temperature by comparing the states of two bodies of water before and after the dissipating tendency has been manifested. At the start of the process the existence of a temperature difference means that the water molecules are distributed with a high degree of order, that is, that they are neatly sorted out into two parts, one hot and the other cold. At the end of the process the entire population is uniformly warm and this order has disappeared. A disordered state is characterized by the fact that we can make a large number of changes in the molecular distribution and leave the bulk state basically the same. In other words, a much larger number of combinations of individual kinetic energies will result in the same warm body of water than the number that will yield the state in which one container is hot and the other one is cold. This affects the probability that one or the other state will occur spontaneously. Because in this case the interactions between molecules are entirely random these odds make all the difference in the world: the state characterizing a warm body of water will have a much higher probability of occurring as a result of random collisions than the one in which they are sorted into hot and cold subpopulations. It is this difference in the odds with which the ordered and disordered states can occur that explains the tendency for one to become the other.[1]

The mechanism of emergence just described for temperature is basically the same for pressure, density, and other *intensive* properties of molecular populations. Despite their relative simplicity these properties are important because the spontaneous flow of energy that takes place as intensive differences cancel themselves can be tapped into to fuel other processes. The whole composed by two containers of water at different temperatures, for example, has the capacity to drive another process partly because the high temperature container stores a lot of energy, much more than the low temperature one, and partly because we can extract that energy by placing the former in contact with the latter.[2] This capacity is relatively short lived, however, because once the intensive difference disappears the energy left behind becomes much harder to extract. But if the difference is continuously refreshed, by placing the first container on top of a fire, for instance, then the whole formed by hot and cold molecular populations can become a component part of a larger whole, playing the role that a gasoline tank or an electric battery play in an automobile or an electronic appliance. The capacity of intensive differences to act as energy storage devices will play such a prominent role in the explanation of emergence in many other examples that it will be useful to have a more compact term for them. We will refer to them as *gradients*.

In addition to serve as energy sources gradients can serve to generate the moving parts of larger wholes. For example, if a gradient is intense enough and if it is prevented from dissipating it can cause a molecular population to self-organize into a circular motion pattern that will persist as long as the gradient persists. The coordinated movement of billions of molecules needed to yield such a pattern is a highly unlikely event and yet it occurs spontaneously in the ocean and the atmosphere every single day. This coherent circulatory flow, referred to as a *convection cell*, is produced by the gradient as the means to cancel itself even as the imposed constraints prevent it from doing so.[3] The mechanism of emergence behind a convection cell can be explained using the same example of a water container: when the container is heated from below it becomes divided into a warm bottom and a cool top; as the bottom water warms up it expands and becomes less dense tending to rise, while the high density cold water on top tends to sink; these up and down movements are counteracted by the internal friction generated by the viscosity of the water, but when the temperature difference becomes intense enough this resistance is overcome and the upward and downward flows join together to form a circular pattern.[4] Because this pattern is very stable it can literally be used as a building block to construct larger emergent entities.

What kind of entities can be built using gradients as fuel tanks and convection cells as moving parts? The most dramatic example is a *thunderstorm*, a typical storm containing five to eight convection cells each a few kilometers in diameter.[5] Viewed from the outside a thunderstorm appears as a large complex cloud with a well-defined form. At the center of the storm is a massive column-like structure called the "central pillar." This vertical structure adopts an asymmetric horizontal shape at its top called an "anvil" for its resemblance to the metal block used by blacksmiths. The central pillar often overshoots the anvil creating a dome at its top. Finally, at the bottom of the pillar there are flanking horizontal clouds lined up in the opposite direction to the anvil. This complex form is one of the emergent properties of a thunderstorm, its directly observable property. But behind its observable form there is the internal machinery of the storm. In addition to gradients and convection this machinery uses *phase transitions*, the transition from gas to liquid or from liquid to solid, as energy amplifiers. One of the differences between a material such as water in its gas, liquid, or solid state is the degree to which its composing molecules move around and therefore the amount of kinetic energy the material contains. In a solid the molecules are relatively confined to fixed positions so their activity is relatively calm. In liquids this confinement is relaxed: molecules still exert some restraining influence over one another but they allow a more energetic movement. In gases the molecules are even more excited since their movement is not constrained at all. A gas therefore contains more energy than a liquid or a solid. When rising vapor becomes rain some of this extra energy becomes available as a surplus that can be exported to the surrounding medium, increasing the amount of energy available to the thunderstorm. This exportable energy is referred to as "latent heat."[6]

To understand the mechanism of emergence behind a thunderstorm we need to explain how these different components are coupled together. First of all, a difference in temperature between the surface of the ocean and that of the atmosphere must exist to get the process started. This vertical gradient causes an upward flow of air and vapor forming one leg of a convection cell. As the warm moist air moves up it becomes cooler eventually reaching the critical point at which vapor becomes liquid water. At first this phase transition produces very small liquid droplets that become suspended in the surrounding air. The concentration of these tiny droplets makes the upward air current visible as a small cauliflower-shaped cloud that becomes the base of the future thunderstorm. Although at this point the air should start turning sideways and head for the downward leg of the convection cell, the latent heat released by the phase transition increases the temperature of the air current adding buoyancy to it and propelling further up. This self-stimulating interaction is repeated several times allowing the updraft to reach great heights eventually becoming the giant cloud described above, with its central pillar, anvil, and dome. The death of a thunderstorm, in turn, is linked to processes that counteract its sustaining gradients: the higher the air reaches the colder it gets, the more saturated it becomes, and the larger the liquid drops and ice crystals that condense from it. When the weight of these drops and crystals reach a tipping point—the point at which the downward force exerted by gravity becomes stronger than that of the updraft—it begins to fall in the form of rain and hail dragging air with it, stealing energy from the updraft and eventually destroying the internal machinery of the storm.

Other features of this emergent meteorological entity are also explained by gradients. A severe thunderstorm is usually accompanied by the production of lightning, either intensely bright flashes created within the cloud or powerful bolts between the cloud and the ground. Lightning is the result of an electrical gradient, a difference in charge between the upper and lower regions of the cloud, or between the cloud and the ground, the brilliant discharge being the form created by the gradient to cancel itself. Thunderstorms are also the birth place of tornadoes, whirling masses of air made visible by the matter (vapor, dust, debris) that they suck into their intensely rapid circulation.

Tornadoes are born from the same vertical temperature gradient that causes the updraft to which a steep horizontal pressure gradient is added. The latter is caused by the fact that the updraft sucks the air from the center of the tornado greatly reducing the pressure inside of it compared to that of the outside.[7] As an emergent whole a thunderstorm is characterized by its properties, such as the heights it reaches or the speed with which it moves; by its tendencies, like its tendency to move in a certain direction or its tendency to consume all its energy and die; and by the capacities it exercises when it interacts with other entities. From a human point of view these interactions are mostly destructive: its lightning kills people and starts brush and forest fires; the heavy rain along its downdraft can result in floods; and the tornadoes it spawns can violently flatten entire towns. These capacities can surely inspire awe and respect at the destructive potential of a thunderstorm but they should not lead to an attitude of intellectual resignation or natural piety toward it: we can explain how it is born, how it lives, and how it dies.

Let's pause to consider the argument so far. The objective reality of emergent properties can be established by elucidating the mechanisms that produce them at a one scale and by showing that emergent entities at that scale can become the component parts of a whole at a larger scale. Mechanisms of emergence may, of course, undergo revision or elaboration, and some are better understood than others, but the possibility of improvement or change in the proposed mechanisms should not force us to take emergence at any scale as a brute fact. There are, on the other hand, aspects of the concept of emergence that this argument does not address. In particular, similar emergent effects can be produced by entirely different mechanisms suggesting that there is more to the emergent properties of a whole than the interactions between its parts. Let's return to the case of convection cells. The self-organized rhythmic flow characterizing convection emerges in many kinds of materials. The flows of molten rock that lie underneath the surface of the earth, for example, exhibit the same coherent circular motion as the air and water above it. More importantly, the same self-organization is displayed by other rhythmic patterns that have nothing to do with the movement of matter in space. A good example comes from the world of chemistry. The gradients in this case are differences in the concentration of certain substances, that is, they are gradients of matter not of energy. The rhythms are the rates at which new compound molecules are synthesized—the chemical reaction switches spontaneously from the production of one type of molecule to the production of another following a perfect beat—not collective circular motions. Yet despite these differences a convection cell and a *chemical clock*, as these reactions are called, are qualitatively the same. This implies that a full explanation of these emergent entities must possess a component that is independent of any particular mechanism.

It could be argued that the similarity in rhythmic behavior is superficial and that it does not demand complicating the concept of explanation, but there are other shared characteristics that cannot be so easily dismissed. In particular, the periodic behavior in both cases is stable against perturbations, that is, if a convection cell or a chemical clock are disturbed by an outside shock they will tend to return to their original period and amplitude after a relatively short time. This tendency is referred to as *asymptotic stability*. Not all oscillating entities possess this kind of stability. A pendulum in which friction has been carefully eliminated, for example, will not react the same way: a small push will permanently change both the duration and intensity of its swing, the pendulum acting as if it "remembered" the perturbation. A convection cell or a chemical clock, on the other hand, quickly "forget" the perturbation acting as if nothing had happened.[8] When we explained convection by the causal mechanism outlined above—a temperature gradient that creates a density gradient that, in turn, amplifies fluctuations into a circular flow—we were giving only part of the explanation because the causal chain behind the emergence of a convection cell does not account for the fact that its properties are stable against perturbations. And similarly for a chemical clock.

Adding to the explanation of emergence a *mechanism-independent* component will involve introducing entirely new ideas so it will be useful at this point to justify the need for the extra complexity. So far the concept of emergence has played an ontological role, showing why it is legitimate to believe in the existence of objective properties, tendencies, and capacities. But once we add the mechanism-independent component the concept of emergence leads to two important epistemological consequences: it explains why we can use partial models to learn about reality and it provides an account for the capacity of those models to mimic the behavior of the processes they model. The first consequence derives directly from the notion of asymptotic stability. When the emergent properties of a whole are stable they can survive changes in the details of the interactions between its parts. A given degree of temperature in a body of water, for example, may result from a number of different interactions between the kinetic energy of its component molecules. This implies that we can take the existence of temperature for granted when explaining the circulatory pattern in a convection cell, that is, that we can legitimately leave out of the explanation a detailed census of the kinetic energy of each of the molecules in the population. To put this differently, a stable emergent property is "indifferent" to local changes in the interactions that give rise to it, and this objective indifference translates into an objective *explanatory irrelevance* of the details of the interactions: including the latter in an explanation would be redundant because many different interactions would yield the same outcome.[9] Being able to take for granted the existence of emergent properties at one scale in order to explain properties at another scale is arguably a basic requirement for scientific research. If scientists had to build models that captured all scales simultaneously no scientific field would ever have succeeded in explaining anything. We would be trapped in a block universe in which every aspect is inextricably related to every other aspect and our incapacity to separate levels of emergence would leave us cognitively powerless.

The second epistemological consequence derives from the very notion of mechanism-independence: if processes as different in detail as a convection cell and a chemical clock can exhibit the same behavior perhaps mathematical equations can also display that behavior. To set the stage for the argument let's first give a simplified account of the relation between mathematical models and laboratory experiments. Let's assume that we want to understand the behavior of the air currents forming the updraft and downdraft of a thunderstorm. We can use a mathematical model of the dynamics of non-viscous fluids that has existed since the eighteenth century: a set of differential equations that relate the properties of density, pressure, internal energy, and velocity to the flow of air. Using these equations we can generate a series of numbers that indicate the course of the modeled fluid at discrete intervals of space and time and then give this series of numerical solutions a visual form, such as a plot in a piece of paper. The expression "the behavior of equations" refers to the pattern generated by its numerical solutions as presented graphically by the plot. Next we move to the laboratory and create an experimental situation in which an actual flow of air is affected only by those same properties, using an apparatus that can exclude any other causal factor from affecting the flow. We run the experiment and take measurements of the airflow at different points in space and instants of time and plot the measured values on a piece of paper. To be able to compare the two plots we must make sure that the values of the variables in the equations and the values of the properties in the apparatus are approximately the same at the beginning of the run, that is, that both the equations and the apparatus are set to the same initial conditions. If the mathematical model captured the real dynamics then the two plots should be *geometrically similar.*[10]

This is, of course, a highly idealized picture of the relation between theory and experiment but it points to the crucial question: the similarity between the two graphic plots suggests that the behavior of the numerical solutions to the equations is isomorphic to the behavior of the physical properties inside the apparatus, a highly improbable behavioral isomorphism that cries out for explanation. Moreover, the advent of computer simulations has allowed scientists to tackle not just simple air currents but entire thunderstorms and the fact that the geometric similarity has persisted has made the underlying behavioral isomorphism even more problematic. In recent decades the equations for non-viscous flow used in the previous example were coupled to another set modeling the phase transitions in water and were numerically solved for every point of a three-dimensional grid, each point representing a box one kilometer wide and half a kilometer high. Enough of these boxes were included in the simulation to fit a regular size thunderstorm. To add a temporal dimension the equations were solved *recursively*, that is, the solutions obtained as outputs at any one instant were used as inputs for the equations to get the solutions for the next time interval. This makes the expression "the behavior of equations" less metaphorical because recursion transforms a static mathematical object into a dynamic computational process.

A set of values to serve as initial conditions was obtained from actual measurements of wind, temperature, and humidity of an area of the ocean where an actual thunderstorm had developed.

After feeding the computer the initial values the recursive procedure took over repeatedly generating populations of solutions for every time interval, the final product rendered using standard computer graphics software. To everyone's surprise a central pillar, an anvil, a dome, and a flanking line of clouds spontaneously emerged despite the fact that none of those features had been explicitly modeled. The updraft and the downdraft forming the internal machinery of the storm also emerged, made visible by adding purely graphic entities (weightless spheres) that followed the simulated air currents.[11] Part of the explanation for the success of the simulation is the decomposability of reality made possible by emergent properties. The microscopic interactions between molecules at the surface of the ocean and those in the air above it, for example, did not have to be modeled in detail. The effect of friction between water and air molecules that starts the process of storm formation was introduced from the outside as a perturbation of the interface between the two fluids. Similarly, macroscopic details like the influence of the earth's rotation were simply ignored. That the correct geometrical form emerged despite these simplifications shows that natural phenomena exhibit a recurrent part-to-whole relation, in which wholes at one scale become parts at the next larger scale, and that interactions between scales can be either left out of a model or added exogenously.[12] On the other hand, the behavioral isomorphism between the solutions to the equations and the physical flows in a real thunderstorm is not explained by the decomposability of reality. This isomorphism has mystified physicists for as long as there has been evidence of its existence, some of them resigning themselves to accept the unreasonable effectiveness of mathematics as miraculous.[13]

But as argued above an explanation of this "miracle" can be given using the notion of mechanism-independence. Let's clarify this notion first for the case of material processes. As mentioned in the Introduction the distinction between properties on one hand and tendencies and capacities on the other is that the former are always actual—actual characteristics of the state of a whole at any given point in time—while the latter need not be: the tendency of liquid water to solidify at a critical point of temperature may not manifest itself if the temperature always remains above that point; and the capacity of liquid water to acts as a solvent may not be exercised if the water never comes into contact with soluble substances. The ontological status of both tendencies and capacities is therefore different from that of properties. As the simple case of temperature or pressure shows the part of the explanation of emergence that depends on mechanisms involves the actual manifestation of tendencies (the tendency behind the objective averaging process) and the actual exercise of capacities (the capacity of molecules to collide and redistribute energy). The mechanism-independent component of an explanation, on the other hand, demands clarifying the status of tendencies and capacities when they are not actually manifested or exercised. We could, of course, characterize that status as that of a possibility but that would be too vague: an unmanifested tendency and an unexercised capacity are not just possible but define a concrete *space of possibilities with a definite structure.*

Let's imagine this abstract space as a set of points each representing a different possibility. The structure of this space can be conceived as the subset of those points that have a much higher probability to become actual. When we described the mechanism of emergence behind the tendency of a gradient to cancel itself we said that it was based on a probabilistic argument: the state in which the gradient is alive is much more ordered than that in which it is dissipated, and in a molecular population in which all interactions are basically random the disordered state is a vastly more probable outcome of those interactions. An alternative way of saying this is that in the space of possibilities for the molecular population there exists a special point, the point of maximum disorder, and that the population is attracted to that state because it is much more probable than the others. A similar idea can be applied to convection cells and chemical clocks. We can imagine that in their space of possible states there is a set of points forming a closed loop that has the highest probability of actually occurring, forcing a physical or chemical process to repeat the same series of states over and over. If the process is subjected to an external shock it will move away from that loop, existing momentarily in less probable states, but then it will tend to return to it. This informal argument points to the solution to our problem: the stability of emergent properties is explained by the structure of a possibility space and the fact that this stability can be displayed by entirely different mechanisms is explained by the fact that their possibility spaces share the same structure.

The concept of a possibility space can be made rigorous using the results of several centuries of mathematical investigation on the nature of abstract spaces. In mathematics a basic distinction is made between metric spaces, the best known example of which is Euclidean geometry, and non-metric spaces exemplified by a variety of other geometries: projective, differential, topological. A relatively simple way of distinguishing metric from non-metric spaces is by the way in which the component parts of a space, individual points, are identified. The metric solution is to give each point an "address" by locating the space relative to a set of fixed coordinates and determining the distance that each point has from those axes. But this familiar procedure is not the only way of individuating points. One can, for example, determine the rate at which the curvature of a space changes at a given point and use this instantaneous rate of change to identify it.[14] When we do this a space ceases to be a set of coordinate addresses and becomes *a field of rapidities and slownesses*, the rapidity or slowness with which curvature varies at each point. The structure of an abstract space, in turn, can be characterized by those properties that remain unchanged when the space is transformed, when it is moved, rotated, folded, stretched. Metric properties like length or area remain invariant under the smallest set of transformations, while those of the least metric spaces stay unchanged under the largest set. For the purpose of understanding in what sense two different mechanisms can share the same structure we need highly invariant structural properties since the metric details of their possibility spaces are bound to be different. A very important example of these invariant properties is the existence and distribution of special or remarkable points (or sets of such points) called *singularities*. This is the concept that we need to make the remarks in the previous paragraph less metaphorical: the possibilities with the highest probability of occurring are topological singularities acting as attractors.

Let's now apply this line of thought to mathematical models. To create a mathematical model the first step is to enumerate all the relevant ways in which the process to be modeled is free to change.

Let's imagine that we are modeling a simple physical process characterized by two changing properties, such as temperature and pressure.
These are called its "degrees of freedom." The process may, of course,
also change in an infinite number of irrelevant ways, the art of mathematical modeling being based in part on the ability to judge what
changes do, and what changes do not, make a difference. Once the
relevant degrees of freedom of a physical process have been identified
the model can be given a spatial form by assigning each of them to
a dimension of a topological space. Each point in this space will be a
combination of values of temperature and pressure representing an
instantaneous state of the process being modeled, while the set of
points as a whole represents the space of all possible states for the
process. For this reason the abstract space is referred to as *state space*
(or "phase space"). Finally, since a given process changing in time
follows a sequence of states its behavior appears in state space as a
series of points, that is, as a curve or trajectory. It was by observing
the tendency of many of these trajectories to converge on specific
areas of state space, to converge on singularities, that the existence of
asymptotic stability was first established.[15]

Using these ideas the explanation for the unreasonable effectiveness of mathematics can be phrased like this: a mathematical model
can capture the behavior of a material process because the space of
possible solutions *overlaps* the possibility space associated with the
material process. The two possibility spaces need not be identical but
merely overlapping because most mathematical models mimic the
behavior of a process only within a certain range of values of their
control parameters. A sufficient overlap can nevertheless exist because
the singularities that structure both spaces are independent of both
causal mechanisms in a process and formal relations in an equation.
This explanation implies an ontological commitment to the autonomous existence of topological singularities, or more generally, to the
structure of possibility spaces. Once this ontological commitment has
been made the term "singularity" ceases to be a purely mathematical
concept and becomes a properly philosophical one. In particular, once
singularities are taken to be as real and efficient as causes the nature
of their reality becomes a problem for philosophers. Do they exist, for
example, as *transcendent* entities in a world beyond that of matter and
energy? Or are they *immanent* to the material world? If all the matter

and energy of the universe ceased to exist, would singularities also disappear (immanent) or would they continue to exist (transcendent)? Although these questions are not mathematical but philosophical the practice of mathematicians can still provide insights into the answers.

If singularities are immanent they must be both irreducible to any particular material process while at the same time requiring that some process or another actually exists. These two conditions are reflected in the way singularities are studied. Topologists, for example, do not study the singularities structuring the possibility space of a model free to change in its temperature and its pressure, but of *all models with two degrees of freedom* whatever these may be. It can be proved, for example, that in a two-dimensional space only certain kinds of singularities exist: four different types of point singularities distinguished from each other by the form of the flow of nearby trajectories (nodes, saddle points, foci, and centers) as well as one type of periodic singularity.[16] In three-dimensional spaces, the four point singularities are still part of the repertoire but now periodic singularities come in three different forms: stable, unstable, and saddle-shaped loops. In addition, a new type of singularity becomes available, one that can be pictured as a loop that has been repeatedly stretched and folded (a so-called chaotic attractor).[17] This implies that topological facts about possibility spaces can be discovered without reference to the nature of the degrees of freedom, only to their number, and without reference to the nature of the gradient (thermal, gravitational, mechanical, chemical) only to its existence.[18] But the fact that the *existence* of a gradient, any gradient, is necessary confirms the immanent status of singularities.

Singularities are, therefore, perfectly acceptable entities in a materialist philosophy. The main problem confronting us now is the extent to which we can generalize from these ideas. State space is only one kind of possibility space, a space useful to study tendencies but not capacities. Capacities involve a much larger set of possibilities than tendencies because entities can exercise their capacities in interaction with a potentially innumerable variety of other entities. The more complex possibility spaces associated with capacities, and the nature of the singularities that structure them, are not nearly as well understood as those of tendencies. On the other hand, computers can supply the means to explore these other possibility spaces in a rigorous way because the interactions in which capacities are exercised can be staged in a simulation and varied in multiple ways until the singular features of the possibility space are made visible. Each of the following chapters will explore how staging a different type of simulated interaction (chemical, biological, social) can tease out the singular structure of their possibility spaces. The first step in this exploration, however, will not address the question of the relation between models and reality. We first need to clarify the concept of emergence in the case of simulations. This is what the following chapter will attempt to do.

CHAPTER TWO
Cellular Automata and Patterns of Flow

Much like the simplicity of temperature and pressure make them an ideal starting point for philosophical reflection on emergence, the question of what is an emergent property in computer simulations can be best approached starting with the least complex cases. The simplest of all computing machines, *finite state automata*, can perform a computation by changing from one state to another in a well-defined sequence without having to store intermediate results. Let's imagine a population of these simple machines embodied physically. One way of letting them interact is to create a large fishing net made of electrically conducting material and to place a finite state automaton wherever two wires cross. The interactions would take place through an electrical current flowing through the wires allowing the state of a given automaton at any one time to be determined by the states of neighboring automata according to some rule. The same interacting population can be created with software instead of hardware if an abstract two-dimensional space is subdivided into "cells" and a simulated finite state automaton is placed in each cell. The cells may be triangular, rectangular, hexagonal, or any shape that exactly tiles the plane so that the cells are connected to one another by sharing edges and corners. Both the physical realization of the population of automata and its simulation in software are referred to as *cellular automata*. The question is whether the same strategy used with temperature and pressure will still work when we replace a population of molecules with one of computing machines. That is, whether we can identify emergent properties, tendencies, and capacities, and whether we can show that emergent entities at one scale can be used to compose emergent entities at a larger scale.

The best known example of a cellular automaton is the so-called *Game of Life*. The cells housing finite state automata in Life are rectangular in shape and the automata are capable of being in only two states, "on" and "off." This is usually expressed as if the two states belonged to the cells themselves which are said to be "alive" or "dead," respectively. Life is not a regular computer game since there is no continuous interaction between the user and the computer: the user merely sets the state of a few cells (that is, makes some of them "alive") and then passively watches as the cells affect and are affected by their neighbors. The interaction rules of Life are deceptively simple: if at a given moment a cell has two neighbors that are alive it will stay in the same state it was in the previous instant, that is, if the cell was alive it will stay alive and if it was dead it will remain dead; if the cell is dead and three of its neighbors are alive, it will come alive; finally, if the cell is alive and only one neighbor is alive, or if more than three are, it will die. The rules are applied to the entire population simultaneously and repeatedly for as long as the simulation is allowed to last. The fact that the interactions are rigidly specified by rules implies that they are *not emergent*. On the other hand, as the population interacts patterns of states in neighboring cells appear and these are indeed emergent since the patterns have properties, tendencies, and capacities that are not present in the individual automata.

The most basic emergent tendencies of patterns of states are the same as those found in real physical processes: the tendency to remain in a steady state and the tendency to oscillate between states. When playing with Life one quickly discovers that most initial patterns disappear after a few generations. So the tendency to maintain the same shape, even though hardly a form of behavior due to the absence of change, is not ordinary. Many patterns in Life display this tendency, the simplest one being composed of four neighboring cells simultaneously alive, a pattern called a "block." These static but enduring patterns are called "still lifes." A second class of patterns, collectively known as "oscillators," displays a tendency to cycle through a series of configurations over and over again. The simplest one, called a "blinker," consists of three neighboring cells in a row that becomes a column in the next generation and then becomes a row again.

The blinker simply switches back and forth between two phases but other oscillators undergo a number of changes before returning to the initial phase and repeating the series again. A third class of patterns, called "spaceships," adds to this rhythmic behavior a tendency to move in space. The simplest one is made of five live cells arranged in a "V" shape that cycle through four phases, the last of which is like the initial one but displaced one cell diagonally. On a computer the pattern seems to glide across the screen so it is referred to as a "glider."[1] Gliders and other spaceships provide the clearest example of emergence in cellular automata: while the automata themselves remain fixed in their cells a coherent pattern of states moving across them is clearly a new entity that is easily distinguishable from them.

Still lifes, oscillators, spaceships, and other emergent patterns can interact and in these interactions they reveal their capacities. As with molecular populations the interactions are simple collisions but the results of a colliding event are so varied that they must be studied empirically. Two gliders, for example, can collide with each other in 73 different ways, the outcome depending on their positions and the phase of their oscillation at the time of the event: 28 of these collisions result in the mutual annihilation of both gliders; six produce a block as their outcome; three result in a blinker; two leave a single glider behind; and the rest produce a variety of still lifes and oscillators.[2] The possible outcomes become more numerous as we increase the number of gliders and while efforts to catalogue them exhaustively continue a more promising route to reveal the capacities of multi-glider collisions is to look for specific combinations that synthesize interesting objects. There is a collision of 13 gliders, for instance, that synthesizes a pattern more complex than the glider itself: a *glider gun*, an oscillating pattern that produces a continuous stream of gliders. There is also an interesting capacity displayed by some still lifes: they are capable of colliding with another pattern destroying it while at the same time reconstituting themselves. This capacity "to eat" other patterns also depends on the capacity of the patterns to be eaten: a still life shaped like a fishhook, for example, can eat most patterns but is not capable of digesting a block.[3]

Knowledge of these emergent tendencies and capacities can be used in the construction of "engineered" Life patterns. Blocks, blinkers, and gliders are referred to as "natural" patterns because when one starts a Life session with a random population of live and dead cells these three patterns (and other simple ones) emerge spontaneously. This spontaneity is explained both by the fact that the patterns are small—patterns made out of a few live cells have a higher probability of occurring than large ones—and by the fact that they can arise following several sequences of predecessor patterns: the more numerous the sequences converging on a pattern the higher the likelihood that one of them will occur by chance. Most large and complex patterns, on the other hand, must be handcrafted. A glider gun is a good example of an engineered pattern. The first gun to be created was based on a "shuttle," a pattern that moves like a spaceship but periodically changes direction. The shuttle is a simple triangular pattern that may occur naturally but it is typically short-lived because as it changes direction it collides destructively against its own debris. But if blocks acting as eaters are positioned at an exact place they will consume the debris stabilizing the shuttle. Once stabilized two shuttles can be made to collide with one another and if their position and timing is just right they will produce a glider every 30 generations.[4] Engineered patterns are important because they hold the key to the other test of emergence: the ability of emergent entities at one scale to become component parts of larger entities with their own emergent properties. Glider guns are already an example of such larger scale emergence but for the test to be significant we would want to determine if using the patterns that emerge in a population of the simplest automata we can build another automaton with much higher *computational capacity*.

The space of all possible automata will be described in detail in Chapter 10 but at this point it can be characterized as structured by singularities in computational capacity: a finite state automaton represents a capacity minimum while a so-called *Turing machine* represents a capacity maximum. The main factor contributing to this greater capacity is access to memory, a degree of access that varies from zero in the case of finite state automata to absolute in the case of a Turing machine and its infinite memory "tape." The gap between the minimum and maximum of computing capacity can be bridged because the different automata stand in a relation of part-to-whole to one another. A Turing machine, for example, needs a finite state automaton as a component part to control the "head" it uses to read the contents of its infinite tape and to write on it. On the other hand, what we need for our second test of emergence is not a way to build a Turing machine out of finite state automata but a means to build it out of emergent patterns of automaton states like gliders and glider guns. There are two different ways of approaching this challenge. One is to actually build a working Turing machine, with its read/write head and its memory tape, and make it carry out a calculation that could not be performed by a finite state automaton. The other is to show that *in principle* such a construction could be performed without actually carrying it out.

Both approaches rely on the fact that computing machines can be built out of basic digital circuits called *logical gates*. An And gate, for example, has two inputs and one output: if the value of both inputs is the number "1" the output will also be a "1"; any other combination yields "0" as an output. A Not gate takes a single input and outputs its opposite: a "0" if the input is "1" and vice versa. Using these elementary circuits as components larger ones can be created, such as a Flip-flop circuit that acts as the simplest type of memory. Any of these elementary circuits can be created out of transistors and in that form they exist in the chips that power most personal computers, but they can also be created out of emergent Life patterns. An And gate, for example, may be built out of a glider gun and an eater. The glider gun produces a continuous stream of gliders that disappears once it reaches the eater. The inputs to the gate are two additional glider streams, produced elsewhere and already coded with information: the presence of a glider in the stream represents a "1" while its absence represents a "0." These two input streams collide destructively with the main stream at 90 degrees before it reaches the eater. If both input streams have a glider in the same position (if both inputs have a value of "1") the first input will collide and eliminate a glider from the main stream creating a hole through which the corresponding glider in the second input can pass. All other combinations do not let any glider through. Thus, the assembly acts like an And gate, the input gliders that manage to make it through the main stream constituting its output.[5] The "in principle" approach stops here because with this And gate and a simpler to build Not gate all the circuits needed for a full computer could be built if we had enough patience.

The second approach, on the other hand, does not aim at simply proving that the construction is feasible but at working out all the difficult details. A current implementation can serve as an illustration: a simple Turing machine capable of being in three different states and using three symbols to write in its memory tape. This implementation is easier to describe starting at the top with the full automaton and working our way downwards. The largest scale components that must be built are a finite state machine controlling the read–write head, the memory tape, and a signal detector connecting the two together. Each of the three main components can be assembled out of simpler ones: a finite state machine can be implemented with nine memory cells; a tape with two stacks; and the signal detector can be made out of colliding glider streams and of units that duplicate each stream, sending the copies to the stacks and the finite state machine. Each of these sub-components can, in turn, be built out of even simpler ones. A memory cell, for example, can be made out of a glider gun and a special type of shuttle (called a "queen bee") that acts as a reflector for gliders, and can be accessed by two streams of spaceships each produced by its own gun.[6] When these and other components are assembled together the result is a working Turing machine that can actually carry out computations. The computations are too simple and the process is too slow for the emergent automaton to be of any practical use, but watching the Turing machine in operation induces in the viewer the same kind of awe created by the emergent thunderstorm discussed in the previous chapter. In this case, however, we are not tempted to view the result as "miraculous" because the mechanisms just described are already part of the explanation, an explanation that may be considered to be *causal* despite the fact that glider collisions and other events are not physical. But this still leaves part of the mystery unexplained: the mechanism-independent part.

What possibility space is involved in this other part of the explanation? Given that the interactions between the finite state automata inhabiting the cells of Life are defined by rules what must be determined is the singularities structuring *the space of all possible rules*. And what these singularities must account for is the existence of natural patterns like blocks and gliders since all the engineered ones used to build the emergent Turing machine depend on them. Strictly speaking we need two spaces, the space of possible rules and the space of possible ways of tiling a space, and not just two-dimensional spaces as in Life but spaces of any number of dimensions. The basic insight, however, can be illustrated by studying cellular automata operating in a one-dimensional space. In this case the cells become points in a line allowing us to ignore the geometry of the tiles and to concentrate on the rules. In the previous chapter we discussed a possibility space (state space) that enters into the explanation of tendencies. The space of possible rules, on the other hand, enters into the explanation of capacities because the rules specify the ways in which automata can affect and be affected by one another. What emerges from the actual exercise of these capacities, one level higher in the part-to-whole relation, is again tendencies: the tendency of certain Life objects to emerge spontaneously.

The size of this space is given by the number of possible rules. It can be calculated from the number of combinations of two variables: the number of states in which a cell can be and the number of neighbors (including itself) with which it interacts. The number of states raised to the number of neighbors yields the combination of possible states in which each neighborhood can be. Each such possible configuration of states for a neighborhood determines in what state a cell can be at the next moment. Since this is all a rule does, defining the transition from one state to the next, the total number of rules is the number of states raised to the number of possible configuration of states for a neighborhood. A one-dimensional cellular automaton in which each cell can be in two states and interacts only with its two immediate neighbors has a total of 256 possible rules. But in a cellular automaton like Life, with two states and nine neighbors, the number of rules is, roughly, the number 10 followed by 154 zeros. This enormous size explains why the first serious investigation of the possibility space for interaction rules was performed in the one-dimensional case. But how does one search for the singularities in such a space?

We saw that to play the game of Life a few of the cells are set by the user to the live state and then the pattern of live cells is allowed to evolve on its own. The same procedure can be used here: we can select one rule from the 256 possibilities, give it a starting pattern, and then follow its evolution. In most cases as the evolution proceeds the number of configurations the states can form decreases approaching in the long run *a limiting pattern*. Four different limiting patterns, associated with four different classes of rules, have been discovered: the first class of rules leads to fixed, homogenous patterns; the second class gives rise to periodic patterns; the third class leads to relatively random configurations; and finally, the fourth class (or "class IV") produces true complexity, including localized structures capable of motion, like the gliders and other spaceships of Life.[7] The huge population of rules inhabiting the possibility space of two-dimensional cellular automata cannot, of course, be explored one at a time but it can be treated just like any other large population: statistically. In other words, the population can be sampled in a systematic way and the limiting patterns discovered by using representative rules from each sampled region. When this statistical analysis has been carried out all four classes have been rediscovered.[8]

The four classes of rules are the singularities structuring the possibility space, with class IV interactions representing a maximum capacity to lead to complex emergent patterns while class III represent a minimum capacity. But as in the case of state space it is important to know not only that the singularities exist but also how they are distributed. This is complicated in the present case because unlike state space that is a *continuous topological space* with well-defined spatial connectivity the space of possible rules is a *discrete combinatorial space* possessing no intrinsic spatial structure: all the possible rules simply lie next to each other without forming neighborhoods or other spatial arrangements. We can, on the other hand, impose a particular order on the rules to reveal the distribution of singularities. One strategy involves arranging the rules in such a way that those belonging to the same class end up as neighbors. A procedure that yields this result starts by defining two extremes, the most homogenous and the most heterogeneous of rules, and then reconstructs the full space by starting at the fully homogenous end and slowly increasing the degree of heterogeneity until the other end is reached.[9] The structure of the resulting possibility space suggests that the four rule classes are indeed distributed in a particular order, with class IV sandwiched between class II and class III and occupying a zone much smaller than the zones on either side of it.[10] This means that class IV rules are not only singular by representing a capacity maximum but also by being relatively rare.

Because the interaction rules for Life belong to class IV the existence and distribution of these singularities gives us the mechanism-
independent component of the explanation for the tendency of
natural patterns like gliders to emerge in it. Gliders are a precondition
for the emergence of a Turing machine but the latter also needs a
whole variety of engineered patterns to serve as its component parts,
and these other components do not emerge spontaneously but are
the result of countless hours of skilled human labor. In other words,
human capacities are also needed for that emergence. Conceivably
we could replace human skills by an impersonal evolutionary process
to discover and assemble the engineered patterns but that would still
not justify the assertion that class IV rules by themselves imply the
emergence of complex automata. This error, caused by a confusion
between mechanisms and mechanism-independent structure, is
compounded by the fact that not only can a Turing machine be built
out of gliders, glider guns, and other patterns but so can a *universal*
Turing machine. The Turing machines discussed so far are special purpose automata built to carry out a specific computational task stored
as a program in their tapes. But a universal Turing machine is an
automaton that can simulate any special purpose Turing machine, its
memory tape including among other things an executable symbolic
description of the automaton it is supposed to simulate. Today's
personal computers are an approximation to a universal Turing
machine, the cheaper and more abundant their memory the closer
the approximation.

The reason why this amplifies the philosophical error of not keeping the two components of an explanation separate is that computer
simulations like that of the thunderstorm, as well as all the others yet
to be described, are carried out on these approximations to a universal
Turing machine. In other words, computational universality is a precondition for the simulation of physical, chemical, biological, and
social processes. This can lead to the mistaken idea that the material
universe itself is a giant cellular automaton using class IV rules in
which all actual processes are the equivalent of simulations.[11] There
is indeed a connection between cellular automata and physical processes but this link needs to be explored more carefully. Physicists did
not take cellular automata seriously until it was shown that a population of finite state automata could mimic the behavior of important

differential equations, equations similar to those used in the thunder-storm simulation except that they also include the effects of viscosity on fluid flow. This different type of cellular automata are referred to as *lattice-gas* automata. While it is relatively uninformative to say that a universal Turing machine built within a cellular automaton can simulate physical processes, to say that a lattice-gas automaton can directly simulate patterns of flow does generate a new insight: it adds the isomorphic behavior of patterns of automaton states to the already known isomorphism between the behavior of solutions to differential equations and the behavior of physical processes. And this added isomorphism needs to be explained.

Before describing lattice-gas automata we need to discuss in more detail the physical processes that are the target of the simulation as well as the modeling strategies that have proved successful in the past and that must be used in conjunction with the simulation. We argued in the previous chapter that scientific models take advantage of the decomposability of reality made possible by emergent properties. One scientific field, for example, can take for granted not only the exis-tence of temperature and pressure but also the tendency of gradients of these two properties to dissipate, as long as it goes on to explain larger processes in which those gradients are component parts, such as the internal mechanism of a steam engine. Another field can then explain how those macro-properties emerge from the interaction among micro-components and their properties (molecules and their kinetic energy and momentum) and why gradients possess the ten-dencies they do. This other field, of course, takes for granted the prop-erties of molecules themselves, treating them as solid spheres endowed with the capacity to collide and redistribute their energy, so another scientific field needs to account for the emergence of these properties in terms of their even smaller components (electrons, protons, neu-trons). These three fields are, respectively, classical thermodynamics, statistical mechanics, and quantum mechanics.

Lattice-gas automata operate at the same level of scale than statisti-cal mechanics and borrows some of its methods. In particular, statisti-cal mechanics must deal with entire molecular populations in order to account for processes like gradient degradation so it cannot deal with molecules individually: even a perfectly rigid sphere has six degrees of freedom being capable of changing its position and momentum in three different directions. In other words, the state space for a single molecule is already six-dimensional, the space of possibilities for the whole population being literally unsurveyable. To reduce the number of degrees of freedom models in statistical mechanics must carefully choose an intermediate spatial scale that is large relative to the size of the molecules but small relative to the physical process being explained, and then use averages at that intermediate scale as its elementary components.[12] This strategy for bridging the micro and macro scales is also used in lattice-gas automata: choosing an intermediate scale that is large enough relative to the size of a single cell but small relative to what emerges from the interactions between cells. The use of intermediate averages as component parts implies that in lattice-gas automata the images displayed on the computer screen are the result of the average behavior of many individual automata not single automata states as in Life. A second difference has to do with the arrow of time. In Life the future of a given cell is entirely determined by the rules but its past is not: a given Life pattern may be arrived at by a variety of sequences of precursor patterns. In lattice-gas automata, on the other hand, the two directions of time must be equally deterministic because the molecular collisions they simulate exhibit this indifference to a direction of time. Classical thermodynamics not only takes temperature or pressure for granted it also assumes the existence of an arrow of time pointing from past to future, that this, it assumes that the temporal order in which a series of events occurs influences its outcome. But if we want to explain the emergence of this dependence on temporal order we must start with component parts in which the arrow of time does not yet exist. In the case of lattice-gas automata this implies that the rules defining the interactions between cells must be fully invertible.[13]

Finally, unlike Life in which a glider's capacity to move is emergent and in which the outcomes of collisions between gliders are also emergent, in lattice-gas automata both the motion of molecules and the results of their collisions are directly specified by rules and are therefore not emergent.[14] On the other hand, the larger scale phenomena that result from these collisions do emerge spontaneously. It is relatively simple, for example, to create a lattice-gas automaton that simulates the dissipation of a gradient and the reaching of equilibrium.[15] But what happens in situations in which the gradient is not allowed to cancel itself, that is, when it feeds on another gradient and exports its own disorder elsewhere? In fluid dynamics these situations are called "instabilities" because the existence of a live gradient is unstable (given its tendency to dissipate) and because the free energy it contains can amplify small featureless fluctuations into complex patterns. The convection cells we discussed in the previous chapter as component parts of thunderstorms are one example of a flow pattern induced by an instability. Another instability familiar in laboratories (the Kelvin–Helmoltz instability) is driven by a gradient of velocity created when two flows of different densities rub against one another, such as air moving over a water surface. The emergent flow patterns in this case are vortices. Yet another well-known laboratory example (the Rayleigh–Taylor instability) is created when a dense, heavy fluid is accelerated by a light one. This density gradient produces characteristic fingering or branching patterns as the heavy fluid invades and displaces the light one. All of these flow patterns have been observed to emerge spontaneously in lattice-gas automata.[16]

Although visually striking the emergence of these patterns is less of a mystery than that which takes place in simulations using mathematical equations. The reason is that while equations do not include any information about the microscopic dynamics behind flow patterns in lattice-gas automata the isomorphism with molecular populations is partially built in. Most cellular automata, for example, rely on strictly local interactions (only cells that are spatial neighbors can affect each other) that are defined by the exact same rules (all cells are treated uniformly). But the properties of locality and uniformity also define molecular populations in which there is no action at a distance and in which every member is identical to every other one. Other properties, such as the invertibility of the rules, are explicitly designed to imitate the reversibility of molecular interactions. This implies that a lattice-gas automaton started with a random configuration will remain entirely random mimicking the fact that in the material world nothing interesting happens if we start a process with a maximally disordered state, such as that of a fully degraded gradient.[17] To obtain the flow patterns just described, for instance, we must start the simulation in a configuration that contains a live gradient.

Two other key properties of molecular populations, conservation and symmetry, also have correspondences in either the rules or in the geometry of the cells. It is well known, for example, that certain quantities (such as the quantity of energy) are conserved in physical processes: energy cannot spontaneously be created or destroyed. The rules of lattice-gas automata map energy into the number of states representing individual molecules and this number is always conserved. Symmetry refers to the indifference that the regularities in the behavior of molecular populations display to being transformed in certain ways. Rotating a population, for example, leaves its behavioral regularities unchanged, otherwise experiments conducted in our spinning planet would give results entirely different in laboratories oriented in different directions. Lattice-gas automata using cells with a square shape do not have enough rotational symmetry (they remain invariant only for rotations of 90 degrees) introducing artifacts into a simulation. Hexagonal cells, on the other hand, have enough rotational invariance to avoid such artifacts.[18] Because some isomorphism is already built into lattice-gas automata their ability to reproduce patterns of flow is less problematic than that of the solutions to the equations of fluid dynamics. Nevertheless, the explanation still provides some philosophical insight because it identifies some key properties (invertibility, conservation, and symmetry) that are shared by the simulations and the equations and that help explain why the solutions to the latter can exhibit the regularities that they do.

In addition, lattice-gas automata complement mathematical models in a novel way. In the models used in statistical mechanics, for example, certain assumptions must be made about the likelihood of different spatial arrangements. In a model of gradient dissipation, for example, we must assume that the disordered state at the end of the process is much more probable than the ordered one at the start, an assumption that must be justified on separate grounds. But with lattice-gas automata we can actually follow the molecular population until it reaches a given spatial arrangement. This is an important capacity of simulations not shared by mathematical equations: the ability to stage a process and track it as it unfolds. Moreover, several runs of the same simulation can be carried out changing the values assigned to certain parameters and tracking the unfolding process to check whether it arrives at the same final state. Since the values of the parameters represent assumptions made about the environment on which the simulated process takes place, varying them in different runs is equivalent to checking whether the outcome is robust to changes in the assumptions. In other words, each run of a simulation is like an experiment conducted in a laboratory except that it uses numbers and formal operators as its raw materials. For these and other reasons computer simulations may be thought as occupying an intermediate position between that of formal theory and laboratory experiment.[19]

Lattice-gas automata provide an important link between the subject matter of this chapter and that of the previous one. It is time, however, to move beyond populations of identical elements whose identity is not altered by their interactions. In other words, we must leave the relative simplicity of physics behind and move to the more complex world of chemistry, specifically, the chemistry of the prebiotic soup. The molecular populations composing the primordial medium in which organisms and their genetic code emerged depart in two ways from the ones examined so far: most of the members of a population change identity in the course of their interactions resulting in the synthesis of entirely new compounds, while those that retain their identity (catalysts) are capable of affecting that synthesis by accelerating it or decelerating it. Controlling the relative rapidity or slowness with which new compounds are produced is a very singular capacity, one that as we will see is as important for the emergence of living creatures as is the capacity for self-replication itself.

CHAPTER THREE
Artificial Chemistries and the Prebiotic Soup

So far we have examined questions of emergence in the relatively simple case of a body of water in which gradients of properties like temperature, density, or speed cause the spontaneous organization of the molecules into collective patterns of flow. We can continue to use a body of water as our basic environment but in order to add a new layer of complexity we must make its composition less homogenous. This means that new gradients must be introduced: *gradients of concentration* of substances other than water. These new gradients are also characterized by a tendency to dissipate but unlike the old ones countering that tendency involves the injection of a flow of matter not just a flow of energy. The effect of that injection will, in turn, depend on the specific chemical substances being injected. Some substances, for instance, have a tendency to donate or export some of their protons, basically hydrogen atoms deprived of their electrons. These substances are called "acids." Other substances have the tendency to act as acceptors or importers of protons and are called "bases." When concentrations of substances with these opposite tendenciess come into contact, forming an acid–base or Ph gradient, a spontaneous flow of protons from one chemical species to another is generated as the means used by the gradient to cancel itself. Another example of a chemical gradient is an oxidation–reduction or redox gradient created when a substance that has a tendency to oxidize, that is, to donate electrons, comes into contact with one that has a tendency to reduce or accept electrons. A redox gradient can drive an electron flow across chemical species when it occurs, for example, in an aqueous environment in the presence of concentrations of metallic substances.

Chemical gradients like these are thought to have played an important role in the dynamics of the prebiotic soup.[1] But in addition to new gradients exploring the primordial medium in which living creatures first emerged involves considering interactions in which different molecules can bond and form a new compound or, on the contrary, in which compounds can be broken down into their component parts. This leads not only to much larger combinatorial spaces with atoms and molecules of different species entering into innumerable possible combinations, but more importantly, forces us to invent new means to explore possibility spaces that are *intrinsically open-ended*: if chemical interactions lead to the formation of a compound not originally present in a mixture, and if this compound is produced in large enough quantities to yield a concentration gradient, then the very nature of the mixture as well as that of its possibility space is changed. In other words, the inherent open-endedness of chemical interactions allows possibilities not originally present in a space to be subsequently added to it. The philosophical interest of the prebiotic soup is that by definition it does not contain any living creatures in it and yet it has the capacity to lead to a novel situation in which such creatures do exist. Thus, both mechanisms and mechanism-independent structure change radically once we reach the level of chemistry and its heterogeneous molecular populations.

What types of molecules in addition to water can we assume were part of these prebiotic populations? The most promising candidates are molecules called *polymers* that are arranged in long linear chains. In contemporary organisms both genes and the proteins these genes code for are polymers differing only in their composition: proteins use amino acids as component parts while genes use nucleotides. Today most proteins are synthesized from instructions contained in genes so we face a chicken-and-egg dilemma when trying to decide what came first: genes are needed to create proteins but proteins are needed to construct and maintain the bodies that carry those genes. Proteins, on the other hand, can also be synthesized without the help of genes and their component parts have a higher probability to form spontaneously than those of genes.[2] So we will assume that polymers made out of amino acids were the type of molecule originally populating the prebiotic soup. These polymers must have been much less complex than those composing living creatures today but they could have increased in complexity simply by adding an extra amino acid at one of their ends. The problem with this route to greater complexity is that the chemical reaction that adds that extra component (called "polymerization") is not favored by an aqueous environment, the presence of water promoting instead the breaking down of long chains into shorter ones. But if we assume that these primordial polymers managed to tap into physical or chemical gradients they could have used that energy to accelerate polymerization producing longer chains faster than the rate at which they were broken down by water.

A chemical reaction may involve several steps, some of which take place in the opposite direction of gradient dissipation and are therefore energetically less favorable. Adding energy from an external gradient can transform a step from "uphill" to "downhill," that is, from a step that does not take place spontaneously to one that does, removing it as an obstacle and accelerating the overall reaction. The only drawback to this solution to the polymerization problem is its lack of specificity: external gradients can accelerate many different chemical reactions, some of which may interfere with polymer growth. So a better solution would combine the energy stored in gradients with some form of *molecular recognition*, the simplest kind of which is a geometrical complementarity between two different molecules, one acting as a "lock" the other as a "key." Putting together these two capacities yields a *catalyst*. Metallic crystals, for example, can act as powerful catalysts: they can attach themselves to a molecule twisting it or otherwise deforming it, pushing it away from equilibrium and creating a gradient. This physical gradient is similar to those that exist in most load-bearing structures, such as buildings or bridges, in which the structural elements carrying the load are typically deformed— stretched if the load is carried in tension, shrunk if in compression— and are for that reason loaded with strain energy. After a metallic catalyst attaches to and deforms its target a step in a chemical reaction that was energetically uphill before the deformation is now downhill and will have a better chance of occurring spontaneously.

We can imagine that with the right metallic catalysts added as ingredients to the prebiotic soup polymerization could have been enhanced allowing the existing polymers to grow in complexity. But an even better solution would be if the polymers themselves had catalytic capacities because as they facilitated their own growth in length and complexity they could also increase their catalytic powers further enhancing their complexification. In other words, if polymers could act as their own catalysts they would generate a self-stimulating process that would increase their complexity exponentially. Some contemporary proteins, called *enzymes*, can act as more powerful and specific catalysts than metallic crystals. They can manipulate the flows of protons and electrons driven by Ph and redox gradients but without relying on intense concentrations of substances that would be harmful to an organism. Some of the amino acids that compose digestive enzymes, for instance, can interact with one another to act as a proton shuttle, transferring positively charged particles to and from a target. These amino acids may form the active site of the enzyme (the part that locks into its target) so they combine the capacity for molecular recognition with that for gradient manipulation. And similarly for redox gradients: if a piece of a metal atom, an iron or copper ion, for example, is inserted into an enzyme it can in combination with the amino acids in the active site act as an electron shuttle. Both proton and electron flows can be used to turn an uphill step in a chemical reaction into a downhill one accelerating the overall reaction with high specificity.[3]

These gradient-manipulation mechanisms bring us closer to a solution to the polymerization problem but there is still an obstacle: both of these mechanisms have been identified in enzymes belonging to contemporary organisms but these are the product of millions of years of evolution, an evolution that presupposes the existence of the genetic code. The spontaneously assembled polymers in the primordial soup could not have possessed these finely tuned capacities since they were much shorter and less complex than their counterparts today. We seem to face another chicken-and-egg dilemma: polymers need gradients to increase in length and past a threshold of length they themselves can acquire the capacity to manipulate those gradients, but it is unclear how they reach the critical length in the first place. One possible way out of the dilemma is *cooperation*: a polymer could catalyze the formation of another polymer which, in turn, catalyses the formation of the first. Once this closed circuit is formed other polymers can be inserted into it if they catalyze a reaction producing one of the existing members and if their own production is catalyzed by another member. In this way an *autocatalytic loop* may spontaneously form and then grow. The closure of such a cooperative network of catalysts would endow it with stability against disruption by perturbations and allow it to concentrate the resources needed for growth (amino acids, short polymers) into itself. To the extent that these resources are used for the benefit of all the cooperating members the loop as a whole behaves as a proto-metabolism, trapping and digesting "food." It is these emergent autocatalytic loops that are the real solution to the polymerization problem and hence constitute the main characters in the prebiotic drama.

Let's summarize what has been said so far. The problem of the emergence of living creatures in an inorganic world has a well-defined causal structure. The mechanisms involved are all chemical in nature: the creation of bonds between amino acids to create proteins; the acceleration of bond creation to compensate for the spontaneous destruction promoted by an aqueous environment, an acceleration explained by the manipulation of gradients; the use of a lock-and-key mechanism to perform molecular recognition and focus the effects of gradient manipulation on specific targets; and finally, the formation of cooperative networks of catalytic polymers acting as proto-metabolisms. Although these chemical mechanisms are relatively well known there are still gaps in our understanding. The recognition mechanism, for example, has only been partly explained. For enzymes to have this capacity their one-dimensional structure must be folded into a three-dimensional shape with the right geometric features. The folding problem has not yet been solved, its study consuming more supercomputer time than any other problem. In what follows the complexities of the folding process will be ignored to concentrate on the increase in length of the chains. In other words, we will assume that longer chains have more complex emergent catalytic and recognition capacities than shorter ones. In addition, as it has been argued in previous chapters, a causal explanation in terms of mechanisms must be supplemented with a mechanism-independent component: an elucidation of the structure of the space of possibilities associated with the prebiotic soup to determine whether its singularities make the existence of autocatalytic loops not just possible but also highly probable.

In fact, we need to examine two possibility spaces: the space of possible polymers of different lengths and compositions and the space of possible chemical reactions that can produce those polymers. The probability that an autocatalytic loop can spontaneously form can then be assessed by a theoretical examination of these two spaces and the actual emergence of such a loop tracked using computer simulations. The first thing that needs to be evaluated is the size of the two possibility spaces. The number of possible polymers of a given length is the number of available components raised to the maximum length. In the proteins used by contemporary organisms the repertoire of components is limited to only 20 amino acids. Nevertheless even a very short polymer five amino acids long can exist in over three million different combinations (the number 20 raised to the fifth power). The number of possible polymers 300 amino acids long, the length of a small contemporary enzyme, is literally infinite. Thus, we are considering possibility spaces that grow explosively as the length of the polymers increases. Next we need to estimate the number of possible chemical reactions that can produce this infinity of combinations, that is, the number of reactions that can glue (or condense) two shorter chains into a longer one, and vice versa, cut (or cleave) a long chain into two shorter ones. For any given polymer there are many different reactions that could produce it: a single amino acid can be attached at one end of an existing chain; or two shorter chains can be condensed together; or three even shorter ones can be used, each perhaps the product of the cleavage of longer ones. The existence of multiple ways to produce each polymer implies that the number of possible chemical reactions grows even faster than the number of protein species as the length of the chains increases.[4]

Finally we need estimate the distribution of catalytic capacities, a task that is impossible to perform without solving the folding problem. A possible way out of this difficulty would be to assume that given the infinity of both possible protein species and chemical reactions the specific distribution of catalytic capacities does not matter much. We can assume random distributions, acknowledging our ignorance of the details, and still reach some valuable conclusions. All that we need to know is the likelihood that a series of catalyzed reactions interconnected to form a closed loop can emerge spontaneously. This can be estimated by creating a graph in which each protein species becomes a point and each chemical reaction between two proteins becomes a edge joining two points. The fact that as length increases the number of possible reactions grows faster than that of protein species means that the number of ways of interconnecting the points grows faster than the number of points. At a certain critical length the number of possible connections relative to that of points is so large that the probability that some catalytic proteins are connected into a closed loop becomes very high.[5] This argument is similar to the one used to explain the tendency of gradients to dissipate. But as in that case, our confidence in the conclusion would be greatly strengthened if we could actually follow the process in a simulation, tracking the population of polymers as they get longer and checking if closed loops have indeed formed. These simulations are collectively known as "artificial chemistries." Some artificial chemistries are discrete simulations that explicitly represent each individual polymer and in which the interactions between chains depend on their composition. Others use continuous differential equations ignoring the details of individual interactions and focusing instead on rates of change: the rate at which cleavage and condensation reactions take place, the rates at which concentrations of polymers of a given length form, and so on.

The continuous approach, called *metadynamics*, models the primordial body of water in which polymer evolution took place as a chemical reaction vessel (or "reactor"). The reactor is driven by a gradient of "food," that is, by an external flow of monomers and short polymers. At any one point in time the reactor contains a large but finite number of chemical reactions, a number that can be reduced if we impose a threshold of concentration below which the presence of a particular species can be considered insignificant. Thus, at any given instant we can model the dynamics of the reactor by a finite number of equations, one for each chemical reaction, the entire set of equations possessing a single state space. Assuming that the chemical reactions are reversible allows us to further simplify things because in that case the possibility space for the reactor is structured by a single singularity: a steady-state attractor defining a stable distribution of concentrations of polymers of different species. On the other hand, unlike the state spaces of physics in which the number of dimensions is given in advance and does not change, in metadynamics the number of reactions does change and so does the number of dimensions of the space. Keeping track of the increase in the number of dimensions can be done by coupling a state space to a graph like the one just discussed, a graph capturing the existing polymer species and their chemical interactions.[6] Thus, metadynamic simulations explore *two coupled possibility spaces*: the graph gives us the structure of the space of possible chemical reactions while the singularities of the state space provide the structure of the space of possible outcomes for a given set of reactions.

A typical run of a metadynamic simulation proceeds like this: inject some food into the reactor to create a gradient and get the dynamics going; follow the process until it reaches the steady-state attractor and check what polymer species are present above and below the threshold of concentration; add to the graph any new species that is above the threshold, erase any old species that is below it, and update the connecting edges to include the new possible chemical reactions; change the set of equations (and its associated state space) to reflect the change in composition of the reactor; follow the new process until it reaches a new steady state, adjusting the graph and the equations to include new polymer species and reactions. This series of steps is then repeated many times until the composition of the reactor stops changing. At that point another steady-state attractor is reached (called a "metadynamical fixed point") but this time it is a singularity representing the long-term tendencies of the entire series of reactions, and it is therefore much more important that all the intervening ones.[7] Once at the metadynamical fixed point we look at the graph to see if it contains nodes connected by edges into a closed network. If such a closed network exists it implies that, had the simulated reactor been populated by individual polymers, they would have formed an auto-catalytic loop. Finally, the simulation is performed several times varying the values of certain control parameters—the degree to which water affects the reactions; the rate at which food is fed into the soup; the distribution of catalytic capacities in the polymer population—to check that the emergence of the loop occurs over a wide range of values and it is not just an artifact.[8] The results of the metadynamic simulations that have actually been performed show that the spontaneous emergence of a proto-metabolism is indeed a likely outcome, one that could have occurred in prebiotic conditions.

To further reduce the likelihood that the result is an artifact we can try to reproduce it using other simulations based on entirely different principles. To be truly different this other simulation should not rely on macro-properties like overall rates of concentration but rather enact micro-interactions between explicit representations of individual polymers and let those interactions generate the concentrations. Like metadynamics the new simulation can exploit the similarity between linear chains of molecules and linear strings of symbols, but it must not employ the strings as mere labels for an entire species of polymers. Instead, it must use them to capture the behavior of individual polymers. In particular, a symbol string must capture the double life of an enzyme: on one hand, an enzyme is simply a chain of amino acids that can be acted upon to be cleaved into parts or be condensed into larger wholes; on the other hand, after this chain has folded into a three-dimensional form, an enzyme is an entity with the capacity to act on other chains breaking them up or gluing them together. The perfect candidate for a symbol string with such a double life would be a small computer program. When a computer program is copied from one hard disk to another, for example, it is treated as a mere chain of ones and zeroes, but when it is executed it becomes a procedure that can perform a variety of operations on other chains of ones and zeroes. Thus, computer programs lead the kind of double life that we need for the new artificial chemistry.

Not all programs, however, lend themselves to this task because we need to consider not only the capacity of a program to affect the data but also the capacity of the data to be affected by the program: programs that perform arithmetical operations, for example, demand that the data consists of numbers not words in English, while programs that perform linguistic operations need words not numbers. Similarly, in an artificial chemistry when a program is treated as a mere string of symbols it must have the right capacities to be affected: the symbol string must be able to undergo random cleavages and condensations and still retain enough coherence to be executed as a program. Programs written in conventional languages contain mechanical recipes specified step by step—using special constructions to repeat series of steps and to transfer control from one recipe to another—and these recipes are completely destroyed if we add to them, or delete from them, random pieces of code. But a different family of programming languages, called "recursive function languages," does not specify computer programs as step-by-step recipes but simply as transformations of inputs into outputs, that is, as functions, and moreover, as functions that can take other functions as inputs and produce yet other functions as outputs. This means that a complex program can be built using a part-to-whole relation: complex functions can be created out of simple functions which are composed of even simpler ones, all the way down to operations that are directly executable. The resulting complex functions can be expressed as symbol strings, with parentheses separating the different nested components, strings that have a much higher chance of remaining coherent after being acted upon by other functions.[9]

Using a recursive function language a folded polymer with catalytic capacities can be represented by a string of symbols with the ability to affect other strings, while the unfolded polymer that is the target of the catalyst can be represented by a symbol string with the capacity to be affected by other strings. When these two strings interact a third string results representing the product of the chemical reaction catalyzed by the enzyme. To simplify the simulation spatial relations are not modeled explicitly, that is, the simulated polymers are not related to one another by relations of proximity. This is equivalent to assuming that the chemical reactor is subjected to a constant stirring motion that destroys all neighborhood relations between polymers. In a well-stirred reactor all collisions between molecules are basically random so interactions between polymers can be modeled by randomly picking two symbol strings from the existing population, treating one as a program (enzyme) and the other as data (target substrate), then releasing their product back into the population. These chance encounters are influenced by the changing concentrations of symbol strings of the same "species," just as in a well-stirred reactor the frequency of collision between two polymers of different species would depend on how many members of each species exist in the chemical soup. Because recursive function languages have the computational capacity of the most sophisticated automata, and because of the random character of the collisions, this artificial chemistry is referred to as a *Turing gas*.[10]

A typical Turing gas simulation starts with a population of randomly constructed functions. The population, consisting of about 1,000 members, is then allowed to interact producing new functions. Some of these products are identical to others already present, others are novel in the sense of not having counterparts in the existing population, while yet others are absolutely novel in that they have never existed in the "history" represented by a particular run of the simulation. The population is deliberately kept constant, by randomly draining excess symbols strings from the gas, and this acts as a selection pressure: the only way for a simulated polymer to remain in the population for extended periods of time is by becoming the product of a stable series of interactions between functions. And, in turn, the only way for a series of interactions to be stable is to display catalytic closure.[11] The simplest autocatalytic loop is composed of a function that acts on a symbol string to produce another symbol string that, when treated as a function, produces the symbol string corresponding to the first function. Such closed sets of interacting functions have in fact been produced in Turing gas simulations and it can be shown that they correspond to singularities (invariant fixed points) of the dynamics of the system.

The results from Turing gases and metadynamics show that autocatalytic loops acting as proto-metabolisms are a recurrent feature in artificial chemistries using very different formal resources. This isomorphism, in turn, may be evidence of yet other isomorphism, one between simulated polymer populations and the real polymer populations inhabiting present day chemical reactors or ancient prebiotic soups. That is, the spaces of possibilities of the simulations and the real environments may exhibit sufficient overlap so that what we learn from the former can be used as the mechanism-independent part of the explanation of the latter. On the other hand, the spontaneous emergence of autocatalytic loops cannot fully account for the origin of life because these loops do not have the means to store information and to pass whatever advantages they may have acquired in catalytic efficiency and specificity to future generations. A possible solution to this problem relies on the fact that the results of these simulations also apply to polymers made out of nucleotides, polymers that do have the ability to act as templates in order to produce copies of themselves. Moreover while some chains of nucleotides, such as those characterizing contemporary DNA, do not have catalytic capacities, the chains composing some forms of RNA do have them, and this means that ancient RNA may have combined the ability to transmit information across generations with the property of catalytic closure. The following chapter will explore this scenario and the new capacity that emerges when a population of self-replicating molecules is coupled to any process that biases that replication one way or another: the capacity to perform a search in a space of possibilities.

CHAPTER FOUR
Genetic Algorithms and the Prebiotic Soup

A choice of a simple but significant starting point for an examination of emergence has proved important in the case of both physics and chemistry. A similar strategy will be useful when we move to the realm of biology. We must remain in an aqueous environment populated by molecules but add a new capacity: the ability to self-replicate. The simplest self-replicating entities are RNA molecules existing in a free state, that is, not encapsulated by a membrane or subordinated to the needs of an organism. To explain their mechanism of self-replication we do not have to consider the complex process used by living creatures, a process in which the genetic code and all its translation machinery are crucially involved. All that we need to account for is the relatively simple process through which an RNA molecule can serve as a template for the creation of a copy of itself. A population of these replicators, in turn, introduces a new kind of gradient, a gradient of fitness. Fitness refers to the differential reproductive success of embodied organisms but it can also be applied to molecular replicators and their different capacities to produce copies of themselves. It can be regarded as a gradient because fitness differences act just like temperature differences: as long as the differences exist they fuel a process of selection favoring the replication of one kind of polymer over another; the moment the differences disappear the selection process stops.[1]

Focusing on "naked" RNA molecules has therefore the advantage of adding only a minimal layer of complexity to the world we are exploring but a layer that already has many of the properties that separate biology from chemistry. An RNA molecule is simply a sequence of four possible nucleotides, each member of the set displaying clear tendencies to bond with just another member. If we refer to the four nucleotides using the conventional letters (A, C, G, U) we know that A's tend to bond with U's, and G's with C's. These tendencies, of course, need to be explained by yet other mechanisms but for the purpose of accounting for self-replication they can simply be assumed to exist. Given these tendencies a sequence of nucleotides can create a copy of itself using a mechanism similar to that of conventional photography: first a "negative" is created as complementary mono-mers attach themselves one by one to the template, and then a "posi-tive print" is produced from that negative. We also know that the amount of energy involved in forming the complementary chemical bonds is not that large, roughly equal to that of thermal fluctuations in an aqueous environment, and this implies that errors in the copy-ing process will tend to occur spontaneously. In other words, the copying errors or *mutations* that provide the necessary variability to prevent fitness gradients from disappearing do not need a separate explanation.[2]

Discussion of the mechanism-independent structure is also simpli-fied by starting with naked RNA because the possibility spaces associated with living organisms can become very numerous as the complexity of their part-to-whole organization increases. In the case of unicellular organisms like bacteria, for example, we must consider at least three different spaces: the space of possible genes; the space of possible structural proteins and enzymes that these genes code for; and the space of possible spatial structures and metabolic pathways that the structural proteins and enzymes can form. In other words, we need one possibility space for the hereditary information (the "genotype") and two possibility spaces for the bodily traits produced from that information (the "phenotype"). In multicellular organisms several other possibility spaces must be added since the phenotype also includes the space of possible cell types (such as muscle, bone, nerve, blood); the space of possible tissues and organs these cells can form; and the space of possible organisms these tissues and organs can compose. Moreover, in large animals the mapping of genotype into phenotype involves a complex embryological process that is only imperfectly understood. By contrast, naked RNA has a very simple relation between genotype and phenotype: the unfolded polymer constitutes the former while the folded version and its catalytic capacities constitutes the latter. This means that we need to consider only two possibility spaces: the space of possible sequences of the four nucleotides, the size of which is the number four raised to the length of the polymer, and the space of folded forms, a smaller space given that several different sequences of nucleotides can end up with equivalent folded forms.[3]

Like other discrete combinatorial spaces the space of possible RNA polymers is intrinsically amorphous. But we can impose an order on it as long as this is justified by reference to the mechanism of replication and as long as it serves to reveal the structure of the possibility space. Thus, knowing that the variation in a population of molecular replicators involves copying errors at specific points in a sequence we can arrange them so that each molecule has as neighbors other molecules differing from it by only one mutation. This space is multidimensional because it must include all the variants that can be created by varying one monomer along the full length of a given polymer, and each of these one-mutant variants must be assigned a different dimension of the space. But while the sheer number of dimensions makes the space very complex it also greatly simplifies the distribution of possible molecules: every possible polymer is in direct contact with all its one-mutant neighbors and a series of neighbors forms a connected path for evolution to follow. In other words, given this spatial arrangement molecular evolution can be visualized as a *continuous walk* from one neighbor to the next driven by events producing one mutation at a time.[4] To complete the characterization of the possibility space we must assign a fitness value to each of the possible polymers. Fitness refers in this case to the consequences for reproductive success of the catalytic capacities that each polymer would have if it were folded into a three-dimensional shape. We showed in the previous chapter how catalytic capacities exercised in cooperative networks can lead to the focusing of resources on a particular set of molecules so we can now take this for granted to concentrate on the effects of catalysis on rates of replication.

A possibility space of self-replicating entities to which fitness values have been assigned is called a *fitness landscape*. The structure of a given landscape depends both on the distribution of singularities, sequences of nucleotides with optimum fitness, and on how fitness varies in the neighborhood of those singularities. For example, if one-mutant neighbors have similar fitness then the singularities will form a distribution of local optima resembling the "peaks" of gently sloping "hills." If fitness varies greatly between neighbors, on the other hand, then the landscape will be more rugged with local optima peaks surrounded by steep "cliffs." Fitness landscapes are important because they complement the traditional model of evolution. In that model scarce environmental resources cause some replicators to be selected at the expense of others, a selection process explained by the capacity of the environment to affect the replicators. But we also need to consider the capacity of the replicators to be affected and this is what a fitness landscape captures. More specifically, in a landscape with many local optima separated by long distances, distance being measured in this case by the number of mutations needed to convert one sequence into another, selection pressures alone cannot account for particular outcomes.[5] An evolving population may, for example, be trapped in a local optimum if the path to a singularity with greater fitness passes through points of much lesser fitness. In this case selection pressures alone cannot dislodge the population from the trap. Thus, to the extent that molecular evolution can be modeled as a walk along a continuous path of one-mutant neighbors the "topography" of the fitness landscape must be part of the model since it facilitates or obstructs those walks.

A precise characterization of this topography would imply knowledge of the exact fitness value of each folded polymer. But even without this quantitative information we can get a sense of the qualitative characteristics of a landscape: whether it has a single global optimum or many local optima, for example, or whether the neighborhood of those singularities is smooth or rugged. An important factor determining this qualitative structure is the degree to which the different components of a polymer interact to determine fitness. When reproductive success is determined by catalytic capacity interactions between components matter because as an RNA polymer folds two or more nucleotides from different parts of the sequence may end up together forming the part of the catalyst that recognizes its target, causing the fitness of the polymer to depend on several components at once. By systematically varying the degree of interaction among components we can determine the effects that this factor has on the topography of the landscape. At one extreme there are no interactions and the landscape is structured by a single global optimum: one best catalyst surrounded by mutants declining smoothly in fitness. At the other extreme, when the fitness of the polymer involves interactions between all its components, the landscape is structured by many local optima around which fitness decreases steeply. The first extreme makes evolution entirely predictable while the second one makes it entirely unfeasible. The interesting cases are, therefore, those corresponding to intermediate degrees of interaction. A particularly important case is obtained when the number of components that interact is small relative to the length of the polymer: in that case there are many local optima with relatively high fitness, their sides slope smoothly, and the highest peaks tend to be grouped together in particular areas of the landscape.[6]

To understand how the structure of the possibility space affects evolutionary walks we also need to determine what exactly performs the walk. Is it, for example, individual replicators competing against each other or is it entire groups competing with other groups? When considering the evolution of large animals and plants the first alternative is more plausible while the second one is more adequate to deal with molecular populations the members of which can be converted into each other by a single mutation. Let's imagine a particular RNA polymer with very high fitness located at a local optimum with smooth slopes. Spontaneous mutations will tend to produce many one-mutant neighbors with similar fitness. These neighbors can also mutate to produce slightly less fit two-mutant neighbors that, in turn, can generate three-mutant neighbors and so on. As we move away from the fittest polymer the number of viable mutants decreases until their number fades to zero, the entire set forming a coherent *cloud of mutants*. Although the cloud contains a fittest member this dominant type may not be the one that reproduces the most, as it would if the competition was among single replicators. The reason is that a non-dominant mutant that is surrounded by very fit ones can out reproduce the dominant one, not because of its own capacity to make copies of itself but because its neighbors can by a single mutation create copies of it. This amplification of reproductive success by nearby mutants means that the cloud as a whole, a so-called "quasi-species", becomes the target of selection.[7]

Let's imagine a mutant cloud moving over a fitness landscape in which local optima of different heights are distributed in relative proximity, the cloud initially clustered around a local optimum with the dominant sequence at the peak. As evolution proceeds part of the cloud may stumble upon another nearby optimum of higher fitness. At that moment the initial cloud will melt and re-condense around the new singularity. This means that when a whole cloud of mutants moves in a fitness landscape the overall movement is not a random walk, as one would expect given the randomness of mutations, but *a search*: not a search with a goal, of course, but a groping in the dark that is nevertheless better at finding local optima of higher fitness than a random walk. A crucial factor behind this searching capacity is the rate at which copying errors are made, that is, the mutation rate. If the mutation rate is zero the cloud does not form while if it is too high the internal coherence of the cloud is destroyed. As before, it is the intermediate values that yield the interesting cases. In addition, the length of the polymers must be taken into account since the longer the molecular chain the more possible mutants it can have. These two factors together determine what is called the *error threshold*, a singularity similar to a phase transition because beyond the threshold the "liquid" cloud tends to "vaporize." The theory of quasi-species predicts that clouds with the capacity to search a fitness landscape will tend to lie near the error threshold, that is, to have as many mutations as possible without suffering disintegration. Evidence that this is in fact the case comes from laboratory studies of the only contemporary organisms that use RNA to store genetic information, viruses. Studies of viral populations, as well as of populations of naked RNA extracted from those viruses, confirm that they tend to form quasi-species existing in the vicinity of the error threshold.[8]

As in previous chapters we can derive further philosophical insight if in addition to considering the theoretical treatment of evolutionary walks on fitness landscapes we could actually follow those walks in a simulation. The replicators in these simulations could be equally "naked," that is, exist in a disembodied state and have the simplest relationship between genotype and phenotype. Simulations using the simplest strings of symbols as genotypes (strings of ones and zeroes) into which potential solutions to phenotypic problems are coded by hand would be adequate for the task. These naked evolutionary simulations, called *genetic algorithms*, are so simple that none of the components of an evolutionary process—fitness, selection, self-replication—is in fact emergent. Fitness can be considered to emerge spontaneously in a simulation if the reproductive success of a given genotype depends on the way the phenotype it codes for actually exercises its capacity to solve survival problems, at the very least the problem of how to extract energy from environmental gradients. In other words, if the phenotype has a simulated metabolism and if the capacity of the genotype to create copies of itself depends on possession of a minimum of metabolized energy, then the evaluation of its fitness is performed within the simulation itself.[9] In genetic algorithms, by contrast, fitness is evaluated from the outside by a procedure to discriminate good from bad solutions to a problem, a procedure called a "fitness function." Once each symbol string has been assigned a problem-solving value another procedure, called a "selection function," uses those values to choose what strings will be incorporated into the next generation and how many copies of each will be produced. In other words, the tendency of different replicators to increase in frequency with each generation does not emerge from competition but is dictated by rules that translate problem-solving ability into reproductive success. Finally, the symbol strings are mostly inert: the copying process is performed for them by another procedure that applies to them a mutation operator to produce variation prior to releasing them back into the population. This means that mutations do not occur spontaneously as the strings create faulty copies of themselves.

The only thing that emerges in simulations using genetic algorithms is specific solutions to specific problems. The fact that the latter are posed by the experimenter makes the problems themselves somewhat artificial but within this limited domain the solutions are indeed found by evolutionary search. A typical simulation of this type takes the form of a cycle: apply the fitness function to the current population of symbol strings to evaluate their problem-solving abilities; use the selection function to decide what fit strings will make copies of themselves; apply the mutation operator to the selected strings to generate variation and form the next generation; repeat all four steps until a globally or locally optimal solution has been found.[10] The problems to which genetic algorithms are applied have often nothing to do with biology. A good illustration in an industrial context is the control of a pipeline for natural gas. A pipeline must link the point of supply of natural gas to its point of consumption or distribution using a series of compressors linked by pipes. The problem is to determine the relation between the suction pressure of each compressor to its discharge pressure (the pressure gradient between input and output) in such a way as to minimize the overall electrical power consumed. In other words, the problem is to find the combination of pressure values for each compressor that optimizes the efficiency of energy use. If for the sake of simplicity we imagine that each compressor can have pressure values between zero and fifteen then a string of four ones and zeroes will be enough to represent it, the string "0000" representing the minimum value and "1111" representing the maximum one. Since we have many compressors several of these "genes" must be concatenated to form the entire "chromosome." Finally, a fitness function must be created to evaluate the power consumption of each combination of values for different compressors as well as to enforce global constraints, such as the minimum or maximum of pressure allowed in the pipeline. When a population of these variable replicators is unleashed in a computer it can find the optimal combination of pressure values for the entire pipeline in a highly efficient way.[11]

Unlike this industrial application using genetic algorithms to model naked RNA in the primordial soup runs into some unsolved problems. While the simulated genotype is still relatively simple to build— the four nucleotides being easily expressed in binary form as 00, 01, 10, 11—creating a phenotype implies transforming a one-dimensional chain of simulated nucleotides into a three-dimensional folded form. But as we saw in the previous chapter a reliable mechanical recipe to perform the folding operation does not yet exist. Neither does a method to evaluate the catalytic capacity that such a folded form would have, an evaluation that would be needed to create a fitness function. So simulations of prebiotic conditions must settle for less: while the full three-dimensional shape cannot be generated an intermediate step in the folding process involving a two-dimensional shape (a "secondary structure") can be reliably produced. And while we cannot calculate the catalytic capacity from this intermediate form we can calculate the energetic stability that the folded form would have.[12] This measure of fitness is justified because an unstable shape would not last long enough to exercise its catalytic capacities. If we think of a folded RNA polymer as the form produced by a gradient as it dissipates, then the stable folded forms would be those that managed to achieve a combination of bonds that fully dissipate the gradient. This stability can be calculated from the secondary structure and used to evaluate fitness.

Given this simplified relation between genotype and phenotype a genetic algorithm can be used to follow a population of simulated RNA molecules across many generations and check whether stable forms emerge that can become the centers of quasi-species. One simulation, for example, started with a population of 3,000 strings, each 70 components long, but in which all components were identical. Since such a homogenous string would be incapable of folding the population started its evolutionary walk at a zone in the landscape that was a "flat plain" of very low fitness, and it had to find and climb a "hill" representing a local optimum. The most important parameter that could be varied in the simulation was the mutation rate, the frequency with which copying errors were made, since as we saw before this partly determines the coherence of the mutant cloud. The mutation rate is normally kept fixed in most applications of genetic algorithms but in this one it had to be varied from one run of the simulation to another to test the existence of the error threshold. The results of the simulation conformed to the theoretical prediction: the population of strings eventually found a local optimum and became capable of folding (as inferred from the secondary structure) but only if the error rate was below the critical threshold.[13] This is a relatively limited result particularly if we consider what the eventual goal of this kind of simulations would have to be: to show how the searching capacity of molecular replicators could have led to the emergence of the genetic code. And not only the code itself, that is, the rigid correspondence between three nucleotides in one type of polymer (genes) and a single amino acid in another type (proteins), but the means to reliably and routinely translate one into the other.

While the naked replicators of genetic algorithms are ideal to model the primordial soup prior to the emergence of the genetic code a different approach is needed to track evolution after that singular event. In particular, we need the means to increase the level of embodiment of the replicators given that the coupling of genes and proteins could not have occurred without the encapsulation of these interacting polymers within primitive membranes. And as we consider more embodied replicators the relation between genotype and phenotype must be modeled in more detail. Even the earliest cellular organisms had to solve metabolic problems by using their limited repertoire of proteins and enzymes as recombinable components to form primitive chemical circuits. So simulations of cellular evolution must have the necessary resources to give rise to simple part-to-whole relations between different levels of the phenotype. And if these relations are to be inheritable the genotype itself must be modeled by symbol strings capable of incremental compositionality. In the previous chapter we saw that simple forms of chemical circuitry (autocatalytic loops) could emerge in a soup of symbol strings belonging to a recursive function language, that is, in a Turing gas. We also saw that those languages allow for complex computer programs to be generated using a part-to-whole relation: the simplest functions can be used to create more complex functions that, in turn, can enter into even more complex ones. The computer programs so generated can be expressed as symbol strings in which the nested functions at different levels are separated by parentheses. The branch of evolutionary computation using these more sophisticated symbol strings is called *genetic programming*.

In fact, in genetic programming the simulated chromosomes are not implemented as strings but as graphs having the form of a tree. This eliminates the pleasing similarity between a chain of molecules and a string of symbols but compensates for it by clearly displaying the part-to-whole relation between problems and subproblems: the overall metabolic task forms the root of the tree while progressively more detailed sub-tasks form the branches of the tree. In industrial applications the power of genetic programming has been clearly demonstrated by going beyond the solution to optimization problems like the gas pipeline discussed above. In particular, genetic programming can tackle more challenging *design problems*. One example is the design of analog electrical circuits, an area in which human expertise has traditionally been required and in which the degree of originality of a given design can be roughly assessed by the fact that a patent office has accepted it. Using genetic programming populations of replicators searching the space of possible circuits have rediscovered several circuit designs that had been previously patented; have discovered novel designs that match the functionality of patented designs; and in at least one case they have found an entirely new design, that is, one not logically deducible from a previously patented invention.[14] This ability to generate non-obvious designs in which components are interconnected in complex ways can be very useful to explore the evolutionary origin of the metabolic circuitry of unicellular organisms.

To show how this could be done let's begin by describing how genetic programming works in applications not involving the modeling of biological processes. First of all, given that complex programs are evolved by recursion, that is, by functions that result from the composition of simpler ones, we need a set of elementary functions to get the process started. These primitive functions form the nodes or branching points of the tree. We also need to specify the variables and constants that those elementary functions use as their inputs (the "leaves" or terminals of the tree). These basic components must be chosen by a designer to match the type of problem to be solved.[15] In the case of analog electrical circuits, for example, the elementary operations include functions that insert a new component (a resistor, a capacitor, an inductor); functions that alter the connectivity of those components (the topology of the circuit); and functions that set the intensity (or sizing) of a component, that is, the degree of resistance of a resistor, the capacitance of a capacitor, and so on. In the case of digital circuit design the elementary functions should be operators like "And," "Or," and "Not." In the case of robotic motion, that is, when the problem to be solved is the synthesis of motion paths, the elementary repertoire must contain functions like "Turn Left," "Turn Right," and "Move Forward." These elementary functions are the component of the evolutionary process that is not emergent since their behavior (the way the functions affect their inputs) is dictated by rules. Any complex function that can be created from the elementary ones by recursion, on the other hand, can be considered emergent if it evolves spontaneously as a specific solution to a design problem.[16]

The final step is to create a fitness function defining the problem to be solved. Since the evolving entities in this case are computer programs evaluating their fitness demands actually running them because what is assessed is the behavior of the program, or the construction capacities with which that behavior endows the program. This evaluation is performed by comparing the running program with a set of test cases that already possess the required capacities, the degree of fitness expressed as a distance from that target. In the case of analog electrical circuits the evaluation of fitness is, in fact, more complex because we need to check not only that a running program can construct the circuit but also that the circuit itself behaves as it is intended to: as a filter, as an amplifier, as a sensor. To do this an "embryo" circuit (an electrical substructure with modifiable wires and components) is placed into a larger circuit in which no component is modifiable. Only the embryo evolves but its placement into a larger functional setting allows it to be checked for viability.[17] As it happens, the insights and techniques developed in the application of genetic programming to electrical circuits can be used to model cellular metabolisms because in many cases there is an isomorphism between the two.

Let's examine a concrete example. The target of a simulation of this type is an actual piece of biochemical machinery that has been studied in the laboratory. This typically includes a network of chemical reactions; a set of enzymes acting as catalysts; and an initial set of concentration gradients of the substances serving as substrates. In traditional biochemistry differential equations are used to model the rates at which the substrates are transformed into either intermediate or final products, as well as the way in which the catalysts affect those rates by accelerating them or decelerating them. These equations are then used to predict the concentration of the final products, a prediction that can be tested by carrying out actual experiments. The question for genetic programming is this: given data about the initial and final substance concentrations can we reverse engineer the chemical network that links the two? This would involve discovering the topology and sizing of the network, that is, the connectivity of the different reactions and the values of the rates at which they proceed.

In one simulation, for example, an actual metabolic pathway using four different chemical reactions was used as a target. The topology of the pathway was complex: it contained an internal feedback loop; a bifurcation point at which one substrate was used for two different reactions; and an accumulation point at which the concentration of a substance was affected by two different sources.[18]

The primitive functions used in this simulation included mathematical equations describing chemical reactions while the terminals were the inputs to those equations, such as substrates and catalysts. Both of these came from models used by biochemists and were therefore not emergent. On the other hand, the initial population of random programs had no information about how many reactions the metabolic pathway was supposed to have, how these reactions should be coupled to one another, or what substrates each reaction got as inputs and what products it produced as outputs. The only information the evolutionary process had about its target was built into the fitness function: the concentration of the final product of the metabolic pathway. The results of the simulation were encouraging. An initial population of 100,000 replicators was able to discover the topology of the chemical network (including the feedback loop, and the bifurcation and concentration points) in about 120 generations, while the sizing of the network (the values for rates of concentration and rates of catalysis) was closely approximated in an additional 100 generations.[19] The evaluation of the fitness of each generation was facilitated by exploiting the isomorphism of chemical and electrical circuits: voltage gradients played the role of concentration gradients, while circuits that performed addition and subtraction represented the production and consumption of a given substance.[20] Once an isomorphic electrical circuit was created it could be tested for fitness using the same approach discussed above: placing an evolving embryo circuit into a larger non-evolving one and using standard software to check for viability.

The conclusion we may draw from this and the previous biological simulation is that the capacity of a population of variable replicators to search a possibility space is indeed real. On the other hand, demonstrating the existence of a capacity is not the same thing as explaining it. The simplest explanation, the one applying to naked RNA, would rely on two assumptions: that the space of possible polymers does in fact possess the order we imposed on it, that is, that the sequences are arranged so that one-mutant variants occupy neighboring positions, and that the search is carried out in parallel by an entire cloud of mutants. But once the relation between genotype and phenotype is taken into account this explanation ceases to be sufficient. Even in the case of naked RNA the topology of the possible becomes more complicated. In particular, to understand how one folded catalyst that targets a certain chemical reaction could evolve into another one with a different target, the path from one phenotype to the other must be also represented in the way the space is ordered. One way of achieving this is to impose an order that ensures that between two molecular sequences, each one occupying a local fitness optimum, there are "ridges" joining the two "mountain peaks," ridges in which the sequences all have the same fitness. This way a mutation could transform one sequence into a neighboring one with the same fitness while keeping the transformation invisible to selection pressures. A series of such neutral mutations could therefore lead from one folded catalyst to a very different one by walking across the ridge even if there are zones of lower fitness between the mountain peaks.[21]

A different kind of problem with the order we impose on the otherwise amorphous space of possible polymer sequences is that in addition to mutation some unicellular organisms use *sexual recombination*. When two different chromosomes are sexually combined each parent contributes half of the genes composing the offspring's chromosome. If we imagine that the ancestors of each parent had climbed a different local fitness optimum the resulting offspring would fall between the two peaks, that is, in an area of lower fitness, and would therefore be eliminated by natural selection. This negative effect may be ameliorated if the landscape has the right topography, that is, if all local optima are grouped together forming a tight cluster of peaks.[22] But a more general solution may force us to rethink how the space of possible polymers should be ordered so that its connectivity is compatible with both mutation and sexual recombination. This is particularly important when giving an account of the emergent searching capacity of simulations based on genetic algorithms or genetic programming because in most industrial applications these favor the use of a *crossover operator* over a mutation operator as a means to generate variation. The crossover operator works this way: it takes two separate simulated chromosomes and picks a particular point in each one of them; it then breaks both at that point crossing one of the two halves from one parent over to the other; finally it reattaches the two parental halves before releasing the offspring into the population. In other words, the crossover operator mimics the effect of sexual recombination.

One plausible explanation for the superiority of crossover over mutation starts with the assumption that the survival problem posed to an evolving population can be decomposed into subproblems each of which can be solved separately. In other words, the assumption is that complex adaptive problems that have a modular structure can be solved *one building block at a time*, with sexual recombination playing the role of bringing separate building blocks together into a full solution. To explore this scenario a special method has been developed to keep track of the propagation of building blocks in simulations using genetic algorithms. If we imagine the simulated chromosomes to be ten bits long, the population containing strings like "1101100000" or "0011011110," we can identify the similarities among strings with a notation using "wild cards." The two strings just mentioned, for example, have similar "genes" at positions four and ten, a similarity that can be represented by a string using a wild card symbol like "#." The string "###1#####0" is called a "schema."[23] Once every generation each member of the population of strings is evaluated by the fitness function for its performance as a solution to a problem. If the population contained, say, 50 strings, that would cover a relatively small area of the possibility space. But if in addition we evaluated the average performance of each schema we would expand the area searched. For example, if the two strings above belonged to the population but not the strings "1001100010" or "0111011100," then the latter two would not be explicitly evaluated. But because these two strings are also instances of "###1#####0" we would get information about them when evaluating the average fitness of the schema.

If we think of each string in the population as a point in a multi-dimensional possibility space then a schema with many instances is like a slice (or hyperplane) of that space.[24] Thus, a population in which strings share building blocks would not be like a cloud of points moving through the possibility space but rather like a set of slices covering a much wider area and therefore increasing the parallelism of the search. The crossover operator, on the other hand, can easily destroy building blocks if the cut point happens to separate its components. This implies that an instance of a schema in which the fixed positions are close to one another has a better chance of preserving its building blocks after many recombinations: instances of the schema "#10#######," for example, have a better chance of preserving the building block "10" than those belonging to "###1#####0." It can be shown that a schema with many wild cards (representing bigger slices of the possibility space) and in which the few fixed positions are clustered together can propagate through a population as long as the fitness of the schema is greater than the average fitness of the population. This result is known as "the schema theorem." The schema theorem, however, says nothing about how building blocks are brought together over many generations to be combined into a full solution to the problem. In other words, the schema theorem explains the propagation of good building blocks but not their accretion.[25] But the latter is equally important because as building blocks come together the evolutionary search is conducted on spaces of ever decreasing dimensionality and ever increasing fitness, that is, each schema represents an increasingly larger slice of the space and contains several partial solutions to the overall problem.

Is there any evidence for the existence of building blocks in real populations of replicators? Two separate but related discoveries in biochemistry and genetics bear on this question. On one hand, biochemists studying proteins and their folded structures have identified those parts of their surfaces that play a role in enzymatic activity: their binding sites and their catalytic sites. Because these sites are relatively compact and exhibit specific folded motifs (sheets, helices, ribbons) they are named "domains." Similar domains in different proteins tend to have similar functions, a fact that suggests that they are indeed reusable building blocks.[26] On the other hand, geneticists have discovered that the genes of unicellular organisms in which the genetic materials are encapsulated into a nucleus are not structured as one continuous unit as they are in bacteria that lack a nucleus. Instead, their genes have a mosaic structure in which sequences of nucleotides that code for proteins (called "exons") are interspersed with sequences that do not code for anything (called "introns").

In many cases one or more exons code for a specific domain in a protein, that is, for a building block, so exons can be reshuffled through sexual recombination to produce novel proteins at relatively low cost, a hypothesis made more plausible by the fact that each protein domain has its own folding capabilities so that new combinations can be expected to fold together neatly.[27] Additionally, the presence of introns should lower the risk of disruption of exons: if the cut point used in sexual recombination lies on an intron then the coevolved components of a building block will not be disrupted.

Despite its more elaborate mapping between genotype and phenotype the replicators used in genetic programming remain disembodied and are not situated in space. And the fact that the evaluation of fitness is performed exogenously, that is, that the target of the search is set by test cases provided by the designer, implies that the process is more like the controlled breeding of farm animals and plants by human beings than an evolutionary process in which some species acts as selection pressures on other species. This means that questions involving the coevolution of species or the emergence of food webs in ecosystems cannot be explored using these simulations. In the following chapter we will remove these limitations by embodying the replicators, situating them in space, and making their reproductive success depend on their capacity to meet their metabolic needs by tapping into resource gradients distributed in that space.

CHAPTER FIVE
Genetic Algorithms and Ancient Organisms

With the emergence of the first living creatures the aqueous environment we have been exploring acquired a new feature: a gelatinous stratum of colonial bacteria at the interface between bottom sediments and water forming the earliest biosphere. This new stratum remained deceptively simple for over two billion years because the motionless microorganisms that composed it hardly changed in their anatomy.[1] But contrary to what a superficial look at their external appearance may suggest those ancient organisms had managed to discover over that period of time all the biochemical processes of energy extraction that exist today. After that, evolution produced many new mechanisms to use energy to perform work, for complex locomotion or for neural control, for instance, but *no new major ways of extracting energy from gradients*.[2] Roughly, the earliest bacteria appeared on this planet three and a half billion years ago scavenging the products of non-biological chemical processes; a billion years later they evolved the capacity to tap into the solar gradient, producing oxygen as a toxic byproduct; and one billion years after that they evolved the capacity to use oxygen to greatly increase the efficiency of energy and material consumption. By contrast, the great diversity of multicellular organisms that populate the planet today was generated in about six hundred million years. Thus the history of the earliest biosphere is a narrative of how the capacity of the environment to sustain life was extended by the discovery through evolutionary search of the biochemical circuitry needed for *fermentation, photosynthesis, and respiration*.

To give an idea of the increased efficiency represented by these metabolic landmarks we can use some numbers obtained from studying contemporary microorganisms. Using the least efficient process, fermentation, 180 grams of sugar can be broken down to yield 20,000 calories of energy. The sugar used as raw material for this chemical reaction was originally taken ready-made from the environment by the earliest bacteria but with the discovery of photosynthesis those organisms could now produce it: using 264 grams of carbon dioxide, 108 grams of water, and 700,000 calories taken from sunlight, they could produce the same 180 grams of sugar, plus 192 grams of oxygen as waste product. With the advent of respiration, in turn, that waste product could be used to burn the 180 grams of sugar to produce 700,000 calories of energy.[3] Thus, adding photosynthesis to fermentation made the growth of the earliest populations of living creatures self-sustaining, while adding respiration produced a net surplus of bacterial flesh (or "biomass"). Given that surplus it became possible to go from mere population growth to increased species diversity through the complexification of food chains. In other words, bacterial biomass itself became a gradient that could be tapped into by newly evolved predatory species, the ancestors of contemporary unicellular organisms like paramecia or amoebae.

Whether predatory or not, more complex living creatures did not have to confront the same metabolic problems that had taken bacteria billions of years to solve. Rather, ancient animals incorporated as a whole microorganisms that had already mastered respiration (the ancestors of mitochondria) while ancient plants absorbed those that had acquired the capacity for photosynthesis (chloroplasts). In other words, the plants and animals that would eventually become multicellular came into being by using bacteria and their metabolic circuitry as building blocks.[4] The interactions between the new creatures and the older bacteria may have started as parasitic and only later developed into a more mutualistic relation as the intimate knowledge that parasites had about their hosts was used for their common benefit. The crucial element in the relation was *simultaneous replication*: the former parasites had to be replicated in synchrony with their hosts so that their reproductive interests did not diverge.[5] In many contemporary organisms there are enduring symbioses in which bacteria in the guts of larger animals allow the latter to digest food they could not otherwise process, but the microorganisms must be re-ingested every generation. The decreased intimacy this implies means that mutations may arise that switch the symbiosis back into parasitism. In the case of ancient animals and their mitochondria, or ancient plants and their chloroplasts, on the other hand, any retained mutation in the absorbed bacteria had to also be beneficial to the host. This deeper form of mutualistic relation is called *endosymbiosis*.

Endosymbiosis is an exotic illustration of the part-to-whole relation in ecology. The more ordinary examples form several levels of organization each one studied by its own sub-discipline: behavioral, population, community, and ecosystem ecology. At the smallest scale the object of study is the behavior of individual organisms in their environment: motile bacteria sensing nutrient gradients in their vicinity and moving in the direction of higher concentration, for example, or ancestral amoebae using flowing protoplasmic extensions to encircle bacterial prey prior to ingesting it. The next scale focuses on the population of which these organisms are component parts and studies the way it grows limited only by the capacity of local gradients to sustain it. Details about the behavior of individual organisms become causally redundant in an explanation of this growth. At the next scale entire communities composed of several interacting populations of different species become the target of analysis. And finally, at the largest scale, the interactions between several of these communities are studied, disregarding the distinctions between species and dealing only with the function they perform, as producers or consumers, in the overall flow of matter and energy in an ecosystem. Although each of these spatial scales is distinct enough to be studied by a different field it is important to emphasize that we are dealing here with differences in *relative scale*, that is, with scale as is generated by the relation of part-to-whole, not with absolute scale: a single contemporary large plant, for example, may house an entire ecosystem of microorganisms displaying all four levels of organization.

A good starting point for a philosophical discussion of ecological issues is the scale studied by population ecology, a level of organization characterized by emergent properties like the pattern of growth of a population. This pattern is produced by two different factors. On one hand, there is the growth rate of the organisms, basically their birth rate minus their death rate, although rates of emigration and immigration also affect the rapidity or slowness of population growth. On the other hand there is the available space, matter, and energy in the location inhabited by the population. These two factors together determine the *carrying capacity*, the maximum population that can be sustained indefinitely without depleting available resources. Since one and the same environment may house many different species the carrying capacity varies depending on the energetic, material, and spatial requirements of each species: a population that can survive on small amounts of energy, for example, will grow to a much larger size than one whose energy needs are higher. Because growth patterns may be affected by overcrowding it is preferable to measure the outcome of growth not in absolute numbers but in densities, that is, by the average population size in a given amount of space. Carrying capacity can then be treated as a singularity in the space of possibilities for the interactions between population densities and resources, the special value of density that ensures a population will be at long-term equilibrium with its environment.

Real populations, of course, need not exist at the singularity but fluctuate around it or periodically overshoot it. How a real population will behave relative to the singularity depends on which of the two factors that determines carrying capacity dominates its reproductive strategy. A strategy based on growth rate implies that a species will tend to produce many offspring quickly, offspring that will tend to be small and short lived. A strategy targeted at existing resources, on the other hand, will produce fewer, larger, longer lived offspring more able to learn to control their environment, more energy efficient, and more capable of fine-tuning its numbers to environmental conditions. Insects and weeds are often used as examples of the first strategy while large mammals and trees exemplify the second one. Given the small size and rapid reproduction of microorganisms one would think that they should always use the first strategy but studies of microbial ecologies have shown that both strategies exist: some populations ignore carrying capacity, overshoot it, then crash—perhaps going dormant as spores or cysts to wait for new resources—while others grow fast at first but then show density-dependent saturation effects and gently converge on the singularity.[6] In addition, changes in the availability of resources can contribute to shaping growth patterns, as when seasonal variations affect resource abundances making the density of a population vary in a periodic way. These cyclic patterns can become even more complex when we move to the level of community ecology because at that point the density of a prey species becomes the main factor determining the carrying capacity for a predatory species.

Using density instead of absolute numbers to characterize a population means that we can think of the latter in terms of gradients: like temperature or pressure density is an intensive property. In this case, the gradient is a concentration of biomass from which energy can be extracted by other species. Ecological relations can, in fact, be defined by the effect that the density of one species has on the density of another. If an increase in the density of one species decreases that of another then the relation is either predatory or parasitic. If the densities of both species decrease there is competition. If they both increase the relation is one of mutualism or symbiosis. And finally, if the density of one population grows without affecting that of the other then their relation is one of commensalism. To study these relations community ecology must add to the mechanisms determining the growth rate of a population a rate coupling mechanism, that is, a enduring interaction making the rates of growth of the two populations depend on each other.[7] Let's use the interaction between predators and prey as an example. In standard models the prey population is assumed to have access to unlimited resources so the primary producers are not explicitly modeled. In the case of ancient food chains the prey population can be imagined to be bacteria using fermentation to consume the organic products of photosynthetic producers. In the absence of predators such a bacterial population would grow exponentially but in their presence its density will depend on the rate of predation. The density of the predator population, in turn, depends on its own growth rate as well as on the rate of prey capture. Finally, the densities of each population affect the probability that they will encounter each other and interact, the higher the densities the more likely the interaction.

In such a scenario it is relatively easy to obtain population densities that do not settle into a steady state but instead cycle repeatedly: as the predator population grows it reduces the population of prey up to the point where there is not enough prey to hunt; this makes the predator population crash allowing the prey population to recover and start the cycle again. On the other hand, a rhythmic pattern of boom and bust in the respective densities does not imply that the space of possibilities for the coupled system predator–prey contains a cyclic singularity (a periodic attractor). This will be the case only if the oscillation in the densities is asymptotically stable, that is, only if the period of the oscillation has a tendency to return to its original value after an external shock. Mathematical models with periodic attractors can be generated if to the previous model we add the assumption that predators can become satiated, that is, that as the prey population becomes more abundant rates of predation slow down because predators are already killing all the prey they need.[8] Data from actual populations in their natural habitats, as well as from populations studied under controlled laboratory conditions, tends to confirm that stable cycles in density are indeed common. In some cases even more complex attractors, cycles on cycles or even deterministic chaos, have been documented.[9] Thus, the interplay of formal analysis and laboratory experimentation is giving community ecologists the means to explore the mechanisms and the mechanism-independent structure of their subject matter. To this it must be added the role that simulations can play as intermediaries between theory and experiment allowing us to follow population densities as they move toward a singularity.

To play this role a simulation must embody its simulated organisms by giving them a metabolism and situate them in a space with a certain distribution of resources. Unlike the uses of genetic algorithms discussed in the previous chapter, in which disembodied replicators were capable of finding a single optimal solution, embodied and situated creatures tend to find a range of acceptable solutions given that resources can vary greatly in their spatial distribution and that the solutions found by evolutionary search need not be optimal for the entire population. In addition, fitness evaluations must not be performed from the outside but need to be *endogenous*: reproductive success must depend on the ability of the simulated organisms to meet their metabolic requirements. Whereas with exogenous fitness an evolutionary search finds solutions to problems posed by the experimenter in these simulations the problems are posed by the environment in the case of population ecology, or by other organisms in the case of community ecology. Let's begin with the first case: simulations of population ecology in which the target of the study is emergent growth patterns and fitness is defined by carrying capacity. On one hand, the growth may take place because the environment has been enriched with new gradients, an injection of mineral resources caused by an external event like a volcanic eruption, for example. On the other, the growth may be caused by the evolutionary discovery of novel metabolic strategies, like photosynthesis or respiration. That is, we want to model the capacity of the environment to affect the organisms as well as the capacity of the organisms to affect their environment.

In one approach, called "Latent Energy Environments" (LEE), a spatial dimension is added to genetic algorithms in two different ways: the simulated organisms inhabit an external space with a certain distribution of resources and they have an internal space (or "gut") in which they can carry resources after ingesting them. In addition, unlike standard genetic algorithms in which a new generation completely replaces the older one and in which population numbers remain fixed, in LEE different generations can coexist and population size can vary, allowing the exploration of density-dependent effects on growth patterns. But the most important feature of LEE is the way in which it enables us to distinguish the effects of resource availability from those of evolutionary adaptations in the fate of a given population. To this end LEE does not distribute resources as ready-made food but rather as bits and pieces that must be combined in specific ways for their "latent energy" to become "useful energy." The possible metabolic combinations of these bits and pieces are predefined in a table, that is, they are not emergent, but they are rich enough to yield not only different amounts of energy but also byproducts that can enter into further combinations. Thus, an experimenter can control the problem that the environment poses to an organism in two ways: by making the possible metabolic combinations more or less complex (changing the entries in the table) or by determining how spatially concentrated or dispersed the food components are. Since the table of reactions is not evolvable and the creatures' gut is a simple container the solutions they must discover are not new metabolic processes but new behaviors. More specifically, they must evolve novel *foraging strategies*. Searching for food in an efficient way is important because movement involves an energy cost. This means that the simulated organisms have an incentive to discover behavioral strategies that minimize the amount of work needed to find the right combination of food bits that will yield a full metabolic reaction.[10]

Although LEE can be used in different ways for the present discussion we should think of these foraging strategies as discovered by an entire population over many generations. We can take the mobile organisms in LEE to represent unicellular predators—the different classes of which are distinguished by their locomotive machinery using cilia, flagella, or pseudopodia—while the static food bits represent different types of immobile bacteria, each providing a predator with different nutrients. Like ancient predators LEE creatures have an oriented body defined by the location of simulated sensors and motors. The sensors range from extremely simple, sensing direct contact with a food particle in the same location, to more sophisticated ones allowing sensing at a distance. The creatures also have "gut sensors" to be able to tell what the current internal contents are and make foraging decisions on the basis of what else is needed to complete a metabolic reaction. These sensors correspond to the role that proteins (diffused in the cytoplasm or embedded on the membrane) play in microorganisms. The component of the simulated organisms that transforms information from the sensors into different types of movement is a simple model of a neuron called a "neural net." This aspect of the implementation has advantages and disadvantages from the present point of view: the advantage is that neural nets can easily be coupled to genetic algorithms, as we will discuss in the following chapter, allowing inherited behavior to evolve over many generations; the disadvantage is that ancient predators did not use neurons to connect sensors and motors but complex biochemical mechanisms. But since we are interested in exploring mechanism-independent questions this way of mapping sensory inputs into motor outputs need not be a problem.

When LEE is used to simulate situations in population ecology what we would like to see emerging is the correct growth patterns. Like ancient predators LEE's creatures are designed to evolve more efficient foraging strategies suggesting a growth pattern in which density is fine-tuned to carrying capacity. That is, the growth pattern of the population should not periodically overshoot the carrying capacity and then crash but approach it asymptotically. And that is, indeed, the pattern observed in actual simulations. In addition, when a novel evolved behavior extends carrying capacity there will be a period of time in which the old equilibrium is replaced by a new one and mathematical models have little to tell us about the dynamics during the transition. LEE on the other hand can track population changes as they adjust to new conditions.[11] Finally, having established its compatibility with traditional models LEE can serve as a means to conduct experiments of different kinds: the table of metabolic reactions, for example, can be changed to reflect the seasonal availability of different resources by making the products of different combinations vary periodically; or the spatial distribution of resources can be altered from relatively uniform to one in which different bits and pieces of food are located in different places, making the solution to the survival problem harder. This way LEE can test whether in environments of increased complexity evolutionary search is able to find solutions that are optimal for the entire population or whether different subpopulations will develop adaptations that are good compromises to their local conditions.[12]

Let's pause for a moment to summarize the argument so far. The earth's earliest biosphere consisted of flat colonies of bacteria with unchanging external anatomies that tended to obscure the momentous changes that were taking place within their membranes: new biochemical circuitry that basically exhausted all the known ways of extracting energy from environmental gradients. These metabolic landmarks eventually led to a net surplus in the production of biomass and to the subsequent emergence of entirely new creatures capable of surviving by consuming that biomass. From then on the interaction between population density and available resources, or that between coupled population densities, became the main source of ecological emergent properties. The main question confronting us now is the evolutionary consequences of these ecological interactions. More specifically, when one species preys on another it becomes a selection pressure on its prey, and vice versa, when a prey species evolves adaptations to counteract predatory abilities it becomes a selection pressure on its predators. This means that over many generations the two species engage in an "arms race" in which a new adaptation by one species stimulates the evolution of a counter-adaptation by the other. And similarly for ecological interactions other than those between predators and prey. Symbiotic species, for example, may come to depend on each other so closely that their evolution becomes tightly coupled, as illustrated by the way in which many contemporary plants have developed an obligatory relation with the insects that pollinate them. Evolutionary interactions are different from ecological ones not only because the latter take place in relatively short time scales—the periods of the oscillations in density, for example, are measured in years—while the former take place in much longer time scales, but also because they are associated with different possibility spaces.

In the previous chapter we saw that an evolutionary possibility space can be conceptualized as a fitness landscape: a space containing all possible gene sequences on top of which a valuation in terms of expected reproductive success has been superimposed. The distribution of singularities (fitness optima) in this space defines the complexity of the survival problem that has to be solved: a space with a single global optimum surrounded by areas of minimum fitness is a tough problem (a needle in a haystack) while one with many local optima grouped together defines a relatively easy problem. In the case of predators and their prey (or of any other ecological relation) we need to couple two of these spaces because although predator and prey species have their own genotypes they influence each other's fitness: when evolutionary search happens to find a new combination of genes that improves the prey's capacity to evade its predator, for example, this will lower the fitness of some existing predator genes, and conversely, a new gene sequence that improves hunting behavior will lower the fitness of some existing prey genes. In other words, the coevolution of predators and prey implies that their fitness landscapes are constantly being deformed with some "hills" being transformed into "valleys."[13] Extending this line of thought to entire food chains implies that many fitness landscapes may become serially coupled, raising the question of how long food chains can be before the coupled possibility spaces contain singularity distributions that make survival problems impossible to solve. These considerations have led theorists to expect that evolution itself may limit the length of food chains to avoid a dead end, a hypothesis made plausible by empirical findings of relatively short food chains in actual ecosystems.[14]

When designing simulations to study coevolution having control of the details of metabolic processes or of the spatial distribution of resources is not as necessary as being able to deploy embodied creatures of different species that can recognize and interact with one another. In one approach, called *Echo*, the internal metabolic machinery of the simulated creatures is made so simple that they in effect "eat genes." In Echo evolution is simulated through a genetic algorithm in which the standard symbol string of ones and zeroes acting as a chromosome has been changed to one using a larger alphabet. The creatures live and move in a simple space containing resources that are symbols from that alphabet and reproduction takes place only when the creatures have accumulated enough symbols to create a copy of their chromosomes. Constructing energetic resources and chromosomes from the same raw materials allows Echo to disregard metabolic processing and include only storage in an internal "gut" while simultaneously making fitness evaluations endogenous. To simulate ecological interactions symbols that are in the guts of other creatures can be captured in the case of predation or exchanged in the case of symbiosis. Echo's creatures are less embodied than those of LEE not only because of the identity of energy and genes but also due to the lack of a transformation of genotype into phenotype: while in LEE the simulated chromosome encodes for a neural net, the inputs and outputs of which act as sensors and motors, in Echo the chromosome acts both as inheritable material and as bodily traits.

More specifically, the chromosome's symbols play the role of *tags* that are "visible" to other creatures. In real microorganisms these tags would be membrane-bound proteins allowing for molecular recognition using a lock-and-key mechanism, or even chemical byproducts of an organism's metabolism through which it can be identified by others, but these details are ignored in Echo. Tags work not only as a means of identification but also as the means to specify the capacities of a creature to affect and be affected by other creatures. This has the consequence that Echo's creatures do not interact with each other directly but need an external program to compare their tags and determine the outcome of an "interaction." The tags are of two types: offensive and defensive. The basic procedure is to randomly pick pairs of creatures inhabiting the same site and then compare the offense tag of one to the defense tag of the other, and vice versa. The comparison aims only at establishing the number of symbols of each tag that match those of another tag at the same position in the chromosome. If the match is asymmetric—the offense tag of one creature matching the defense tag of another but not the other way around—the first creature is taken to be a predator and the second one its prey. If the match is symmetric, that is, if both the offense and defense tags of each creature match each other, then the two are considered symbionts. The number of matches determines the amount of resources that are captured by the predator (it can "eat" the entire prey or simply take a "bite" from it) or the amount of resources that are mutually exchanged in symbiosis. This allows for complex ecological relations to emerge: one species may prey on another that is symbiotic with a third one that, in turn, preys on the first.[15]

In a more complex version of Echo the chromosome is divided into two parts, one acting as tags the other performing the role of condition-action rules, that is, rules specifying that if a given condition obtains a particular action is taken. In this more complex version the interactions are still not performed by the creatures but the tags are compared through the condition-action rules allowing for outcomes that are more flexible: the creatures can "refuse" to interact if the conditions specified in their rules are not met, for example.[16] The relative lack of embodiment of Echo's creatures reflects the emphasis of this approach on the long-term outcomes of interactions (structure of food chains, relative species abundances, arms races) rather than the interactions themselves. As in LEE the first task to be performed is to calibrate these emergent outcomes to those of either mathematical models or data from community ecology. For instance, in many cases the relative abundance of different species has a distinct statistical shape: many species have a few representatives while a few have many representatives. Experiments with Echo designed to test whether it can produce these abundance patterns have been conducted and the initial results are encouraging. The experiments attempted to match not only a target statistical distribution but also tried to answer the question of whether the outcome was produced by coevolution. To test this hypothesis two versions of Echo were ran for each experiment, one in which interactions were mediated by tags and conditions (hence subject to coevolution) and another in which interactions took place randomly. The tag-mediated simulation fit the data better than the purely random one.[17]

From the point of view of simulating the ancient biosphere Echo provides a means to explore the very different ways in which the descendants of the earliest microorganisms evolved. There were two distinct evolutionary dynamics depending on whether or not a microorganism possessed an inner membrane encapsulating its genetic materials within a nucleus. Lacking such a nuclear membrane allows the free sharing of genes by entirely different organisms. It is well known, for example, that transferable sets of genes called plasmids are responsible for the spread of antibiotic resistance in bacteria in the past 70 years, but this genetic promiscuity is nothing new. Ancient bacteria may have engaged in this form of horizontal gene transfer from the start using plasmids and other movable genes as combinatorial building blocks to rapidly acquire capacities they previously lacked. The ancient predators of those bacteria, on the other hand, did possess a separate nucleus and were not capable of sharing genes that way. They compensated for that by acquiring the capacity for *reproductive isolation*. In larger organisms the formation of new species occurs largely through the isolation of their gene pool from flows of genetic materials from other species. This mechanism of speciation (the birth of a new species) is a major evolutionary force promoting divergence and anatomical differentiation. The evolutionary histories of microorganisms with and without a nucleus (eukaryotes and prokaryotes) testify to the importance of this distinction: while the former went on to form all the different plants and animals that exist today, the latter followed not a divergent but a convergent path. That is, instead of yielding a plurality of gene pools more or less isolated from each other they generated what is basically a giant gene pool spanning the entire planet.[18]

In addition to the presence or absence of speciation the other major determinant of early evolutionary outcomes was endosymbiosis, the already mentioned absorption of entire microorganisms and their metabolic capacities. Simulating endosymbiosis and speciation can be done in Echo simply by adding new tags or condition-action rules. The first modification is to add a new tag mediating adhesion interactions and a means to manage the boundaries or membranes of the interacting creatures. In a simulation of ancient microbial ecosystems adhesion tags could play several roles depending on the outcomes of the interactions and the resulting boundaries. Allowing adhesion between similar organisms can easily yield colonies arranged in layers, much like the mat-like structures that non-motile bacteria formed in the first two billion years of evolution. With this spatial organization the evolution of individual creatures may be influenced by the environment provided by similar creatures on the same layer, or by different creatures in a neighboring layer, promoting specialization. Endosymbiosis, on the other hand, can be simulated if the result of adhesion interactions is not the creation of a single boundary around many creatures but the absorption of one creature by another in which the absorbed creature keeps its own boundary.[19]

To simulate speciation the obvious choice would be to add a new tag to simulate expressions of species identity. This choice would be justified by the fact that many organisms achieve reproductive isolation through the possession of special markings (colors, odors, pigmentation patterns). But in Echo selective mating is achieved by adding a new condition-action rule that uses an existing tag (the offense tag). Whenever two creatures occupying the same site are ready for reproduction, that is, when they have ingested enough symbols to make a copy of their chromosomes, the condition part of their mating rules are compared to their offense tags and if both conditions are satisfied copies of their chromosomes are made, crossed over, and two new offspring are added to the population. This procedure resembles that used by paramecia the ancestors of which were among the earliest eukaryotes. By varying the specificity of the mating condition lower degrees of reproductive isolation can be achieved to yield the equivalent of prokaryotes.[20] The distinction between the types of evolution that result with and without the possibility of speciation must be kept in mind when testing Echo's evolutionary outcomes. One experiment, for example, attempted to check whether Echo's simulated evolution displayed the same open-ended character as real evolution or whether it remained bounded within limits. The results failed to match the degree of divergence that is evident in the fossil record after the great burst of differentiation known as the "Cambrian explosion."[21] But the experiment did not control for the degree of reproductive isolation. Since the fossils of eukaryotes predominate in that record a simulation of evolution that matches its open-ended character should be conducted with populations that can speciate through strong reproductive isolation.

Once our simulations reach the post-Cambrian period we need to enrich them with new resources. So far the simulated unicellular organisms have been able to learn how to solve survival problems only as a species. That is, the solutions are reached by an entire population over many generations. But after eukaryotes underwent their explosive divergence changes in their composition created the conditions for the emergence of problem solving abilities that could be exercised during a single organism's lifetime. LEE's creatures, in fact, can be used in this mode by allowing the strength of the connections of their neural nets to be established not by a genetic algorithm but by the training the creatures get as they move around searching for food. The next step in this investigation should therefore be a discussion of the nervous system and of the emergent learning capacities with which it endows living creatures.

CHAPTER SIX
Neural Nets and Insect Intelligence

The explosive divergence that multicellular organisms underwent six hundred million years ago had many consequences. The diversity of the survival problems that these organisms had to solve, for example, increased enormously as their environments filled with other living creatures capable of affecting and being affected by them. To confront this diversity organisms began to develop internal models to guide their behavior. Even humble motile bacteria, as they swim up a gradient of nutrients toward the point of maximum concentration, can be said to have an internal model of their environment.[1] This internal model is not, of course, based on representations of any kind and it is not a model of the world at large but only of the concrete opportunities and risks afforded to bacteria by their immediate surroundings. In other words, from the beginning of life the internal models mediating the interaction between a primitive sensory system and a motor apparatus evolved in relation to what was directly relevant or significant to living beings. With the advent of multicellular organisms and the progressive differentiation of their cells into multiple kinds the scope for internal models was greatly enlarged. In particular, a new kind of biological material, neuronal material, began to grow and interpenetrate the living jelly accumulating at the bottom of the ocean. And with the availability of neurons the capacity to distinguish the relevant from the irrelevant, the ability to foreground only the opportunities and risks pushing everything else into an undifferentiated background, was vastly increased.

Simple multicellular organisms, like the hydra or the jellyfish, have a few separate neurons linked together into a network. In the hydra this network is concentrated around the mouth while in the jellyfish it is linked to simple receptors for light and chemical substances. These assemblies of neurons, in turn, sustain the emergent capacity to modulate inherited behavioral responses during the lifetime of an organism. The simplest of these capacities is called *habituation*: it operates on sensory-motor activities that are innate but it allows organisms to control their intensity. An organism like a hydra, for instance, can gradually decrease its response to a stimulus—can become habituated to it—as experience finds it harmless or avoidable. In other words, habituation transforms a significant stimulus into an insignificant one. The opposite capacity, sensitization, allows these organisms to behave toward a previously irrelevant stimulus as a potential source of an opportunity or a risk, that is, it makes the stimulus behaviorally relevant. In a sense these two ancient forms of learning mark the emergence of subjective gradients: before a hydra becomes habituated to a novel stimulus, for example, it may be thought of as being "surprised" by it, a proto-subjective state that slowly diminishes until it disappears as it reaches equilibrium. Behind these subjective gradients, on the other hand, there are objective ones: concentration gradients of electrically charged substances constantly produced and maintained in the fluids inside and outside neurons. The capacity to become habituated to external stimuli can serve as a useful starting point for a philosophical investigation of animal learning because explaining it demands looking only at what happens inside a single sensory neuron as it interacts with a single motor neuron.

The standard model of neurons places the manipulation of gradients of metallic ions, potassium or sodium ions, for example, at the heart of their functioning. Manipulating these chemical gradients—keeping potassium at high concentrations inside the cell and at low concentrations outside of it—produces yet another gradient, one of electrical potential. The key to the conversion of one gradient into another is the selective permeability of a neuron's membrane to metallic ions: as membrane permeability changes ions flow in and out of the cell creating variations in the gradient of electrical potential. Neurons use these smooth low-level variations to record the electrical signals acting as their input. Producing an output involves changing the electrical gradients from continuous to discrete, transforming them into a chain or train of practically identical electrical spikes. This spike train is used to produce a chemical signal that, when received by other neurons, increases the permeability of their membranes if the chemical substances are excitatory or decreases it if they are inhibitory.[2] To provide a mechanism for habituation in simple creatures all we need to assume is that the supply of an excitatory substance in a sensory neuron becomes progressively depleted after successive stimulations, so that less and less of this substance crosses the gap to affect the permeability of a motor neuron's membrane leading to a decrease in its response. A similar mechanism can account for sensitization if we add a second sensory neuron interacting with the first causing it to increase production of the excitatory substance and therefore the amount of the latter that reaches the motor neuron.[3]

The capacity to become habituated or sensitized implies only the possession of innate internal models. But with the advent of more complex assemblies of neurons new forms of learning emerged that made possible the creation of internal models during the lifetime of an organism. In particular, ancient insects were capable of the kind of learning referred to as *classical conditioning* in which an inherited association between a stimulus and a response provides the basis to form a novel association with a previously insignificant stimulus. Studying this form of learning in a laboratory involves identifying a particular behavior (salivation in a dog, for example) that is always triggered by given stimulus (food odor). If the trigger is presented immediately preceded by a neutral stimulus (the sound of a bell) the latter becomes capable after many presentations to elicit the desired response alone. Although mammals were originally used to prove the existence of this associative capacity it became clear later that insects also possess it. When the antennas of honey bees, for example, are touched by a drop of sugar in solution the bees reflexively extend a part of their mouth toward the sugar and lick it. If an odor or a color which was previously irrelevant to the bees is made to coincide with the presence of sugar it will after some training trigger the licking behavior alone. Technically, the stimulus to which the animal is genetically predisposed to respond is called the "unconditioned stimulus" while the ones that may be associated with it are referred to as "conditioned stimuli."

Outside the laboratory this associative capacity has survival value only if the conditioned stimulus is in fact predictive of the presence of the unconditioned one. Parasitic wasps, for example, have hunting reflexes triggered by the odor of the caterpillars on which they feed but they can learn to display the same behavior when stimulated by the odor of the plant the caterpillar feeds on.[4] In other words, the wasps can learn to predict the presence of their prey through a conditioned stimulus. The evolutionary relevance of conditioned stimuli is sometimes ignored by psychologists who are interested only in the link between a stimulus and a response. But behavioral ecologists know that evolution can build biases as to the kinds of stimuli that may or may not be successfully associated, and that ecologically sensible explanations can be given for those biases. Food search in honey bees, for example, implies learning to recognize different flowers, that is, objects that are colorful, have a special aroma, and have geometric arrangements of petals. This suggests that they should be able to associate not sounds but odors, colors, and many-pointed shapes with the presence of food. We can also expect an ordering of these stimuli relative to their usefulness to make predictions: floral odors should be easier to learn than the shape of flowers since the latter varies with the angle of observation and is thus less predictive of the presence of food. Experiments with honeybees confirm these two hypotheses.[5] Classical conditioning in insects illustrates the beginning of a true internal model: while the behavior of a honey bee may not be affected by a flower as a whole but only by a set of stimuli that tend to co-occur in the presence of flowers, the fact that there is a causal link between each of these stimuli and their source suggests that a simplified model of the flower (a set of linked stimuli) is indeed created in the bee's brain.

Unlike the hydra and the jellyfish insects possess a more elaborate nervous system in which many individual neurons form the component parts of larger wholes, like a primitive brain or the ganglia that coordinate their articulated limb movements. Nevertheless, we need not consider their entire nervous system to explain their capacity for classical conditioning. It is well known, for example, that many insects can learn to avoid certain limb positions by associating them with an electrical shock but the same association can be achieved by an isolated insect leg together with its ganglion.[6] Thus, it is the properties of local assemblies of neurons, not entire nervous systems, that sustain this capacity, properties like their connectivity and the strength of their connections. These two properties are related because a connection or synapse between two neurons becomes stronger the more often the neurons on either side of it are active simultaneously. Or more exactly, simultaneous activity influences a connection's strength although not necessarily in a constant way. Classical conditioning, for example, is characterized by a learning curve that displays a clear deceleration: while at the beginning of the training the joint presentation of the conditioned and unconditioned stimulus has a large effect on behavior the effect becomes less and less pronounced with time. This suggests the existence of a state of expectation in the animal's mind so that the more surprising the stimulus the larger the conditioning effect.[7] In addition to this subjective gradient a new kind of entity may be needed to fully explain classical conditioning: a mental representation. Theorists have traditionally been ambivalent about what exactly becomes associated when an animal is trained: is the animal linking the conditioned stimulus with a pattern of behavior (the reflexive response) or is it associating it with a representation of the unconditioned stimulus? While behaviorist psychologists favor the former explanation laboratory experiments suggest that the latter is the correct one: if an animal is artificially paralyzed during training, so that the reflexive behavior cannot occur, an association still forms and affects the animal's behavior once its ability to move has been recovered.[8]

Given that we don't know what a representation in an insect's mind is like, other than the fact that it cannot possibly be a symbolic representation, it will be useful to explore the question of insect intelligence at the mechanism-independent level. That is, we need simulations that display an emergent capacity for classical conditioning even if the mechanism of emergence is entirely different from that of real neurons. On the other hand, to make sure that we are exploring a space of possibilities that overlaps that of real neurons we need simulations in which the computing units interact with one another through excitation and inhibition; in which some form of learning takes place as these interactions modify the strength of their interconnections; and in which non-symbolic representations of relatively simple patterns emerge spontaneously from the dynamics. The type of simulation that satisfies these requirements is called an *artificial neural net*. A typical neural net consists of many computing units connected to each other in a certain pattern, each computing unit being much less sophisticated than the central processing unit inside a desktop computer: all it must be able to do is calculate its own degree of activation given the excitatory or inhibitory signals it receives from other units. The computing units interact through connections that can vary in their ability to transmit excitation or inhibition, increasing in capacity if the interconnected units are active together or decreasing if they are simultaneously inactive. The variable capacity to transmit excitation or inhibition is called the strength or weight of the connection.

The simplest neural net has computing units arranged in two layers, the input layer and the output layer, a design known as a "perceptron." Simply put, a perceptron is a device that maps an input pattern into an output pattern.[9] One pattern may be, for example, a simple sensory stimulus while the other may be a simple motor response, although in practice neural nets are studied in a disembodied state ignoring the details of the sensors producing the input pattern and those of the actuators that convert the output pattern into a motor action. The association between input and output patterns is created by *training* the neural net. The training process consists in repeatedly presenting a pattern to the input layer, activating some units but not others, while fixing a desired activation pattern at the output layer. Or in more embodied terms, the training involves stimulating the neural net's sensors while simultaneously showing it the desired motor response. Once both activation patterns are set the computing units in each layer begin to interact with each other, increasing or decreasing the weight of their connections depending on whether the units at both ends of a connection are active or inactive. The simultaneous presentation of input and output patterns is performed many times until a stable configuration of weights in the connections is produced. After the training is over the fixed output pattern is removed and the neural net is tested to check whether it is able to reproduce it whenever it is presented with the original input pattern. This emergent capacity is explained by the fact that the connections have now specific weights and will transmit activation from the input layer to the output layer in just the way needed to reproduce the output pattern. In more embodied terms the final product of the training process is the ability to recognize a stimulus, a recognition expressed by the production of the correct motor response.

Before discussing the more complex neural net designs needed to simulate classical conditioning it will be useful to give an example of how simple perceptrons can be used to model the inherited reflexes that are the basis of that kind of associative learning. By definition innate reflexive behavior is learned by a species over many generations not by organisms during their lifetime. This situation can be simulated by coupling neural nets to genetic algorithms allowing the configuration of weights that constitutes the product of the learning process to be discovered not by training but by evolutionary search. In one simulation the emergence of innate locomotive behavior in insect-like creatures was captured with perceptrons playing the role of the ganglia that control the different articulated limbs of real insects. The bodies of the creatures were made of several parts (torsos, limbs, heads) articulated in a variety of ways: some articulations acted like hinges constraining rotational motion in one direction; others were like a ball and a socket allowing rotation in all directions. Each body part was specified by a single "gene" coding information about its size, the type of joint that it had with another body part, and the constraints on the extent to which these joints could move or rotate. The simulated gene also specified the properties of the perceptron needed to control each articulation: the number of units in its input and output layers, their connections, and the evolvable weights of those connections. The simulation, in fact, did not use genetic algorithms but genetic programming, so the chromosome was not a simple string of ones and zeroes but an executable program specifying how to build a body part and its neural net. This way if a body part was built twice as a result of genetic variation each copy could be grown with its own internal neural net and would be immediately functional.

The input layer of each neural net received sensory information not from the external environment but from the insect's own body, that is, proprioceptive information. Simulated sensors in each articulation provided information about joint-angles and about whether contact had been made between one body part and another, or between a body part and a portion of the environment. The output layer, in turn, controlled the movement of the joints themselves (pushing, pulling, rotating, bending) through simulated actuators.[10] In addition to being embodied the creatures were situated in a space that mimicked the physical characteristics of either water or dry land. This mattered because evolution always takes place in physical environments that provide organisms with opportunities and risks, like a cluttered space that affords the opportunity to walk in some directions but not others or a cliff that affords the risk of falling.[11] At the start of the simulation a population of randomly assembled creatures incapable of coherent motion was unleashed in the computer. The type of locomotive behavior to be evolved was then decided: for swimming behavior gravity was turned off, water viscosity turned on, and the fitness function was made to reward greater speed in both horizontal and vertical directions; if walking behavior was the target a static ground with friction was added, gravity was turned on, viscosity off, and horizontal speed was used to evaluate fitness. After many generations the result was the spontaneous emergence of a large variety of successful locomotion strategies: snakelike sinusoidal motion; the use of paddles, symmetrical flippers, or even sets of many flippers for swimming; a variety of terrestrial gaits based on leg-like appendages. Some of the locomotive styles resembled those used by real insects while others seemed entirely alien.[12]

The outcome of this simulation showed that complex coordinated movements could emerge without the need for central commands from the brain. That is, each body part and its articulation (with its own neural net, sensors, and actuators) played the role of a reusable building block allowing overall body motion to emerge in a completely decentralized way as building blocks coevolved together. As mentioned above, insect limbs and their ganglia seem to have a similar degree of autonomy. On the other hand, insects also have brains that can exercise centralized command over the behavior of the entire body, and although isolated limbs can be conditioned to learn simple associations a complete simulation of classical conditioning needs neural nets that display the abilities of a simple brain. To do this two improvements must be made to the basic design: increasing its computational power and giving it the capacity to generalize. The first change is needed because animals may be conditioned to predict an electric shock from two different stimuli (a light and a sound) when presented individually but not when presented together. That is, they will produce the reflexive behavior when exposed to either the light or the sound but not to both. This ability is isomorphic with that needed to learn some elementary logical functions (the logical function "exclusive or") that early critics of neural nets correctly pointed out was beyond the computational power of simple perceptrons.[13] The second change is necessary because when insects learn through classical conditioning it is very unlikely that they will find the exact same conditioned stimulus on every occasion. This implies that, in however simple a form, insects must be able to organize their experience through the use of general "categories" of which similar stimuli are particular instances.

Both improvements can be achieved by supplying a perceptron with one or more intermediate layers between its input and output layers. Because these extra layers are not accessible from the outside they are referred to as *hidden layers*. A neural net with hidden layers is called a "multilayer perceptron." Although this change may seem simple it took years to be properly implemented because no one knew how to train a neural net with multiple layers. The core of the training process is the learning rule, a procedure to adjust the connection weights to ensure a progressive convergence on the stable configuration that can produce the target output pattern. An effective learning rule for multilayer perceptrons is based on a simple but powerful idea: instead of only allowing activation to flow forward from the input to the output layers, information about the degree of mismatch between the currently produced output pattern and the desired final pattern is allowed to flow backward. In other words, the rule allows learning through the back-propagation of error ensuring the convergence on the target pattern through the progressive minimization of this error.[14] A training process guided by back-propagation constitutes a search in the space of possible weight configurations, a search process known as "gradient descent" for its resemblance to the dynamic through which a physical gradient cancels itself.[15]

As in the case of simple perceptrons training a multilayer one involves supplying it with a sensory stimulus and a desired motor response. As several different but similar input activation patterns are presented to it, and as information about the correctness of its current output pattern flows backwards, the units in the hidden layer develop their own pattern of activation. Unlike the input and output patterns the pattern in the hidden layer is emergent and its composition is influenced by similarities in the different sensory patterns included in the training set: as the input layer is stimulated by different patterns and as this activation travels to the hidden units those parts of the patterns that resemble each other have a larger effect on the shape of the emergent pattern than those that are different. At the end of the training the connections between the input and the hidden layer have acquired a configuration of strengths that can produce the emergent activation pattern whenever the neural net is presented with a similar stimulus even if does not belong to the training set. The hidden units, in turn, will cause the right motor response using the stored weight configuration in the connections between the hidden and output layers. This implies that a trained multilayer perceptron has the capacity to generalize from the sensory stimuli it received during training to many other similar stimuli. And this, in turn, suggests that the emergent activation pattern behaves like a non-symbolic representation of sensory stimuli, a representation that can be used to recognize related stimuli. Or to put this differently, during training the hidden layer slowly *extracts a prototype* from the different patterns contained in the training set, a prototype that it can use to produce the right motor response after training.[16] These emergent non-symbolic representations and the way they capture similarities in what they represent are exactly what we need to understand in what sense insect brains can build internal models of their environment.

We are now in a position to show how multilayer perceptrons can be used to simulate learning through classical conditioning. Existing designs can be quite complex because they attempt to reproduce all the different characteristics of this kind of associative learning: the shape of the learning curve; the capacity to associate many conditioned stimuli (odors, colors, flower shapes); and the increase in associative strength for conditioned stimuli that have more predictive power.[17] But the basic idea can be explained in a straightforward way. We need a design consisting of two multilayer perceptrons, one to generate a non-symbolic representation of the unconditioned stimulus and the other to generate one of the conditioned stimulus. The first neural net plays the role of an inherited reflex so its configuration of weights must be rigidly fixed as if it had been found through evolutionary search, while the second one must be able to learn from experience, that is, the weights of its connections must be found through gradient descent. Finally, the hidden units of each neural net should be connected to each other laterally in such a way that their non-symbolic representations can interact with one another. During training, as each neural net is stimulated with the patterns corresponding to the two stimuli, the emergent representations that form in the hidden units will increase the weight of some of the lateral connections and decrease the weight of others. After training, the lateral connections will possess a configuration of weights able to produce the representation of the unconditioned stimulus if given that of the conditioned one and vice versa. This means that when the input layer of the second neural net is presented with the conditioned stimulus it will create in its hidden units a pattern of activation capable of producing the extracted prototype of the unconditioned stimulus in the first neural net which, in turn, will trigger the inherited motor response.

The concept of a prototype extracted from experience and stored as a non-symbolic representation will play such a crucial role in the explanation of animal behavior in the following two chapters that its nature should be made very clear. First of all, an emergent representation is not explicitly stored as such, the product of the learning process being a configuration of connection weights that can recreate it when presented with the right input. In other words, what is stored is not a static representation but the means to dynamically reproduce it. Second, unlike a photograph these representations are dispersed or distributed in all the hidden units and are thus closer to a hologram. This means that they can be superimposed on one another so that the same configuration of weights can serve to reproduce several representations depending on its input, simulating the ability of insects to associate several colors or odors with the presence of food. The dispersed way in which extracted prototypes are represented is so important for the capacity of a neural net to generalize that these emergent representations are usually referred to as distributed representations.[18] Finally, unlike the conventional link between a symbol and what the symbol stands for, distributed representations are connected to the world in a non-arbitrary way because the process through which they emerge is a direct accommodation or adaptation to the demands of an external reality. Thus, multilayer perceptrons offer a plausible account of the intentionality of mental states.[19] When neural nets are studied in a disembodied way, that is, when their input is preselected and prestructured by the experimenter and their output is simply an arbitrary pattern of activation that has no effect on an external environment, this emergent intentionality is not displayed. But the moment we embody a neural net and situate the simulated body in a space that can affect it and be affected by it, the creatures behave in a way that one feels compelled to characterize as intentional, that is, as oriented toward external opportunities and risks.

There is one more question that needs to be addressed when considering the applicability of neural nets to simulate insect intelligence. When a simple perceptron is trained the desired motor behavior is given to them by the experimenter. This implies that, unlike insects in their natural environment, neural nets do not train themselves. This exogenous training is even more problematic in the multilayer case because the neural net is supplied not only with the desired output pattern but also with the degree to which its current output fails to match the target pattern at any point during training. Moreover, in both cases it is the experimenter who decides what patterns to include in the training set and this may introduce statistical biases in the input that artificially facilitate a learning task. Any of these problems can cast doubt on the extent to which the neural nets themselves are creating a link between their internal representations and the external world. The situation is similar to that of exogenous fitness evaluations in the case of genetic algorithms. In that case too the fact that the problem that evolution must solve is posed by the experimenter (through the design of the fitness function) may introduce unwanted biases into the search process. When neural nets or genetic algorithms are used in industrial applications these biases need not be a problem and may even be desirable if they shorten the amount of time needed to perform the training or to conduct a search. But when used as biological models exogenous training and exogenous fitness can be problematic. A way out of this dilemma has already been suggested: embody the simulated genes or neurons and situate them in a space that provides them with opportunities and risks.

One of the two simulations discussed in the previous chapter, latent energy environments (LEE), illustrates how humans can be replaced not only as animal breeders but also as animal trainers. When describing

LEE's simulations of population ecology we focused on only one of the two ways in which it can use neural nets: link them to genetic algorithms and let evolution find the configuration of weights that improves foraging behavior. But LEE's neural nets can also be configured to allow its simulated organisms to learn to forage for food during their lifetimes. LEE endogenizes the training process through a clever adaptation of back-propagation: the output layer of the neural nets produces not only motion instructions (move forward, turn left, turn right) but also predictions regarding the possible location of food. Those predictions are compared with the results obtained from further exploration of the environment and the degree of mismatch is propagated back to the other layers.[20] Ideally, these two uses of neural nets—simulating learning by the species and learning by the organism—should be used together so that something like the classical conditioning design outlined above could emerge. The first of the two neural nets, the one that creates a distributed representation of the unconditioned stimulus, should be slowly evolved within an environment that can constrain and enable action to yield reflexes linking sensory stimuli to adequate motor responses. The second neural net, the one with distributed representations of the conditioned stimuli, must arrive at a final weight configuration during the lifetime of the creatures, but the rest of its architecture could be evolved using predictive success as part of the endogenous evaluation of fitness. This way the biases built by evolution on what can play the role of a conditioned stimulus—color, floral aroma, petal arrangement, but not sound in the case of honey bees—could emerge spontaneously in a simulation.

Moving beyond the learning capacities of insects demands a more radical strategy that simply embodying multilayer perceptrons and situating them in space. In particular, larger animals with more elaborate nervous systems are capable of learning to develop novel behaviors. Unlike classical conditioning in which the existence of an inherited reflex to anchor an association is necessary, new learned behaviors can be developed through their association with rewards or punishments. Some insects may, in fact, have access to this more sophisticated learning capacity. Honey bees, for example, use classical conditioning to learn to predict the presence of food but they must also learn by trial and error how to exploit a flower blossom once it has been identified.[21] Nevertheless, the capacity to learn novel behaviors is greatly amplified in animals like birds and mammals because in their case perception and memory go beyond the world of mere stimuli. Providing evidence for this claim and examining the kind of neural nets that can display these perceptual and memory capacities will be the task of the following chapter.

CHAPTER SEVEN
Neural Nets and Mammalian Memory

As populations of neurons grew and proliferated inside living creatures, gathering into layers and folding into elaborate three-dimensional structures, they provided an ever richer substratum for the growth and proliferation of more ethereal entities: memories. The memories that birds and mammals form of actually lived episodes, for example, are more or less vivid re-experiences of events or situations in which objects play specific roles (such as agents or patients) and in which their interactions make sense to the animal. The content of autobiographical memories in animals must be thought of as endowed with significance not with signification, which is a linguistic notion. The significance of a scene or event is related to its capacity to make a difference in an animal's life, to its capacity to affect and be affected by the animal's actions, while signification is a semantic notion referring to the meaning of words or sentences. Birds and non-human mammals may be incapable of dealing with signification but they surely can attribute significance to the opportunities and risks that their environment affords them.

Evidence for the existence of different types of memory comes mostly from their dissociation in amnesic human patients or in animals that have undergone surgery to produce specific lesions in the brain. The type of memory involved in classical conditioning, whether in insects, birds, or mammals, is referred to as "procedural" because of its content's lack of accessibility outside of the sensory-motor associations that it enables. Memories whose content is accessible are referred to as "declarative," a category further subdivided depending on whether the content of the memory is events and situations that have actually been experienced, a type of memory referred to as *episodic memory*, or whether it consists of linguistically expressed facts, that is, semantic memory.[1] Damaging certain areas in animals' brains can seriously disable their capacity for declarative memory while leaving procedural memory intact. Similarly, humans suffering from certain kinds of amnesia can retain their capacity to remember linguistic information but be incapable of recalling autobiographical events, and vice versa, they can recall actually lived scenes but are unable to remember what has been said to them.[2] The very fact that episodic and semantic memory can become dissociated suggests that human sensory experience and the memories we form of it are independent of language and strongly related to one another. But for the purpose of this chapter we do not have to settle the controversy over the thesis of the linguisticality of experience: non-human mammals and birds do not posses language so their sensory experience and autobiographical memories cannot possibly be structured by it.

Unlike the perception of atomized stimuli in insects the perception of objects with an enduring identity is a complex task, involving the synthesis of features from different external as well as internal senses. Predatory mammals, for example, must guide their searching behavior by the information they get from different senses, using smell to bring them into close proximity to their target then switching to sight or sound. And they must constantly calibrate the information they receive from the external world to that generated by their own proprioceptive senses so they can distinguish between a change in their visual field produced by a prey's movements and the apparent motion created by the movement of their own head or body.[3] The synthesis of information from different sensory modalities is thought to be performed in an animal's hippocampus and related areas, an organ also involved in the formation of episodic memories. Damage to the hippocampus, for example, impairs performance on tasks that involve comparing one memory to another or using the content of a memory in a novel context.[4] Until the mechanisms behind these capacities are fully understood a philosophical exploration of avian and mammalian memory is best conducted at the mechanism-independent level. Much as the multilayer perceptrons discussed in the previous chapter helped us develop a better idea of what a representation in an insect's brain could be like—despite the fact that the simulated mechanisms, like the back-propagation of error, have no anatomical counterpart in real brains—the capacity of neural nets to recognize enduring objects and make sense of interactions between objects can be a great aid in fine-tuning our philosophical intuitions about what goes on in the minds of larger animals.

Given the complexity of the subject it will be useful to break it down into two different capacities, object recognition and scene analysis, give examples of the evidence that animal psychologists have gathered for their existence, and then discuss the currently existing neural net designs that can approximate them. The clearest laboratory evidence for the existence of the first of these two capacities comes from experiments called "two-way classifications." Two-way classification experiments were first conducted with pigeons but were later extended to monkeys and other mammals. Pigeons were shown projected photographs and trained to peck at a switch that activated a food dispenser if certain kinds of objects appeared in the pictures. In one experiment, for example, over a thousand slides of urban and countryside scenes were used, half of which contained humans in different positions (sitting, standing), with different appearances (clothed, naked), and shot from different angles. This variety eliminated the possibility that the pigeons were reacting to simple stimuli, such as color or brightness. After a few weeks the pigeons had acquired the capacity to classify pictures into those that contained one or more humans and those that did not. This result strongly suggests that the pigeons were able to extract a prototype from their perception of human figures and then use it to assess the degree of typicality that different images had relative to the prototype. Pigeons were also shown capable of performing two-way classifications of pictures with pigeons versus pictures with birds other than pigeons; of pictures with and without trees; and of pictures with and without a body of water.[5]

Before showing how multilayer perceptrons can display similar object recognition capacities one aspect of their design should be clarified. Unlike the neural nets discussed in the previous chapter in which the input layer received sensory stimulation while the output layer controlled motor behavior, we are dealing here with partial models of a more complex nervous system. This implies that a neural net's input may not come directly from sensors but from other neural nets, while its output may be subject to further processing before it is converted into a bodily action by actuators. In many cases the neural nets directly connected to either sensors or actuators are not incorporated into the design but just assumed to be there. If the neural net that receives sensory information is not included, for example, then the one whose pattern recognition behavior is being studied can have its input units labeled with words, words that stand for the objects that the latter would receive if it were actually connected to the former. Similarly, if the neural net that controls movement is not part of the design the output units of the one being studied can be labeled with words for motor actions. In the present case using words to label the input units would defeat the purpose of the experiment given that what we need to simulate is a bird's capacity to recognize objects from the visual information provided by images. The output units, on the other hand, can be labeled linguistically since in a real bird this output would be the input to many other assemblies of neurons before becoming a motor action.

A good illustration of the use of neural nets for this purpose is a simulation designed to recognize human faces. The input layer consisted of a two-dimensional array of units, 64 units on each side, into which an image could be projected. Each input unit was connected to a one-dimensional hidden layer consisting of 80 units that, in turn, were connected to an output layer containing eight units labeled with words. During training the input layer was presented with pictures of 11 different human faces (as well as of objects that were not faces) while its output layer was given an activation pattern the meaning of which was given by the labels: one unit was labeled "face," being active if the input was indeed a face and inactive if it was not; two units were labeled "female" and "male," their activity signifying gender recognition; and the remaining five units were labeled with a name and a number assigned to each face. After being trained the neural net was not only able to perform a two-way classification of pictures into those that contained and did not contain faces, but also to correctly assign face pictures to the right gender category and even to identify faces belonging to specific persons. To test its ability to generalize the neural net was tested with pictures of the same people that were not part of the training set and it performed almost flawlessly.

Moreover, it could correctly identify faces in which 20 percent of the content was deliberately obscured by completing the facial pattern with information from the distributed representations in its hidden units.[6]

The presence of labels in the output units designating linguistic categories like "male" and "female" had no effect on the ability of the neural net to recognize faces. The explanation for this capacity lies instead in the 80 units of the hidden layer. Before training all the possible patterns of activity that could occur in this layer formed an unstructured space of 80 dimensions. As the neural net was trained it first subdivided this internal space of possibilities into two regions, one corresponding to faces and the other to non-faces. Further training led the neural net to partition the face region into two subregions, one for female the other for male faces, which were then further subdivided into even smaller regions for individual faces. The "center" of each region corresponded to a prototype—the easiest to recognize faces in the training input or the easiest to recognize views of an individual face—while the borders between regions corresponded to ambiguous inputs, such as pictures in which the content could not be determined to be a face, or in which a face was displayed in such a way that it was impossible to decide whether it belonged to a male or a female.[7] This simulation provides a powerful insight into how an objective category can be captured without using any linguistic resources. The secret is the mapping of *relations of similarity into relations of proximity* in the possibility space of activation patterns of the hidden layer. That is, objects that resemble each other become neighboring points in the internal possibility space, and vice versa, objects with a high degree of dissimilarity (faces and non-faces) end up as points that are far away from each other in the space of possible activation patterns.

One limitation of this simulation is that even though the linguistic labels of the output units do not play any explanatory role their presence indicates that we are dealing with a partly disembodied neural net. We could eliminate the need for labels by adding other neural nets using the output layer's activity pattern to generate motor behavior. This behavior could be relatively simple, the simulated equivalent of pecking on a food dispenser. In laboratory animals this kind of behavior is not achieved through classical conditioning but through a different training process called *instrumental conditioning*. Instead of using a reflex as its starting point instrumental conditioning starts with a behavior that tends to occur spontaneously using rewards to increase its frequency or punishments to decrease it. The positive or negative reinforcement must be contingent on changes of behavior: if the frequency of occurrence does not change the reinforcement is not given. In addition, laboratory experiments must include a signal, a simple sound or light, to help the animal tell which one of its possibly many behaviors should be associated with the positive or negative reinforcement. This signal is called a "discriminative stimulus."[8] Outside of the laboratory reinforcement learning can lead to the development of routine behavior that helps an animal cope with the complexity of a situation but it can also lead to the formation of superstitious habits bearing no relation to real opportunities and risks. The role of discriminative stimuli is precisely to allow an animal to distinguish the behavior that is being rewarded from co-occurring behaviors that are irrelevant.

The typical laboratory outcome of instrumental conditioning, an animal that learns to press a lever to obtain a pellet of food, gives a very poor idea of the types of behavior that can be learned through this kind of training. This simple behavior is used because of the ease with which increases or decreases in the frequency of lever-pressing can be measured. But with careful manipulation of reinforcement schedules and changes in discriminative stimuli complex patterns of behavior can be generated as exemplified by the elaborate tricks that can be taught to circus animals. The target behavior may be, for example, a rat standing on its hind legs in a given corner of the cage. The experimenter must first reward going to that corner, a behavior that takes place spontaneously once in a while. If this chance behavior is rewarded and a discriminative stimulus is used to let the rat know what is being rewarded, it will increase in frequency. At that point it stops being rewarded and a different low-frequency behavior, such as moving the head to an upright position, is rewarded and linked to another discriminative stimulus until its frequency increases. The procedure continues one behavioral pattern after the next (raising the left paw, raising the right paw) until the desired final behavior is obtained. This process is called "successive approximation."[9]

The main obstacle to the design of neural nets able to learn this way is not capturing the capacity of reinforcers to affect but the capacity of an animal to be affected by them. Using food as a reinforcer, for example, implies that an animal is hungry or at least not fully satiated. But simulating hunger would seem to involve reproducing aspects of its phenomenology, such as the pangs of an empty stomach. Early explanations of hunger, in fact, took stomach contractions to be part of the mechanism through which hunger motivates food seeking behavior. This hypothesis was shown to be false by experiments in which the stomachs of rats were removed, attaching their esophagi to their small intestines, leaving the behavior associated with hunger intact.[10] In the previous chapter we argued that the degree to which an animal is surprised or startled by a novel stimulus is a subjective gradient that can be dissipated by habituation but its existence presupposes that of an objective gradient, a concentration of excitatory substances in the neural substrate. And similarly for hunger: contractions of the stomach and other components of the experience constitute a subjective gradient but one that is also underpinned by an objective one, such as concentrations of glucose in the animal's blood stream. Removing a rat's stomach eliminates the former but not the latter. This means that all a neural net must capture is the motivational effect of hunger not anything about its phenomenology.

Implementing the capacity for instrumental conditioning can be done by adding to the neural nets handling sensory and motor activities others acting as a source of motivation for behavior. In one relatively simple implementation four neural nets were linked together, two for internal reinforcement (pleasure and pain) and two for motor behavior (approach and avoid). Lateral inhibitory connections ensured that only one member of each pair was activated at any one time. External reinforcement was connected to the internal reinforcement neural nets through fixed connections to capture the fact that animals do not have to learn to respond to external sources of pleasure and pain. Simulated animals equipped with these four neural nets were able to master some tasks, such as navigation through a maze, that normally require training through instrumental conditioning in laboratory animals.[11] In other simulations the positive reinforcement centers were further differentiated so that their output activation patterns denoted a given degree of hunger or thirst. This increased the degree to which the behavior of the simulated organisms was goal-oriented, seeking not just positive reinforcement in general but food when they were hungry or water when they were thirsty.[12]

Once we embody and situate neural nets with the capacity to recognize enduring entities the next step would be giving them the ability to analyze scenes in which those entities interact playing the roles of agent or patient. Laboratory evidence for the capacity of birds and mammals to perform scene analysis is more difficult to obtain because of our complete lack of access to their phenomenology. In some cases we can compensate for this limitation by teaching an animal how to express its experience through external means. It is well known, for instance, that chimpanzees can be taught to use a relatively large vocabulary in sign language. They can also be taught to use not hand gestures but colored plastic objects of different shapes arbitrarily paired with referents, that is, paired in such a way that neither the shape nor the color of the plastic object bears any resemblance to its referent—a blue triangle, for instance, associated with an apple. Chimpanzees are not only able to associate the plastic objects with real entities and actions but can also arrange them in sequences that give us information about how they make sense of a scene. Given the plastic objects associated with the trainer, with itself, with the action "to give," and with the entity "apple," for example, a chimpanzee can arrange them in what seems to be requests like "Trainer Give Apple Chimp." The chimpanzee can also be trained to understand requests like "Chimp Give Apple Trainer."[13] These results do not show that chimpanzees can learn to use language because the sequences of plastic objects do not have a real syntax, that is, they do not have the combinatorial productivity of human words. But the outcome does show that they can place entities and actions in relations that are significant to them: they can understand and memorize scenes in which one participant acts as an agent, another as a patient, and in which certain actions link the two together.

Given the scarcity of evidence about the neural substratum and phenomenology underlying the capacity for scene analysis in animals, and about the related ability to memorize actually experienced scenes, the subject must be approached indirectly. We will first discuss the kinds of models that have been created for human episodic memory, a case in which we do have access to the phenomenology, and then work our way back to the animal case. Current simulations of human episodic memory use propositions, the meaning of sentences that express (truly or falsely) facts about the world. Propositions are used as component parts of more complex wholes called *scripts*, structured representations capturing the regularities of routine situations.[14] Scripts can be used, for example, to represent the regularities in activities like going to a restaurant. The space of possible actions in restaurant scenes has a structure—with some actions being causal preconditions for the occurrence of others—a structure that allows us to make inferences like "If the customer does not know what food is available she must ask for the menu" or "If the customer is finished eating he must pay the check." The hypothesis behind scripts is that this structure must be captured by our minds if we are to successfully and routinely anticipate action possibilities using our episodic memory of past visits to restaurants. The restaurant-going script was created by first subdividing the possibility space into types of restaurant (fancy restaurant, cafeteria, fast-food joint) since the action opportunities in each of these types is quite different. Then the different restaurant types (called "tracks") were subdivided into scenes "Entering," "Ordering," "Eating," "Exiting," each of which was defined by a sequence of simple actions. Each track was also given a set of characteristic objects (tables, menus, food) and roles (customer, waiter, cook, cashier). The typical conditions of entry to the situation (hungry customer with money) as well as its typical outcome (satiated customer with less money) were also included.[15]

Scripts and other structured representations of scenes were created in the symbolic school of Artificial Intelligence so it is not surprising that there is a linguistic bias built into them. Specifically, the content of episodic memory was assumed to be language-like, an assumption that may be defended on a variety of grounds. We may argue, for instance, that human experience is structured linguistically, a thesis that has little experimental support but that has been very influential in philosophical circles in the past 200 years. A weaker but more defensible argument would be that we have no access to other people's episodic memories except through verbal reports. This is indeed true but it may be argued that those reports are only a pale shadow of the more or less vivid re-experiences constituting autobiographical recollections. Finally, this way of modeling episodic memory may be defended in terms of the goal of a particular simulation. The above script, for example, was created to give simulated agents the capacity to understand short stories taking place in restaurants, the agents displaying their understanding by answering questions about, or paraphrasing passages from, those short stories. Because short stories typically leave out many details the ability to paraphrase them or to answer questions about them involves inferring those missing pieces of information using as an aid something like a script. Given the goal of endowing a simulated agent with this emergent capacity the concept of a script may be accepted as being useful for explanations of episodic memory at the mechanism-independent level.

The first step toward adapting this explanatory strategy to the case of avian or mammalian memory involves creating a neural net implementation of scripts, one that displays the same capacities to paraphrase and answer questions about short stories. Unlike the scripts created by the symbolic school those using neural nets do not have to be handcrafted by their creators: the scripts are learned by example extracted from statistical regularities in actual stories much like multilayer perceptrons extract prototypes from sensory stimulation. In other words, unlike the symbolic version of scripts those implemented with neural net are emergent.[16] The modules that compose this implementation differ in important ways from the neural nets discussed so far so a description of their design will be necessary before explaining how the entire assembly works. The two novel architectures are *recurrent neural nets* and *self-organizing maps*. Recurrent neural nets are like multilayer perceptrons augmented with feedback connections. In regular multilayer perceptrons there is backward movement of information about the degree of discrepancy between current and desired output patterns but this feedback operates only during training. After the weights of the connections have converged on their final values the neural net ceases to use any feedback. Recurrent neural nets, on the other hand, use feedback during actual operation. The simplest version adds to a multilayer perception an extra set of units, called "context units," linked to the hidden layer by connections with unchangeable weights and operating at full strength. This means that the context units receive an exact copy of the activation pattern that the hidden layer had immediately before its current one. This copy is then fed back to the hidden layer (along with the activation coming from the input units) causing its present state to be related to its immediate past. The result is an emergent capacity to extract *temporal regularities* from sensory stimulation, a capacity that can be used, for example, to analyze spoken sentences and predict the next word in a series.[17]

The second type of neural net needed to implement scripts is the self-organizing map. In its simplest version this design uses only two layers one of which, the input layer, functions just like in multilayer perceptrons. The second layer, the map itself, is made of computing units arranged in a specific spatial pattern, such as a two-dimensional rectangular array. This design is said to self-organize because unlike multilayer perceptrons it is not given a target output during training or the degree of mismatch that its current output has relative to the target. In other words, the training of a self-organizing map is unsupervised. The way in which the training proceeds is as follows. Every unit in the input layer is connected to every unit in the map layer, the weights of the connections set to random values at the beginning of the process. An activation pattern from a set of training examples is then presented to the input layer. Because an activation pattern is simply a list of intensities that can be expressed as numbers, and a configuration of weights in each set of connections is a list of strengths that can also be numerically expressed, the activation pattern of the input units can be compared for its degree of similarity to the weight configuration of each set of connections to the map layer. After stimulating the input layer a comparison is performed for each set of connections and the weight configuration that happens to be more similar to the input pattern is selected. That is, at the start of the training whatever similarity there may be is completely by chance but it nevertheless allows us to pick a particular unit in the map layer as the "winner."

After selecting the winner the weight configuration of the set of connections to the winning map unit is changed so that it resembles the input activation pattern a little bit more. The connections of the spatial neighbors of that map unit are also adjusted to become more like the input, the degree of adjustment diminishing the further away the map units are from the winner. Then the process is repeated with the same input pattern, the winner now being the same map unit as the previous iteration since the weights of its connections have already been made more similar to the input. The weights of the connections to this unit are made even more similar as are those of its neighbors except that now the size of the neighborhood is decreased. This process is repeated until the size of the neighborhood has been reduced to a single map unit. At that point the configuration of weights associated with the winning map unit are almost identical to the input activation pattern, while those of its neighbors are very similar to it. This means that if we activated the winning unit and allowed this activation to travel backwards through its weighted connections it would recreate the original pattern at the input layer. And if a neighboring unit was activated it would recreate a pattern similar to the original one. Through this unsupervised training procedure the activation pattern in the input layer is effectively "stored" in a region of the map layer, or more exactly, the means to reproduce it are stored in the configuration of weights between the winning map unit and the input layer.[18] This training procedure can be repeated many times for different input patterns each one "stored" in a different region of the map.

When discussing the face recognition neural net above we saw that similar faces were mapped into nearby regions in the space of possible activation patterns of the hidden units, and that this transformation of similarity relations into relations of spatial proximity was crucial to the ability of the neural net to recognize objects. A similar effect takes place in self-organizing maps except that in this case the similarity between inputs is mapped into proximity relations in the map layer itself. In other words, the relations of proximity are now between regions of a concrete actual space not an abstract possibility space. This changes the degree to which the "stored" distributed representation is accessible by other neural nets. The prototypes that a multilayer perception extracts are available only to itself, a limited access that makes them useful to model procedural memory but not declarative memory, whether episodic or semantic. But once these prototypes are made explicitly spatial they become publicly available: other neural nets that can activate the winning map unit in the self-organizing map and that can read the resulting activation pattern at its input layer will be able to retrieve the distributed representation. In addition, the "stored" distributed representation is made simpler and more compact because a self-organizing map can perform a reduction of the number of dimensions of the possibility space of activation patterns.

If the number of hidden units in a neural net is, say, eight, then its possibility space has eight dimensions. This number can be reduced to only two when the activation pattern is projected into the two spatial dimensions of the map. The self-organizing map itself selects the two dimensions that have the most variability, that is, the two that are most likely to be relevant for the ability to recognize patterns. The other six dimensions are approximated by the way in which different distributed representations are placed in the map, a placement that may develop an intertwined form resembling the way in which a one-dimensional fractal curve tries to approximate a two-dimensional surface by repeatedly folding on itself.[19]

Combining recurrent neural nets and self-organizing maps to implement scripts has been done in a simulation called "Discern." Discern uses eight separate modules, six of which are used for processing propositions and two for memory storage. The first processing module uses a recurrent neural net to parse sentences, that is, it inputs a temporal sequence of words (subject, verb, object) and outputs a series of roles: agent, patient, action performed, instrument used in the action. A second recurrent neural net uses those roles as an input to parse stories, that is, it maps the series of roles into the categories of a script. Two other processing modules perform the reverse operations: one takes scripts as inputs and outputs a series of roles, the other inputs the roles and outputs a sentence. Finally, two additional processing modules are used for the specialized tasks of answering questions and producing paraphrases.[20] The two memory modules are self-organizing maps used for the storage and sharing of distributed representations, one corresponding to semantic memory the other to episodic memory. The former is needed because the ability to understand short stories presupposes a previously acquired lexicon while the latter is where the structure of scripts is memorized. The episodic memory uses several maps arranged in three different layers: one layer for scripts (going to a restaurant, shopping, traveling); another for tracks (different places to eat or shop, different means of transportation); and one to store the patterns corresponding to the incumbents of roles (who is doing the eating, shopping, or traveling; where these activities are performed; what is being eaten or bought). The multiple maps form a pyramidal structure in the sense that each unit of the top map is connected to a separate track map, and each unit of a track map is connected to a larger map in which roles are bound to their incumbents. This pyramidal structure greatly facilitates the extraction of the inherently hierarchical structure of scripts from the different short stories included in the training set.[21] The end result is a modular neural net that exhibits the emergent capacity to answer questions about short stories, or paraphrase parts of them, by inferring missing pieces of information using its episodic memory.

Using Discern to guide philosophical thinking about mammalian and avian memory involves simplifying some aspects of its design as well as complexifying others. On one hand, the design must be made simpler because the animal capacities we need to reproduce are not as sophisticated as those that Discern simulates. If we think of scripts as internal models that explain actually lived scenes then the needed simplification would boil down to this: whereas human beings use as explanatory resources not only physical causes but also reasons (social conventions, cultural values) and motives (personal goals), birds and mammals need only frame their explanations in terms of causes since they are not capable of ascribing mental states to others nor understand how shared conventions or values shape behavior. When, for example, a chimpanzee uses colored shapes to make a request ("Trainer Give Apple Chimp") it is merely trying to causally affect the behavior of the trainer not to influence his or her mind. On the other hand, we would have to make Discern more complex because in its current form it makes use of linguistic information that would not be available to animals. Its interface to the external world is implemented through images of letters transformed into activation patterns, that is, it extracts scripts from printed texts not from sensory experience. This greatly facilitates the task of assigning the roles of agent and patient to objects in a scene using the syntactic and semantic structure contained in printed sentences, a structure that is not automatically provided by visual experience.

The changes necessary to break the linguistic dependence of scripts should be easier to implement in Discern than in the original symbolic version because the task of making sense of situations is carried out in the former with emergent distributed representations used as building blocks to compose equally emergent hierarchical taxonomies. Those distributed representations could, for example, be supplied by a video camera using the face recognition neural net discussed above.

But the real problem is not so much the kind of information used as sensory input as the fact that Discern is entirely disembodied. The lack of a body situated in space leaves Discern without the resources needed to distinguish what is relevant in an image for the purpose of assigning perceived objects to the roles of agent and patient, or to understand the connection between a cause and its effect. As we suggested in the previous chapter possession of a body gives animals a variety of ways to filter out irrelevancies. First of all, learning at the level of the species builds into an animal's body a variety of inherited behavioral tendencies that have evolved in connection with a real environment and that are therefore relevant to operating in that environment. Habituation, in turn, allows animals not to spend cognitive resources on stimuli that required an active response prior to getting used to it, in effect transforming a stimulus that was relevant into an irrelevant one. Classical conditioning permits inherited reflexes to be triggered not only by a stimulus that has survival value but also by a previously irrelevant stimulus that is nevertheless predictive of the presence of the first.

These simple forms of procedural memory represent assessments of significance made by the species as a whole over many generations, assessments that can be further modulated or adapted during an animal's lifetime. To these irrelevancy filters already available to insects we must add the habits acquired through instrumental conditioning in larger animals, habits that are less constrained by genetics. The flexibility of habits comes at a price since as it was argued above learning through reinforcement can lead to the formation of superstitious habits bearing no relation to the capacity of an environment to affect and be affected by the animal. Nevertheless, when animals learn good habits they can not only automate a series of actions to be executed without any conscious planning but they can also learn to anticipate the routine consequences of their actions. Considering that much of what makes up a script is routine and repetitive procedural memory in the form of good habits can considerably narrow down the range of experience that must be deliberately considered by the animal to make sense of situations. In other words, an embodied agent can let different forms of procedural memory take care of filtering out insignificant details while it focuses its attention on the most important aspects of a complex scene.

In addition to giving Discern a body we must also situate that body in space. When simulated agents are modeled without a body they are treated as smart planners but dumb executioners, planning everything in their heads prior to performing an action. When they are simulated without situating them in space they are treated as if they had no information about their immediate surroundings.[22] This information is referred to as *indexical knowledge*. Knowledge about an external object's position, for example, can be expressed indexically, the object is in front of the agent and to its left, or in a context-independent form by giving its latitude and longitude. While indexical knowledge comes from an agent's situated point of view—a ground-level view of reality, as it were—the source of context-independent knowledge in simulations is the godlike aerial point of view of the designer.[23] In the particular case of scripts indexical knowledge is necessary because at the lowest level of the taxonomy there are specific roles that must be bound to their incumbents, the incumbents being in most cases entities known only indexically. A possible obstacle in this regard is that neural nets are not good at solving binding problems, whether the problem is binding pronouns to proper names in a linguistic context, variables to their values in a mathematical context, or roles to their incumbents in a scene-analysis problem. One way of overcoming this limitation is suggested by the experimental observation that groups of neurons in real brains, each of which extracts different features from the same object, tend to fire in synchrony with one another when perceiving that object. In other words, temporal simultaneity in the firing behavior of neurons can act as a dynamic binder. This insight has already been successfully exploited in some modular neural net designs that perform script-like inferences.[24]

Even though we are still far from understanding how avian and mammalian memory and perception work the ideas we have derived from simulations suggest that the key ingredient in the explanation of those capacities continues to be the extraction of prototypes from sensory exposure and the "storage" of those prototypes in the form of distributed representations. In the case of scene analysis the prototypes must be extracted not only from similarities in the spatial configuration of the defining features of sensed objects but also from patterns in their temporal behavior, such as the regular co-occurrence of linear causes and their effects. The more enduring form of memory needed for autobiographical recollections, in turn, must be implemented through the use of self-organizing maps or similar designs in which the number of dimensions of the map is not fixed in advance.[25] Finally, we must provide these neural nets with the necessary irrelevancy filters with which evolution supplies embodied animals. These are particularly necessary for the operation of self-organizing maps because the mechanism through which they achieve the storage of distributed representations presupposes a criterion of similarity provided exogenously, and similarity is a very problematic relation: two objects that are dissimilar to each other visually may be similar in their auditory, olfactory, or haptic properties. Even more problematic is the fact that any two entities may be similar to each other in an infinite number of perceptually irrelevant ways: in being inhabitants of planet Earth, for instance, or in moving slower than the speed of light.[26] Evolution has filtered out many irrelevant dimensions of similarity from the neural machinery used by animal brains but disembodied neural nets do not have access to these automatic filters.

It is time now to move beyond simulations of individual agents and their individual minds to consider entire communities of agents. While in the former case we are concerned with how an embodied and situated agent makes sense of the opportunities and risks provided to it by its environment, in the latter we must add the opportunities and risks supplied by its interactions with members of the community of which it itself is a component part. Since we will now be concerned with larger wholes with their own emergent properties the details of how individual agents perceive and memorize can be taken for granted. This means that simulations can use linguistically expressed rules and procedures to generate agent behavior without begging the question. The following chapter will tackle this subject starting with multiagent simulations of the social behavior of our closest relatives in the animal world and moving on to consider how the more complex social behavior of our hunter-gatherer ancestors could have emerged.

CHAPTER EIGHT
Multiagents and Primate Strategies

As the psychological life of animals became richer and their behavior increasingly determined by their membership in a community their interactions provided the medium for the rise of a new kind of entity, social strategies, and generated new possibility spaces in which the singularities defined sets of mutually stabilizing strategies. Although some insect species have an elaborate social life within colonies or hives their interactions do not involve recognition of individual conspecifics and take place by indirect communication, that is, by alteration of the physical and chemical properties of a shared environment. Monkeys and apes, on the other hand, are capable of recognizing each other not only as unique individual organisms but also as belonging to a certain kinship group and occupying a given rank in a dominance hierarchy. The likelihood that a young monkey or ape will start a fight with another, for instance, depends not only on memories of the outcomes of previous aggressive encounters but also on the presence or absence of an older relative acting as a social ally. Other examples of the kind of social problem-solving performed by these animals include coalition formation—a lower ranking animal may be able to challenge a rival if he or she has previously established an alliance with a higher ranking one—as well as reconciliatory behavior to undo the damage of previous aggressive encounters.[1] The observed social capacities of contemporary non-human primates provide us with the best guide to speculate about how our last common ancestors could have affected (and be affected by) one another. More specifically, they provide us with insight into the mechanisms behind the emergence of reciprocal altruism, a social interaction involving the exchange of favors in which there is a temporal delay between the provision of a service and its reciprocation. Reciprocal altruism, in turn, may have been the point of departure for a long process that would eventually lead to the emergence of communal solidarity in ancient hunter-gatherer communities.

Solidarity in contemporary human communities acts as a social gradient that varies among different groups endowing them with different capacities for political mobilization and other forms of collective social action. The mechanism of emergence of solidarity in these communities depends on the existence of a dense network of connections among their members. In a community in which everyone knows everyone else word of mouth travels fast, particularly if the subject of conversation is the transgression of a local norm: an unfulfilled promise, an unpaid bet, an unreciprocated favor. This rapid transmission of linguistic information allows the community to act as a reputation-storage mechanism. If in addition ridicule and ostracism are used to collectively punish those who dishonor commitments then the community has the capacity to act as an enforcement mechanism. The question to be explored in this chapter is how the transition between the reciprocal altruism of the common ancestors of humans and chimpanzees and the communal solidarity of the earliest hunter-gatherers could have occurred without the use of linguistic resources. Some experts believe that the first emergence of language (glottogenesis) took place between thirty and fifty thousand years ago when burial rites, sophisticated stone tools, and regular trade were already well established. Others believe that glottogenesis occurred in an earlier period, the middle paleolithic, that began about two hundred and fifty thousand years ago.[2] Either way, by the time language appeared the ancestors of modern humans had already spent hundreds of thousands of years as members of communities in which a dual economy of hunting and gathering involved new role assignments, public monitoring of relations, and collective evaluation of resource allocations. In other words, a complex social life preexisted the emergence of language.

Reciprocal altruism among non-human primates involves strategic interactions between two animals supplying one another with an opportunity to cooperate—to groom parts of the body that are inaccessible without help, for example—but also with the risk of being cheated, since the delay before reciprocation means that there is no immediate assurance the service provided will be repaid. This is an example of a *social dilemma* a social interaction that can have collective benefits but that is endangered by the possibility of greater individual gains. In the simplest social dilemmas interactions between pairs of agents are structured by two opportunities and two risks: the tempting opportunity to cheat a cooperator gaining at its expense (called "temptation" or simply "T"); the opportunity of mutual gain by cooperators (a "reward" or "R"); the risk of mutual cheating (a "punishment" or "P"); and the risk for a cooperator of being cheated (being made a "sucker" or "S"). The field of mathematics that studies strategic interactions models them as games so these opportunities and risks are referred to as the "payoffs" of the game. What makes a strategic interaction a social dilemma is the ordering of the payoffs. In the situation referred to as the *Prisoner's dilemma* the payoffs are arranged like this: $T > R > P > S$. If $R > T$ then there is no conflict between individual and collective gains so all dilemmas must have $T > R$. But this particular arrangement also implies that the worst thing that can happen is to be a cooperator that is cheated ($P > S$).[3] A different dilemma can be generated by the arrangement $T > R > S > P$. This is called "Chicken"—after the game in which two drivers on a collision course play to see who swerves out of the way first—because unlike the previous case the worst outcome is when neither driver swerves and both crash ($S > P$). Like all opportunities and risks the payoffs of strategic interactions structure a space of possibilities, an objective possibility space shared by the interacting agents.

In addition to this objective space we must also model the subjective space of possibilities, that is, the strategic choices available to the agents. In the simplest case these are simply the choices to cooperate or cheat but in more complex situations the subjective possibility space contains not only choices but strategies. Because in the latter case the value of one agent's strategy depends on its relation to the strategies of other agents what we need to explore is the structure of an intersubjective possibility space. This intersubjective space is structured by singularities called *Nash equilibria* defining combinations of strategies that stabilize one another because no agent can get a better payoff by unilaterally changing to a different strategy. When the opportunities and risks are arranged as in the Prisoner's dilemma and the interaction occurs just once the only Nash equilibrium is for both agents to cheat: they would be better off if they cooperated, since R > P, but neither one can choose cooperation unilaterally without risking being cheated and getting S. If the interaction is repeated many times then mutual cooperation becomes a Nash equilibrium except in the very last encounter in which mutual cheating pays best. But if the agents know when the last interaction will occur then it pays to cheat in the previous one as well, and for that reason in the one prior to that one, and so on all the way to the very first one. So the interesting case from the point of view of modeling the emergence of coopera- tion in primate communities is a repeated (or iterated) strategic inter- action in which neither agent knows when the last encounter will take place. This is called the *indefinitely iterated* Prisoner's dilemma, a version characterized by the fact that the "shadow of the future" (the probability of future interactions) helps to stabilize cooperative out- comes.[4] While social dilemmas involving only a single interaction represent the conflict between individual and collective interests, the iterated version adds a temporal dimension that captures the tension between short- and long-term interests.

The simplest strategies are those that do not take history into account: Dove the strategy of always cooperating and Hawk the strat- egy of always cheating. Next in complexity are strategies in which an agent's choices take into account only the previous action of the other agent, cooperating if it cooperated or cheating if it cheated, for exam- ple. If we add to this that in the very first encounter, when there is no history on which to base a choice, an agent always cooperates we get the famous strategy known as *Tit-for-tat*, winner of the first simulated competition between strategies.[5] Next in complexity are strategies that involve remembering not only the other agent's previous choice but also an agent's own previous choice. An example would be a strategy instructing an agent to cooperate in the next encounter if its previous cooperation was reciprocated; to shift back to cooperate if both previously cheated; to cheat again if it cheated while the other one cooperated; and finally, to shift back to cheat if it cooperated while the other one cheated. This strategy is referred to as *Pavlov* (or Win-Stay, Loose-Shift) and differs from Tit-for-tat in that it takes advantage of unconditional cooperators (Doves). More complex strategies can be generated by increasing the amount of memory that agents must bring to bear remembering, for instance, not just the previous action but the previous two actions. An example would be a more "forgiving" version of Tit-for-tat (called "Tit-for-two-tats") in which an agent must be cheated twice in a row before cheating back.

These ideas can be used to model the social strategies of non-human primates in the case of dyadic interactions, such as the reciprocation of grooming or food sharing between two animals, and only when the interacting pair is not related by kinship, since kindred animals may be genetically predisposed toward cooperation. Some triadic interactions, like starting a fight in the presence of an ally, may be broken down into two dyadic ones: the interaction with the ally, who may have been groomed in advance and its being present at the fight is its way of reciprocating, and the agonistic interaction itself, a ritualized contest in which opponents assess each other's strength. In this contest using the Hawk strategy means to escalate the level of violence until injured while using Dove means to make aggressive displays (such as bearing one's teeth) until escalation starts then withdraw.[6] In addition to restricting the application of the model to pairs of unrelated animals there is the question of whether non-human primates can in fact analyze each other's behavior and base their own responses on the results of those analyses. Evidence in favor of this hypothesis comes from experiments using dyads of unrelated tamarin monkeys placed in a situation in which one of them has an opportunity to provide food for the other without itself getting any reward. In one experiment some tamarin monkeys were previously trained to use the Hawk and Dove strategies—some would never pull the lever that provided the other one with food while others always pulled it—and then they were paired with untrained monkeys. The results were clear: the untrained monkeys pulled significantly more for the Doves than for the Hawks.

This result, however, does not necessarily imply that the untrained monkeys were reciprocating past behavior that was mentally analyzed and determined to be altruistic, so a different experiment was carried out to rule out the possibility that mere satiation was the motivating factor. Two untrained monkeys were placed in the above situation but alternating in roles, each having several chances to deliver food for the other without immediate benefits to itself. The rate at which they cooperated in these interactions was recorded and then they were made to interact in a situation in which each pull of the lever resulted in food for both of them. Finally, they engaged in another session of alternating altruistic food exchange. If their rate of cooperation depended on mere satiation then the intervening situation in which both got food should have increased the rate of cooperation. If on the contrary, the rate depended on their memory of the other's past behavior then the intervening situation should have had no effect. The results were compatible with the latter hypothesis: the monkeys seemed to be responding to prior intentional acts of food giving by their conspecifics.[7] Finally, there is the question of whether monkeys and apes have the cognitive capacity to use behavioral strategies like Tit-for-tat or Pavlov as part of a larger community in which each animal must remember the last outcome of every interaction with other members, literally keeping score of all its strategic interactions. Laboratory studies indicate that only chimpanzees have the cognitive sophistication to do this while other species may be using simpler behavioral strategies, such as mirroring each other's behavior or favoring those with whom they spend time in close proximity.[8]

Given that all we need in this chapter is a way of modeling the social strategies of the common ancestors of humans and chimpanzees this evidence is enough to allow us to assume that they could memorize partner-specific contingencies, punish cheaters, and perform score keeping. The next step is to find a way to explore the emergent consequences for an entire community of many indefinitely iterated dyadic interactions. In particular, we need to be able to track a changing composition of strategies over many generations. If some strategies come to dominate the community in the long run and if these strategies involve some form of reciprocal altruism (like Tit-for-tat or Pavlov) then social cooperation can be considered a stable outcome and thus one likely to have actually occurred among our ancestors. The simplest way of exploring this question is by coupling models of strategic interaction to genetic algorithms. Coding a given strategy into the simulated chromosome of a genetic algorithm is relatively straightforward because the choices that make up a strategy are binary (cooperate or cheat) as are the bits that compose the genes: four bits can code for the binary responses to an agent's previous move while an added two bits can tell the agent what to do in the very first move.[9] The outcome of the simulations, on the other hand, can be quite complex because the fitness of a particular strategy is frequency-dependent in the sense that as a strategy becomes more frequent in a population it can create the conditions for its eventual demise. In other words, the relative success of a strategy depends not only on its intrinsic properties but on the proportion of agents that are using it as well as on the proportion of agents using other strategies.

Frequency-dependency creates such complex dynamics that the results from one simulation may change when one of the parameters—initial proportions of strategies, initial mix of strategies, number of generations, mutation rate—is changed. This is clearly illustrated by the fate of the very first simulation of this kind in which Tit-for-tat came to dominate the population after 50 generations in a large number of runs. This result was viewed as a watershed in the study of reciprocal altruism and also carried some moral comfort because, to use psychological metaphors, the winning strategy was "nice" since it always cooperated in the first move; it was "forgiving" renewing cooperation if a former cheater cooperated; and it was not liable to be abused because it was "retaliatory," punishing cheaters by cheating.[10] In the original simulation the initial mix contained only Hawk, Dove, and Tit-for-tat as alternatives. Hawks performed well at first by taking advantage of Doves, but as the Doves began to disappear from the population so did the Hawks, leaving only Tit-for-tat. But when the same simulation was allowed to run longer than 50 generations frequency-dependent tendencies became manifest: a mutation transformed one copy of Tit-for-tat into Dove and because all Hawk strategies were gone Doves were able to slowly spread as more mutations accumulated at random; and once the Dove strategy had acquired a critical mass a mutation producing a copy of Hawk had again a chance to get a foothold and then invade the population. It is now well known that Pavlov will do better in this scenario because unlike Tit-for-tat it can take advantage of Doves and prevent them from creating the conditions that lead to the spread of Hawks. Pavlov, on the other hand, does not do well against Hawks so to spread through the population it needs to use Tit-for-tat as a stepping stone.[11]

In these simulations the behavioral strategies were modeled as if they were inherited in a rigid way, that is, as if the agents did not learn during their lifetimes. When learning is performed by the species over many generations a Nash equilibrium refers to a population of strategies that is stable against invasion from mutant strategies. These are referred to as *evolutionary stable strategies*, strategies that perform successfully when interacting with others as well as when interacting with copies of themselves. In some cases it is easy to establish whether a strategy is evolutionary stable: the Hawk strategy, for instance, is clearly not stable because even though it is good at exploiting others it does not do well against itself. But as the case of Tit-for-tat shows a strategy previously thought to be evolutionary stable may turn out not to be so in the long run and this complexity calls for a complementary approach using both computer simulations and mathematical analysis.[12] While mathematical analysis reveals the singularities that structure the intersubjective possibility space computer simulations can actually follow the path toward the singularities. We have already encountered this complementarity between the two different approaches in earlier chapters but in the case of simulations of interacting agents being able to track a historical trajectory is even more important because many interesting events occur during *transients*, that is, during the period of time before a singularity is reached. In some cases a frequency-dependent dynamic may spend most of its time in long transients. This implies that giving an explanation of the long-term consequences of strategic interaction involves showing not only that a Nash equilibrium exists and that it can be reached but also providing an estimate of the time scale necessary to reach it.[13]

Simulations can also complement mathematical analysis by helping to clarify some conceptual assumptions. There are two aspects of the concept of a Nash equilibrium that need clarification. One has to do with the maintenance of equilibrium, that is, with the mechanism that restores stability after an external shock, while the other relates to the selection of one Nash equilibrium over another in the case of possibility spaces structured by multiple singularities. The selection problem can be solved through a mechanism that performs a search of the possibility space to converge on one of the several available Nash equlibria. In earlier chapters we have seen that biological evolution constitutes a powerful search mechanism and the simulations just discussed shows how useful they can be to fine-tune our intuitions about the selection process.[14] The maintenance problem, on the other hand, needs a different approach. In traditional mathematical models the problem is solved via an assumption of full common knowledge on the part of all agents: it is not enough that a strategy is such that no one can switch unilaterally to a different one and be better off but, in addition, every agent must know that all other agents know this. The assumption of common knowledge, however, demands postulating cognitive capacities that the ancestors of humans and chimpanzees could not have had. So the solution to the maintenance problem must be sought in the development of good habits that achieve the same result.[15] In the case of our primate ancestors those good habits may have been developed through reinforcement learning in times of scarcity, times in which it was in everyone's self-interest to cooperate by sharing food, but being habits as opposed to rational decisions they could have survived into times of plenty.[16]

Using computer simulations to clarify the maintenance problem implies the use of agents that can acquire habits in their lifetime and this, in turn, involves making several changes in the assumptions built into the models. In particular, unlike the case of disembodied strategies in which the payoffs can simply be assumed to act as incentives, reinforcement learning implies relating to the opportunities and risks of strategic interaction as rewards and punishments. Thus, the first change that needs to be made is to introduce a cutoff point in the series of payoffs to make some unambiguously rewarding and the others punishing. Placing the cutoff point in the middle, so that, $T < R < 0 < P < S$, yields the most interesting results.[17] Next we need to create neural nets that can relate to these payoffs as positive and negative reinforcement. As we saw in the previous chapter this involves a certain degree of embodiment in the form of neural nets performing motivational roles, such as simulated hunger or thirst, but in the simplest case all we need to assume is that the agents have a (non-emergent) tendency to avoid the risk of unreciprocated cooperation. This boils down to the unproblematic assumption that agents dislike being cheated but it also carries the implication that every member of a dyad has an incentive to try to get the other member to cooperate. Thus what is needed is a population of neural nets that train one another on a continuous basis as they attempt to elicit cooperation from their partners: the input units receive information about the previous outcome (or outcomes) while a single output unit yields a binary choice to cooperate or cheat in the next encounter. The weights of the connections are changed only if the previous interaction was negative, that is, if the payoff was P or S, and in proportion to how negative it was, more for S than for P.[18]

In one simulation an initial population of 100 neural nets was paired at random and the repeated interaction between dyads followed to observe the sequence of changes that led to mutual cooperation. Depending on the strategy different sequences were followed: two Pavlov strategies, for example, eventually locked into cooperation following the sequence unilateral defection-bilateral defection-bilateral cooperation. If we imagine that biological evolution had already brought a community of strategists near a Nash equilibrium, the addition of learning may be seen as a means for the community to return to the singularity after a forced departure from it. In other words, the habit of trying to elicit cooperation from a partner would be a way of solving the maintenance problem. On the other hand, without coupling neural nets to genetic algorithms the ability to learn by itself is not a solution to the problem. This is illustrated by the effect of mistakes on the collective outcome. Errors can be made when one agent incorrectly "perceives" the other's last move or when it mistakenly responds to it. When Tit-for-tat confronts itself, for example, and one of the dyad members mistakenly responds by cheating after a cooperative act, the second member will retaliate by cheating and the two will lock themselves into a feud that can only be ended by another error. Pavlov, on the other hand, is not only able to recover from an error after a single round of punishment, but it can use its own errors to spot Dove-like strategies once it discovers that it need not fear retaliation. When the strategies are fully inherited errors help stabilize cooperation by allowing pragmatic reciprocators (Pavlov) to spread through the population.[19] But without inheritance this effect disappears. The reason is that a population of learning dyads is, in effect, searching the space of possible strategies by itself. In the case of neural nets that take into account the last two previous moves there are 21 possible strategies and hence 21 squared (441) possible pairs. The effect of mistakes is to complicate the search of this large space and to make it harder for cooperation to spread.[20]

There are two more factors to consider when evaluating the chances that reciprocal altruism can become established in a population: the role of spatial relations and of kinship. The former is important because opportunities for interaction are affected by proximity, an effect ignored in all the previous simulations in which pairs of strategies were picked at random to interact. The latter must be included despite the fact that generosity among relatives is not the result of a strategic interaction because it can act as an exogenous source of cooperative behavior and influence the overall outcome. The effect of both factors is to create groups of cooperators within a larger community within which reciprocal altruism can become stable. One relatively simple way of developing intuitions about spatial effects is to couple models of strategic interaction with cellular automata. As discussed in Chapter 2 these simulations involve populations of finite state automata that interact only with their neighbors capturing proximity effects directly. The task of programming any of the above strategies into a finite state automaton is quite straightforward: the input to the automaton is the outcome of the previous encounter (or encounters) while its output is the choice to cooperate or cheat in the next interaction.[21] Unlike the classic model of iterated Prisoner's Dilemma in which only the ordering of the payoffs matters (T < R < P < S) a crucial factor in the cellular automaton version is how much larger the payoff for unilateral defection is relative to that for mutual cooperation. For low enough values cooperation prevails while for large values cheating always does so it is in the intermediate range that the interesting results lie. One of these results is that while a population of cooperating neighbors can be invaded if a single cheater arises, a population of cheaters needs a large enough cluster of neighboring cooperators to be invaded.[22]

A less abstract way of exploring the effect of proximity can be implemented by making the choice to cooperate or cheat to be about the use of resources located in space. In one simulation it was found that groups of cooperators can form if the distribution of food is patchy and if there are costs associated with moving between patches, such as an increased risk of predation. The inheritable cooperative behavior in this simulation was restraint in the consumption of food to prevent the over exploitation and exhaustion of the resource, and the outcome was that groups of cooperators emerged but only as long as the food patches were small and widely spaced.[23] Kinship is another way of generating cooperating groups for two different reasons. First, biological evolution can give rise to altruistic behavior between closely related animals by a mechanism known as *inclusive fitness*: any gene predisposing an animal toward altruism can propagate if the animal itself reproduces or if close relatives with which it shares those genes reproduce, so altruistic gestures toward relatives can have similar evolutionary effects as self-interested behavior. Second, kinship can influence the formation of groups because the benefits of kin-directed altruism can only be enjoyed if relatives stay in close spatial proximity. Both of these possible effects have been tested in simulations using genetic algorithms coupled to neural nets in which evolution fully determined the final weight configuration.

In one simulation a population of 100 multilayer perceptrons was evolved, using information about kinship as an input and the decision to share or hoard food as an output. The population was broken down into 20 groups of relatives and fitness was measured by the amount of food gathered during a lifetime. The outcome conformed to the inclusive fitness hypothesis: while altruistic behavior toward strangers was weeded out altruism between relatives was not. Then a second simulation was performed in which the food was given a spatial distribution and the neural nets were provided with additional units to allow their behavior to be shaped by spatial position: for "young" agents two input units gave the position of their parents (one for angle, the other for distance) while for "adult" agents the input was the position of food items. For both age groups additional output units allowed the agents to perform simple movement decisions (to move forward, to turn right, or to turn left). Parents had to decide whether to feed themselves, feed their existing offspring, or save food for future offspring since they could reproduce several times during their life. The results were that in "young" agents a tendency to stay in ever closer proximity to their patterns evolved, and with it the emergence of clusters of cooperators. For adults the results were more complex because their choices involved compromises. In particular, if they were too altruistic and did not sufficiently feed themselves they had shorter life spans and less overall offspring; if on the contrary, they were not altruistic enough their offspring tended to die. So reproductive success belonged to those that stroke the right compromise.[24]

Let's pause to consider what has been argued up to this point. Existing laboratory evidence suggests that chimpanzees can not only remember the outcomes of past encounters with individual members of their community but also analyze scenes involving social interactions to detect tendencies to cooperate or cheat. The discussion of episodic memory in the previous chapter makes the existence of these capacities rather unsurprising but a new twist has been added in this one: the responses of chimpanzees in future interactions tend to be correlated with the results of those analyses making their behavior an instance of a social strategy. Using these capacities for social problem-solving as a guide the question we set out to answer was whether some form of reciprocal altruism could have become established in the communities of the last common ancestors of humans and chimpanzees. Although the conclusion we reached was not unambiguous it seems plausible to assume that sets of cooperative strategies of changing composition could have become established in prehuman communities through an interaction of several factors: genetic predispositions coupled to good habits; formation of clusters of cooperators living in close proximity; and the effects of inclusive fitness. In other words, stable solutions to social dilemmas involving indefinitely repeated dyadic interactions could have been arrived at collectively and then maintained in a community. The next step is to use the ideas developed so far to model the transition from our primate ancestors to pre-linguistic hunter-gatherers as a historical event that involved arriving at solutions to new social dilemmas.

One way of approaching the emergence of cooperative hunting (or gathering) is to model it as a transition from the two-person Prisoner's dilemma—in which a whole community may be involved but interactions are dyadic—to the multi-person Prisoner's dilemma in which each member strategically interacts with the rest of the community. Another name for social dilemmas involving a plurality of agents is public good dilemmas. In the case of cooperative hunting the public good is the meat obtained at the end of the hunt, a public good involving a cost to cooperators but not to those who refrain from hunting but enjoy its rewards when the meat is redistributed. In this case the opportunities and risks structuring the objective space of possibilities become more complex to calculate since they must be a function of the number of cooperators, the costs of cooperating, and the degree to which cooperation amplifies (or multiplies) individual efforts. These three factors can be used to calculate the public good that is produced, a number that must then be divided by the number of people into which the spoils are redistributed. Since a cheater gets the same amount of meat as someone who participates in the hunt its payoff is simply the result of that division, while the payoff for a cooperator is that amount minus the costs of cooperating. For there to be a dilemma the multiplication factor must be larger than one —else there are no benefits to collaborative hunting over and above those of individuals hunting alone—but it must also be less than the number of persons into which the spoils will be redistributed. The reason is that while cheaters always do better than cooperators because their payoff never includes costs, if the multiplication factor is large enough cheaters can improve their payoff by switching to cooperation.[25]

An important difference between dyadic and communal interactions is that strategies like Tit-for-Tat are not part of the intersubjective possibility space because of the difficulty of focusing retaliation. A good illustration of this difficulty is the so-called *tragedy of the commons*, a situation involving a community of agents exploiting a common resource that is vulnerable to depletion by overexploitation.[26] If a single cheater overexploits and a former cooperator attempts to retaliate by also overexploiting, as Tit-for-tat would do, this not only unfairly penalizes those who refrained from selfish behavior but it may also trigger a wave of further retaliations in which everyone overexploits the resource with a predictably tragic outcome. Thus, viable strategies must find a way of replacing the individual punishment of cheaters by the collective enforcement of cooperation. In addition, while in the case of dyadic interactions it is up to the members of a dyad to detect and remember departures from cooperation, when an entire community is involved such individual memories are not enough. This means that we need a way to replace the individual recognition of cheaters by the collective storage of reputations. As mentioned above these two mechanisms are implemented in contemporary communities by the rapid spread of word of mouth about violations of local norms and by the use of ostracism and ridicule to punish violators. But in the present context we must model the emergence of both collective mechanisms without presupposing the existence of language.

The problem of storing reputations can be solved by replacing word of mouth with the shared experience of violations of cooperation. For entire communities it would be unrealistic to assume that every violation can be witnessed by all members. But if a community tended to sort itself out into distinct groups and if members of these small groups tended to stay in close proximity to one another then the episodic memories of group members would suffice to keep a record of the past behavior of other group members. As we just saw, both ecological and genetic factors can bring about the formation of such groups so we can take those results as indications that there is a solution to this problem. The problem of collective enforcement, on the other hand, is not so easy to solve because of the existence of frequency-dependent effects. This can be illustrated with a simple example. Let's assume the existence of certain inherited tendencies that would influence the outcome of a public goods dilemma, behavioral tendencies like vengefulness, the tendency to punish those that are caught, and boldness, the tendency to cheat relative to the chance of being caught. We can code degrees of boldness and vengefulness into the simulated chromosomes of a genetic algorithm and track the resulting collective dynamic. In one simulation a population of agents started with genes determining intermediate levels of both tendencies. After a few generations the degree of boldness began to fall because even without very high vengefulness being caught cheating was costly. As the proportion of bold agents decreased genes for vengefulness also began to disappear because with only a few cheaters enforcement costs become a liability. But as the average degree of vengefulness in the community fell and with it the costs of being caught, boldness made a comeback.[27]

Simulations like this show that the existence of certain personal characteristics is not enough to yield the desired outcome because the activity of *punishing cheaters is itself a public good*: if some cooperators refrain from punishing because of the costs associated with it then they are cheating those that do punish. In other words, any behavior that promotes a public good is itself a second order public good. This suggests that the solution to public good dilemmas must involve both primitive norms—inherited or habitual patterns of behavior leading to the punishment of cheaters—as well as *metanorms*, the tendency to punish those that do not punish.[28] This possible solution must be coupled with that for cheater detection, that is, with the formation of small groups within a larger community. In one simulation, for example, agents were matched into groups using the norm "do not choose cheaters as members" and the metanorm "do not choose those that choose cheaters." Both degree of cooperativeness and degree of vengefulness were coded into a genetic algorithm and a population was allowed to evolve different strategies as the agents made decisions about group formation and choices to cooperate or cheat. The outcome depended on three conditions affecting group formation. The first condition related to the way in which membership was decided, that is, whether a unilateral choice by an agent who wanted to join was enough or whether acceptance or rejection of membership depended also on the group (mutual choice). With unilateral choice there was no room for metanorms so the outcome was predictably that low cooperators cheated on high cooperators. The second condition involved the possibility for vengeful members to split from a group to express their dissatisfaction with those who refused to punish. Without this possibility genes for high vengefulness could not get established and low cooperators continued to cheat. Finally, the third condition involved the possibility that agents who may have departed from a previous group could reenter another group allowing resilient groups of cooperators to recruit new members and grow at the expense of other groups. The strategy combining mutual choice, splitting, and rejoining performed best as a solution to the multi-person Prisoner's Dilemma.[29]

We may conclude that when the emergence of metanorms allowed communities to solve the public goods dilemma involved in collective hunting and gathering the transition from animal to human communities was complete. As mentioned at the start of this chapter these novel communities embodied a new resource gradient, a gradient of solidarity. From that point on the further development of human sociality began to depend not only on the interactions of small groups within a community but on the interactions between distinct communities, the outcome of which was determined in part by the solidarity gradients that each of them could exploit. More specifically, when the practices of early human communities began to include the production of stone tools, changing the ways in which hunting and gathering were conducted, new Nash equilibria that were improvements over the old ones appeared in their possibility spaces. A greater degree of solidarity in a community could have made the transition to the new singularity smoother by increasing the degree of social coordination needed to move through the possibility space while staying in the cooperative payoff region of that space. Communities that were able to successfully make that move would have therefore increased their chance of survival relative to communities that failed to do so.[30] Thus, what future simulations must allow us to do is to track many communities of agents as they move from one Nash equilibrium to another in an ever changing space of possibilities. In the following chapter we will examine one of the sources of new Nash equilibria, stone tool technology, as well as a new social gradient that emerges from the interactions between communities: the gradient represented by the gains from trade.

CHAPTER NINE
Multiagents and Stone Age Economics

As communities of early humans began to spread over the planet their activities added to its surface one more layer of complexity. On one hand, their members, on whose bodies ancient communal habits had already sedimented, acquired the capacity to transform stone into manufactured tools. On the other, the tools themselves and the debris produced during their manufacture slowly accumulated leaving behind a record not unlike that of fossils embedded in geological strata. Most of the knowledge we have about the culture of those early communities comes from those deposits of stone artifacts. Next to them archeologists have also found the bones of animals that died at different ages, giving us information about hunting techniques, as well as ashes from wood or bone, providing us with evidence for the routine use of fire. Nevertheless, it is the stone artifacts themselves that are our richest source of data about the way of life of our ancestors. One of the safest conclusions that can be drawn from the strata in which these deposits are arranged is their great longevity: the oldest stratigraphic sequence (the Olduvai sequence) is about one and a half million years old.[1] Much of the content of this and other sequences is relatively uniform but as we approach more recent times the tool and debris deposits begin to diversify: the variability in tool types increases in the middle paleolithic (two hundred and fifteen thousand to forty thousand years ago) and reaches a peak in the upper paleolithic (forty thousand to ten thousand years ago).

Tools from these more recent periods display a complexity that bears witness to the increased sophistication of the manual operations used to produced them: from the oldest method of percussion, the deliberate breaking of a stone into pieces by a few strong blows; to the more recent technique of retouching, using lighter but more frequent blows; to the use of pressure flaking, first for the creation of sharp blades, then for the precision shaping of a tool by controlling the thickness of its different parts, the sharpening of its ends, and the elimination of curves.[2] If habits promoting cooperation constituted the first form of human cultural content transmitted across generations, the manual skills involved in the manufacture of stone tools greatly enriched this cultural heritage. The distinction between habits and skills is like that between tendencies and capacities: habits are repetitive and limited in variation while skills are more flexible and open ended. Like all capacities to affect skills must be adapted to a capacity to be affected: percussion blows must aim for cracks or fractures; edges must be created in a rigid stone capable of holding on to a shape; flaking operations must be applied to fine-grained stone; production of large tools must use rocks of the right dimensions. Both manual skills and the complex procedures to which they gave rise are certainly older than spoken language suggesting that *the hand may have taught the mouth to speak*, that is, that ordered series of manual operations may have formed the background against which ordered series of vocalizations first emerged.

Variability in tool and debris deposits is evidence not only of the progressive differentiation of skills but also of cultural enrichment within communities and even of contact between different communities. The latter follows from the fact that good quality stone was not always available locally so that it had to be imported. Reliable methods to determine the provenance of different materials have been developed by archeologists who have shown that a great amount of movement of high-quality flint took place in the middle paleolithic. Roughly, if a given material has traveled less than five kilometers it is assumed to be of local origin; if the distance is between five and twenty kilometers it is said to be of regional origin; and if the material has been transported over distances greater than 30 kilometers it is deemed exotic or imported.[3] While in the middle paleolithic the longest movements seem to be of the order of a hundred kilometers by the upper paleolithic they have increased to 400 kilometers. What is not clear is whether the long-distance movement of flint and other materials was effected through some form of trade or by another mechanism. One possibility is that the movement began with a traveling delegation carrying an offering that was then entrusted to a variety of intermediary communities none of which ever left its own territory.[4] This would imply that some form of cooperation between different communities had become stable enough to support such a multistaged transport mechanism but, as was argued in the previous chapter, the stability of cooperation is hard to achieve within a single community let alone between several different ones. So trade remains a possibility even if it involved only a very primitive form of barter with no clear conception of profits.

Evidence from contemporary hunter-gatherers indicates that within communities the only type of stable exchange is in the form of transactions internal to kinship groups: mutual aid or gifts not immediately reciprocated. The interactions between such groups within a tribe can become less personal but it is only in transactions between different tribes that social distance increases enough for impersonal exchange to exist.[5] This evidence can serve only as a rough approximation to think about middle paleolithic communities because today's hunter-gatherers already possess spoken language. But this is less of a limitation than it may seem because the existence of a complex language has never been a prerequisite for trade even in relatively recent times: in areas of intense commercial activity between communities of different linguistic backgrounds simplified languages, called "trade pidgins," are often created in a relatively short time and they disappear as the contact situation ceases to exist. For simpler forms of barter a few gestures and unarticulated sounds could have sufficed to carry out a transaction. The main question then is not so much about linguistics but about economics, that is, about situations in which choices must be made due to the scarcity of raw materials and the alternative uses to which they may be put. Scarcity is a concept that must be handled carefully because it is easy to introduce ethnocentric prejudices in an analysis. Judging contemporary hunter-gatherers as suffering from resource scarcity as compared to agriculturalists, for example, is mistaken. The former may have less possessions than the latter but that is a condition that perfectly fits their migratory life style, possessing only as much as they can carry with them.[6]

The concept of scarcity, therefore, must always be used relative to specific resources. The typological diversity of tools in middle paleolithic deposits and the differential intensity with which the tools were worked is evidence that their producers had an awareness of the limited availability of high-quality materials and were forced to make choices between possible uses: if the raw material was imported it was used to create a wider variety of tools and to create more complex forms (such as double-edged tools) than if it was of local origin.[7] Incentives to trade were also created by environmental factors that limited the mobility of early humans constraining their access to geological sources of raw materials. The middle paleolithic lasted so long and witnessed such dramatic climatic fluctuations (from full temperate to full glacial) that in the cold periods such incentives to trade must have been common. Finally, there were plenty of distinct communities to provide the degree of social distance necessary for impersonal exchange. Although archeologists label similar deposits of stone tools recovered from different sites with names like "Mousterian" or "Aurignacian" these terms should not be taken to refer to self-identified ethnic groups occupying large territories. Rather, the transition from the middle to the upper paleolithic involved many small bands inhabiting favorable areas with large empty zones between them, similarities in tool design being the result of cultural contact.[8] It is plausible that some of these contacts involved trade but this hypothesis is normally resisted by anthropologists because orthodox economic models make certain assumptions—personal self-interest, optimal decision-making, cost-free information—that are clearly inadequate in the context of contemporary hunter-gatherers let alone middle paleolithic humans.[9]

On the other hand, several simulations of barter have been created that dispense with these assumptions removing at least one source of objections. To the extent that these simulations are used to model hunter-gatherers the agents deployed in them should not be considered to be persons but bands or tribes since trade does not take place within communities but between them. Simulated agents can be used to model entire communities because, like the persons composing them, they are individual entities. The term "individual" has come to be used as synonymous with "person" but that is misleading. As an adjective it can legitimately be used to speak of individual organizations, individual cities, individual nation-states, or any other entity that is singular and historically unique. Another reason why communities can be modeled as agents is that once they have acquired emergent properties of their own, properties like solidarity or internal cultural homogeneity, they can play an explanatory role independently of the persons that compose them. When two communities interact, for example, the actual interactions may be performed by individual persons but the details of their personal interests and preferences will be explanatorily irrelevant if any other two community members could replace them and leave the outcome invariant. In other words, if the outcome of an inter-community interaction is not altered by changes in the identity of the persons that performed it then the defining features of their personal identity can be left out of an explanation. Because we are modeling individual communities notions like that of a community's self-interest or of its cultural and material preferences are perfectly valid. The persons composing these communities can still be conceived as possessing their own self-interest but one that is subordinated to that of the entire group with definite costs associated with the breaking of that bond.

Thus in what follows the term "agent" will refer to an entire community and the term "subjective" to the shared preferences characterizing that community. Let's first describe the objective and subjective possibility spaces involved in a trading interaction between two communities. The subjective space contains all the possible combinations of quantities of the objects to be traded. In the simple case of paleolithic barter we can assume there would be only two such objects: high-quality flint and partially worked stone tools. A two-dimensional possibility space in which every point is a combination of a certain quantity of flint and a certain quantity of tools can be used to express the preferences of each agent, the subjective preference for one of the objects in terms of a number of units of the other object: one agent may be willing to let go of one piece of high-quality flint in exchange for two partially worked tools, for example, while another may prefer a different combination. If an agent cannot choose between, say, two pieces of flint and three tools because both quantities are equally desirable then that point in the possibility space is a combination that makes no difference to the agent. Joining several such points by a line defines an *indifference curve*.[10] Each agent may have several indifference curves differing in desirability. While desires or preferences cannot be compared quantitatively—we cannot judge by exactly how much more one object is desired over another—we can nevertheless arrange preferences in an order making rigorous judgments about an object's greater or lesser desirability. Using these qualitative judgments to rank many indifference curves yields an indifference map capturing the structure of the subjective possibility space for each agent.

The objective possibility space can also be defined by different combinations of the two trade objects but now the actual amounts of high-quality flint and partially worked stone tools that the agents have available to them must be taken into account. That is, unlike the subjective space is which only desires are mapped in the objective space we must include the initial endowments of each of the traders, since these define what can actually be traded. In a space of all combinations of trade objects the initial endowment of both agents are each a single point: one agent may have all the partially worked tools while the other has all the high-quality flint, for example, or they may each bring to the trading situation a given amount of each object. The other objective component is the "price" at which the two objects are exchanged. Since there is no money involved these prices are simply the amount of one object that is customarily exchanged by an amount of another object. From the endowment point (the point representing the initial state of the interaction) price lines may be drawn showing the ratios of the two goods that could be traded at a given price. Finally, because both objective and subjective spaces define possible combinations of quantities of the same objects the endowment points and price lines of the former can be integrated with the indifference maps of the latter to yield a single composite diagram called an "Edgeworth Box," a beautiful geometrical construction condensing in two dimensions up to 12 different concepts from economics.[11]

Because this composite diagram includes subjective and objective factors it allows us to define the two gradients that drive trading interactions. On one hand, the sets of indifference curves arranged by increased desirability define two subjective gradients of satisfaction, one for each agent. An important feature of these gradients is pairs of indifference curves that just touch each other. At these points of tangency the amount of satisfaction that each agent would get from an additional unit of the traded object are identical and hence there is no further incentive to trade. These are the points at which the subjective gradients have been "dissipated." On the other hand, an objective gradient defining the potential gains from trade is captured by the diagram as a region containing combinations of the two goods that are more desirable than the initial endowments. If we could exactly quantify desire we would be able to establish that in a given transaction the loses of one agent were more than compensated by the gains of the other and that the trading interaction had achieved unambiguous gains. But since we cannot quantify it the only unambiguous judgments we can make about interactions that improve satisfaction are outcomes involving gains for one agent and no losses for the other. Using these qualitative judgments we can divide the diagram into two areas, one containing allocations that make at least one agent worse off and another containing those that do not and that therefore act as an incentive to trade. Within the second area there is a singularity, called a "competitive equilibrium," defining the point at which all potential gains from trade have been exhausted, that is, the point at which the objective gradient has disappeared and cannot longer drive interactions.

Like any other diagram capturing the mechanism-independent component of an explanation the Edgeworth Box says nothing about the actual process that would drive two agents toward the singularity. When modeling this dynamic process economists usually make two assumptions which are unjustified in the present context. First, it is assumed that the agents have the calculational capacity and the necessary information to make optimal choices between alternative combinations of the two goods. Second, the interactions between the traders are assumed to be guided by an auctioneer who does not allow the transaction to proceed until it can take place at the singularity: the auctioneer proposes a price and the traders answer by giving the quantities of a good they would be willing to trade at that price; if these quantities leave gains of trade unrealized (if there are wasteful excesses or deficits) then a second price is proposed, quantities offered, and the process is iterated. In this way the auctioneer gropes its way toward the competitive equilibrium and authorizes the trade only when the singularity has been reached. This mechanism is clearly not realistic in most trading situations, even in contemporary ones, and it does not show how prices can emerge endogenously from actual negotiations. So from the point of view of modeling paleolithic trade we would have to get rid of the auctioneer and of agents possessing unrealistic calculational capacities (optimizing rationality).[12]

Both of these problematic assumptions have been addressed in multiagent computer simulations. In one of these the assumption of optimizing rationality was tackled directly and radically: the agents had no awareness of the trading situation; no memory of past transactions; no notion of profits; and only enough intelligence to avoid losses. These agents were appropriately called "zero-intelligence traders." Instead of an auctioneer the simulation used a double auction: agents did not respond to exogenous prices by providing information about the quantities they were willing to trade but supplied prices directly: "bids" if they wanted to buy or "asks" if they wanted to sell. The bids and asks were matched continuously even if the singularity had not been reached. In other words, unlike the process directed by the auctioneer in which transactions take place only at the competitive equilibrium in a simulated double auction they can occur anywhere within the area defining the gains from trade, that is, transactions can take place away from equilibrium. When zero-intelligence traders were placed in an Edgeworth Box they were able to move toward the singularity and come close to it using only local information to climb the gradients of satisfaction. What the outcome of this simulation showed was that the crucial ingredient in the mechanism was not the calculational abilities of the traders but the structure of the interaction, an interaction that came close to the haggling that takes place in marketplaces or bazaars.[13]

Similar results were obtained in another simulation called "Sugarscape" in which the totally disembodied zero-intelligence traders were replaced by agents that had a body (that is, a metabolism) and that were situated in a space with a certain distribution of resources. The behavior of both agents and resources was entirely determined by rules and was therefore not emergent, but the use of rules is an advantage in this case because if the actions of the agents had been produced by a neural net it would be hard not to view those actions as implying personal agency. With rules, on the other hand, no assumption about underlying mechanisms is made so agency can be attributed to larger units, like entire households or communities.[14] Nevertheless some care must be taken when interpreting the rules since these specified the range of vision of agents—defined as the number of grid squares of the space they inhabited within which they could detect the presence of food—as well as their metabolism, the amount of resources they had to consume to continue moving and prevent death. In our case "vision" and "metabolism" must be taken to refer to the perceptual capacities and alimentary needs of entire communities: the consensus view reached after many personal observations and the subsistence activities needed to keep the entire group alive. Rules also specified the behavior of resources in the simulation: at each point in time each square in the two-dimensional space had both a given quantity of sugar, a rate at which it replenished itself, and a limit on the maximum amount that could exist there. Agents used their vision to inspect all squares within their range, identified those unoccupied squares with the most sugar, and moved to the nearest one to gather the resource. Through this simple rule they acquired the emergent ability to climb resource gradients.[15]

Although the agents in this simulation had (non-emergent) preferences, to move to the nearest square containing more sugar, for example, they did not yet have to make choices between alternative resources. To allow for this to happen a second resource together with a second metabolism was introduced: spice. Now as the agents moved around they confronted choices between squares more or less rich in sugar and those with a greater or lesser abundance of spice. Since the resources were defined by rules it would be relatively simple to change them to simulate choices between "high-quality flint" and "partially worked tools," but this would not make a difference in a simulation designed to explore the mechanism of emergence of prices. Let's therefore stick to the original formulation. To determine an agent's decisions its preferences for different combinations of quantities of sugar and spice had to be charted, that is, each agent had to be assigned an indifference map. Several factors entered into the determination of the indifference curves in Sugarscape: the agents' metabolisms for sugar and spice; the current amounts of each good they currently possessed; and the current degree to which their metabolic needs were satisfied. These factors determined the relative desirability of sugar and spice at any given moment for each of the agents as a function of their relative internal scarcity and their current endowments. Finally, the agents were given the (non-emergent) capacity to trade by adding a new rule. The trade rule can be described in Edgeworth Box terms: if the indifference curves of a given pair of agents were tangent to each other there were no incentives to trade so the couple did not interact; if the curves were not tangent then a direction of trade was established, one agent may have needed sugar and the other spice, so sugar moved in one direction and spice in the other. Then a ratio of sugar to spice was established (via a bargaining rule) and the quantities of each good that would be traded at that price were checked to see if no agent was made worse off, that is, if the transaction was within the area defining the gains from trade, in which case the transaction was carried out.[16]

To see whether after many such trading interactions an entire population could collectively reach the point of competitive equilibrium 200 agents were unleashed in a space with a certain distribution of both sugar and spice. At the start of the simulation there was significant variation in prices across the population but as it proceeded there was a tendency to converge toward the equilibrium price, never quite reaching the singularity but coming quite close and staying within a small neighborhood around it. In other words, prices emerged spontaneously away from equilibrium without the need for an auctioneer.[17] The mechanism of emergence depended on the fact that as agents repeatedly interacted their internal valuations for the two resources became more and more alike; and the more similar their valuations became the closer they all got to a single price. On the other hand, some degree of price dispersion survived until the end of the simulation, a degree of dispersion that was increased by any factor that interfered with the intensity of the interaction: reducing the range of vision of the population (since this made agents less able to locate potential traders); allowing agents to die even if they met their metabolic needs (shorter lifetimes reduced number of interactions); and allowing agent preferences to change in response to noneconomic factors (since this increased the time needed for internal valuations to become similar).[18] In the case of paleolithic trade a large degree of price dispersion is something to be expected so the outcome of the simulation supports the thesis that the gains from trade could have been realized in that context without making any of the usual assumptions that anthropologists find so objectionable.

Let's draw some conclusions from what has been argued up to this point. Multiagent simulations can guide us in the search for solutions to archeological problems as defined by the available evidence: deposits of stone tools and the debris left behind during their production. In some cases the problem is to account for a particular distribution of these deposits, a problem to be discussed below, but there is also the question of explaining how rare imported materials got to the place where they were found. Because we do not know the method of transport that was used multiagent simulations can help fine-tune our intuitions about those unknown transport mechanisms. While the currently preferred explanation is some kind of ceremonial transport, an account that draws its plausibility from the fact that instances of it have been observed in some contemporary hunter-gatherers, there is also the simpler mechanism of trade between communities. This option has been underestimated by archeologists partly because of the presuppositions built into economic models. But if the latter are taken to address only the mechanism-independent component of an explanation, that is, the singularities structuring the possibility space of a trading situation, and not the actual mechanisms involved in the making of decisions or in price negotiations then the assumptions become less problematic. Although simulations also operate at a relatively mechanism-independent level the capacity of computational process to track historical paths toward a singularity, and the added advantage of using embodied and spatially situated agents, makes them ideal to explore potential candidates for the transport mechanism that accounts for the available evidence.

To go beyond this relatively humble role and tackle archeological problems like explaining the actual distribution and composition of deposits of stone artifacts in a specific geographical area, we need a more explicit way of modeling the different elements of a multiagent simulation: the resource landscape, the behavioral rules, and the temporal scale of the subsistence activities. This is a highly interdisciplinary task but archeology itself has long relied on other fields (chemistry, geology, ecology, ethnology) to reconstruct subsistence activities and settlement patterns from stone tools, fossilized pollen, animal bones, and hearth remains. Simulated reconstructions of the subsistence economy of hunter-gatherers vary in the degree of detail of both behavioral patterns and resource gradients. In the earliest simulations the type of plants and animal prey assumed to be the target of foraging activities were guessed either from contemporary hunter-gatherers in the same region or from the fossilized remains found in a cave or another site. Then the conditions affecting the relative abundance of those resources today (rainfall for plants, population dynamics for animals) were modeled to create statistical series of good, bad, and average years to be used in the simulations. Although the resource distributions generated this way were clearly more realistic than those of the Sugarscape simulations just discussed, extrapolating from present conditions can be problematic if the landscape is not temporally stable, if target species are now extinct, or if ecological diversity has been greatly reduced.[19]

To avoid these potential sources of error data and techniques from multiple disciplines must be used to reconstruct ancient landscapes: using the information stored in ice sheets, tree rings, sediment, and rocks paleoclimatology can help to recreate the temperature and precipitation conditions of a given time period; geomorphology can be used to understand the history and dynamics of land forms, and to recreate the effect of rivers, volcanoes, and glaciers on the distribution and quality of soils; ecology can furnish information about the succession dynamics of different plants and this, together with the output from palynology (the study of pollen, spores, and particulate organic matter), can guide the reconstruction of ancient distributions of plants of a given species.[20] Once the spatial component of resource distributions has been worked out we need to add a temporal dimension to the simulations. This is simplified by the fact that the subsistence activities of hunter-gatherers tend to have a cyclical structure. In some cases the plants that are the target of foraging activities ripe in different seasons and this gives the activities a yearly cycle, sometimes accompanied by settlement patterns that display a similar periodicity. In other cases a much shorter period may be used such as a daily cycle divided into diurnal and nocturnal activities.[21] This periodic repetition of activities can be used to give temporal structure to a simulation and to correlate its output with time series for temperature and precipitation changes, the rise and fall of available groundwater, and the changes in soil quality created by the deposition of sediments.

The next step is to make more realistic the behavioral and metabolic rules that capture the decision-making and consumption activities of agents. Ethnological studies of contemporary hunter-gatherers can be a valuable source of information in this regard but we must be careful not to reify particular cases into a timeless set of properties. In the 1960s, for example, the consensus view of contemporary hunter-gatherers characterized them as living in groups of 25 to 50 members, with no material possessions to constrain their high mobility, a sexual division of labor, flexible membership, and very egalitarian authority structure. But a decade later other tribes were found that did not match this list of properties, being sedentary part of the year, living in larger groups, and storing some possessions.[22] These two cases can be used to define the two extremes of a continuous possibility space and the behavioral rules for the simulations can be derived by making educated guesses about the likely position of paleolithic hunter-gatherers in this continuum. Several simulations may be performed with rules derived from different parts of the continuum to check the sensitivity of the results to different assumptions. Finally, to be able to use these simulations to make specific predictions about the distribution of deposits of stone artifacts the latter must be available in a well preserved state. In general, the further back in time we go the more disturbed the archeological record is so most detailed simulations have focused on more recent periods, such as the mesolithic, the transitional period between the upper paleolithic and the already agricultural neolithic. This period differs from the ones discussed so far in one crucial respect, the availability of language, a change reflected in the simulations by the need to incorporate the flow of semantic information among the agents.

In one simulation, called "Magical," the goal was to reproduce the distribution and composition of stone artifacts on an island of Western Scotland where mesolithic hunter-gatherers once foraged for hazelnuts. In this simulation resource gradients were modeled in detail using the paleoenvironmental approach just discussed, including competition among typical temperate forest trees (oak, birch) with hazel. Yearly, monthly, and daily time scales were included. The activities on a yearly time scale were determined by the life cycle of the trees themselves: one season with a hazelnut harvest and one without. This, in turn, was assumed to affect human activities like gathering on a base camp followed by dispersing around a given area of the island. The monthly time scale was determined by decisions reached by consensus about the location of the base camp: whether or not to move it to a new place with better chances of increasing the productivity of foraging activities. Finally, on a daily basis agents foraged or explored during the day and got together at night to share the results of their activities.[23] Unlike the previously discussed simulations in which the agents were entire communities here the agents were taken to be individual persons so the nightly reports had to be modeled explicitly. The solution to this problem was very ingenious. Since the activities of the agents had to take place in a simulated space with the same characteristics as the original island, a standard format for the storage of spatial data, called a Geographic Information System (or GIS), was used. A GIS is basically a map on which multiple layers are superimposed each containing information about a particular landscape property (soil composition, distributions of plant species, water availability). In Magical these maps were given an additional use: to represent the knowledge that the agents acquired about the landscape. In other words, the cognitive maps that the agents formed of resource distributions, maps that would have been created by real hunter-gatherers through a combination of episodic and semantic memory, were each represented by a GIS map. That way when the agents gathered at night to report their daily findings the linguistic exchange among them could be modeled by merging all the individual GIS maps to form a composite one that was then redistributed among all the members of the group.[24]

Unlike the agents in Sugarscape the use of simulated visual information did not form the basis on which movement decisions were made, the agents of Magical using instead their internal GIS maps for that purpose. But as in Sugarscape, Magical's agents were heterogeneous in this capacity: while in the former they possessed different ranges of vision in the latter they analyzed differently sized portions of the map around their current position before moving to a neighboring location. Agents who made decisions based on a smaller portion of the map were being "conservative" in the sense that they were trying to reduce risk and improve their short-term gains; those using larger portions took more risk by moving to locations with unknown hazelnut abundance but could benefit from longer term gains if they discovered new sources of food. Finally, the stone artifacts were divided into different categories (waste from production processes, small tools, larger scrapers) and probabilities that the agents would discard them were assigned according to their position relative to the base camp and the stage of the yearly season.[25] So far the main results of using Magical have been to reduce the likelihood of some previous scenarios proposed to account for the existing archeological data. In particular, the hypothesis that the only determinant of land use was the gathering of hazelnuts, an admittedly important resource, has lost some credibility. Many runs of the simulation were performed, each run representing about ten years of foraging activity, using different landing sites around the island as well as different distributions of risk-taking behavior. Yet, none of the outcomes managed to repro-duce the existing distribution of deposits of stone artifacts.[26] Although the simulation's results were negative its contribution was clearly positive: it showed that other spatial constraints must have been in operation, such as the availability of high-quality flint near the coast that may have been an incentive to create specialist base camps used for the production of tools. In other words, the simulation's results pointed to useful alternative hypotheses.

Similarly negative but highly informative results have been obtained in a Sugarscape simulation in which resource distributions were reconstructed using paleoenvironmental models. The simula-tion tackled an even more recent period, the Neolithic, a period in which agriculture was already practiced and the nomadic lifestyle of hunter-gatherers had been abandoned. While stone tools continued to be used and their increased sophistication and functional differen-tiation left behind a richer archeological record, the Neolithic intro-duced a more sensitive medium: pottery. The plasticity of clay gives pottery a greater range of stylistic variation and this together with the fact that it was typically produced locally supplies us with evidence about regional groupings and about the interactions between neigh-boring communities.[27] Another source of information from this period is settlement patterns. Settlements leave mineralized remains arranged in separate strata: some layers may show that for a while most of the population was concentrated in one large village, for example, while other layers may reveal that at other times the settlers dispersed and lived in many small villages. For archeologists trying to explain these variations the question is whether they can all be attributed to changes in resource gradients (soil productivity, availability of water) or whether cultural changes were also involved. Multiagent simulations can be used to tackle this question for specific historical cases. One particular case is the Anasazi culture that inhabited the Long House Valley in northeastern Arizona, first as hunter-gatherers (before 1800 BC) then as agriculturalists surviving on a economy based on the cultivation of maize until they abandoned the region in AD 1300 for reasons still unknown.

Unlike the static resource landscapes of the Sugarscape simulations discussed above those of the Long House Valley had to be modeled dynamically because the productivity of maize crops, the main gradient driving the process, undergoes change at several time scales: it is influenced by relatively short-term variations in the moisture and temperature of the atmosphere as well as by longer term variations in the dynamics of rivers, affecting the availability of groundwater and the creation and destruction of new fertile soil. The time scale for the simulation was determined by the agricultural cycle, that is, the simulation proceeded in yearly periods. The agents in this simulation were not individual persons but individual households, composed of five members each, whose metabolic requirements were calculated using anthropological studies of other subsistence agriculturalists: each member of a family was assumed to consume 160 kilograms of maize per year, storing whatever was left for up to two years. Families were given behavioral rules the most important of which was a resettlement rule: at the end of each year each family calculated on the basis of the current harvest and their stored grain the chances that there would be enough food next year; if it decided that there would not be enough it made a decision to relocate constrained only by the availability of unoccupied farm land and proximity to drinking water. If the wrong decision was made and not enough food was produced the family disappeared from the simulation.[28] Each run of the simulation generated, as the emergent cumulative effect of the movement decisions by many families year after year, a possible settlement history between the years AD 800 and 1300. To capture statistical trends many such possible histories were generated starting from different initial conditions and varying certain parameters. The output was both a geographical representation of settlement locations that could be compared with maps created by archeologists, as well as statistical series on population growth and aggregation patterns that could be checked against those in the archeological record.

The comparisons, however, were not intended to be exact and quantitative: it would be unrealistic to expect agreement on overall population sizes, number of households, or size of settlements. In fact, the simulation consistently generated quantities that were too large packing many more households in a single residential zone than is consistent with the evidence. But the qualitative agreement was striking: for population growth, for instance, the qualitative features of the statistical series, the periods of growth and decline, as well as those in which numbers remained constant, were mostly reproduced.[29] Similarly, the responses of the simulated agents to environmental changes—to aggregate in a large village to perform intensive agriculture when groundwater was scarce and to disperse into many small ones when plentiful groundwater allowed cultivation in many places—generated settlement patterns qualitatively similar to those in the data. The main discrepancy between the simulation and the archeological record was itself highly informative. Around the year 1250 long- and short-term variations in environmental factors coincided to produce a subsistence crisis in the Long House Valley and by the year 1300 the Anasazi had abandoned the area. The simulation failed to reproduce this event suggesting that the decision to emigrate was not necessarily linked to gradient degradation. In fact, the simulation indicated that the available resources could have supported a smaller population dispersed into smaller communities. That the real Anasazi did not take advantage of this opportunity suggests that the cultural and social factors that were not included in the simulation must have played an important role in their decision.[30] In particular, when dealing with agents that already possess language we must assume not only that they can exchange factual information but also that they can form and share magical beliefs that can play an equally important role in their own explanations about resource availability, and hence on their decisions to stay or to emigrate abandoning the area altogether.

We will return in Chapter 11 to the role that magical beliefs play in the determination and explanation of human behavior, and to the way in which the effect of those beliefs can be incorporated into multiagent simulations. But before we tackle that problem we must confront the one that ultimately gives rise to it: the emergence of language. Although hunter-gatherer communities during the hundreds of thousands of years they spent skillfully working stone may have already developed simpler forms of communication, based perhaps on hand and facial gestures, the gradual development of articulated language marked a threshold beyond which an entirely new world became possible. The crucial property of language is that from a finite set of words an infinite number of sentences can be produced. Thus, what needs to be explained is how this infinite combinatorial productivity could have emerged starting with a few monolithic symbolic artifacts incapable of entering into complex part-to-whole relations. It is to this task that we now turn.

CHAPTER TEN
Multiagents and Primitive Language

When humans first began to shape flows of air with their tongues and palates the acoustic matter they created introduced yet another layer of complexity into the world. The production of sound relied on the same mechanism used by other animals—a source of oscillating air shaped by a vocal cavity acting as a filter—but in humans this mechanism underwent several important evolutionary changes. The source, the larynx and its vocal chords, lowered its position relative to the bone at the base of the skull extending the range of vowels that could be produced, even at the cost of losing our ability to swallow and breathe at the same time. The filters, in turn, constituted by all the different organs that can change the form of the resonating cavity (tongue, lips, teeth) became capable of manipulating pressure gradients with ever greater precision: resonances in the vocal cavity concentrated the energy of the airflow around particular frequencies and these concentrations (called "formants") became the building blocks that in different combinations would eventually yield all the different sounds of language. Since evolution has no foresight neither of these evolutionary changes was aimed at making language possible. The descent of the larynx may have occurred, as it has in other species, due to sexual selection: a lower larynx can produce sounds that mimic the effect of a larger body size, an effect that animals exploit during territorial disputes.[1] And the greater control of the organs producing formants was most likely a byproduct of the increased size of the brain. Life in the savanna had long ago changed dietary patterns—adding new nutrient sources (tubers, meat) and new techniques for food preparation (the use of tools to crush tubers and fire to cook meat)—increasing the amount of energy consumed and making its digestion more efficient. The extra metabolic energy available, in turn, was invested in a longer embryological development, with a more elaborate folding of neuronal layers packing more brain matter into a given volume.[2]

But if there was nothing uniquely human about the biological evolution of the sound production mechanism, the acoustic matter itself was unique because as soon as it emerged it became part of an evolution that was separate from genetics. Pre-linguistic hunter-gatherers possessed learned habits and skills that were transmitted across generations and that could therefore play the role of replicators in a cultural evolutionary process, a process into which the newly born linguistic sounds could be instantly grafted. The details of what happened to those early sounds may never be known but we must assume that linguistic evolution began with monolithic symbolic artifacts. That is, we must assume that the first "words" were not made out of parts that could be recombined to form other words, and that the words themselves were not parts that could enter into larger sentences. The only communicative function that those monolithic symbolic artifacts could have had is that of labels that referred to directly experienced objects and actions. Simple concatenations of those artifacts could have later on been used to express the observed constant conjunction of linear causes and their effects, an observation that had been made routine by the practices associated with stone tool production. The next evolutionary step, going from a set of monolithic sounds to one of words that could be combined into an infinite set of possible sentences, is much more difficult to explain. We need not only to account for the capacity to combine a set of words like "the prey" and "runs away" into a sentence like "The prey runs away." We also need to account for the ability to feed this simple sentence back as an input, together with another set of words like "the hunters" and "chase," to produce a complex sentence like "The prey the hunters chase runs away." In other words, we need to explain the unique human ability to use recursion.

To get a sense of the problem that had to be solved by cultural evolution it will be useful to consider the space of all possible languages. The structure of this space can be explored using automata theory, a theory in which memory, recursion, and language complexity are closely intertwined. Automata can be classified into a series of increased computational capacity determined by their degree of access to memory resources: finite state automata, pushdown automata, linear-bounded automata, and Turing machines. This series, in turn, can be related to a series of languages of increased complexity. Finite state automata possess no memory and can handle only languages without recursion: *regular languages*. The next type has access only to the last item stored in memory (the others being "pushed down" a stack) but this gives it the ability to handle simple recursion and master *context-free languages*. In particular, pushdown automata have the ability to keep track not only of embedded clauses ("the hunters chase") but to match verbs and nouns separated in a sentence, that is, to match "the prey" to "runs away." The next level of computational capacity involves a more powerful memory in the form of an infinite tape on which symbols can be stored but access only to a small portion of it. This is enough, however, for linear-bounded automata to handle the stored symbols together with their immediate context and master *context-sensitive languages*. Examples of the more complex recursive constructions that this allows are rare in natural languages but do exist, as illustrated by cross-dependencies in which verbs are not matched to nouns in the order they appear. Finally, the most powerful automata, Turing machines, have unlimited access to the memory tape, can take as much context into account as needed, can handle any form of recursion, and master *phrase-structure languages*.[3] A typical desktop computer lies somewhere between a linear-bounded automaton and a Turing machine approximating the latter ever more closely as memory gets cheaper and more abundant.

As mentioned in Chapter 2 automata theory is important philosophically because it provides for capacities what state space and its attractors do for tendencies: a clear and rigorous way of exploring the structure of a possibility space. The singularities in this case are constituted by the four automata, with finite state automata and Turing machines constituting a minimum and a maximum of computational capacity, respectively. The term "language" in automata theory refers not only to the approximately 6,000 currently existing natural languages but also to all the programming languages used to create software for the different automata, as well as many languages that are possible but have never been used. Like many of the combinatorial possibility spaces that have been discussed so far this space is infinite in size but for the purpose of exploring the evolution of natural languages we can concentrate on the region containing context-sensitive languages. This implies the assumption that the part of the human brain that handles language must have the computational capacity of a linear-bounded automaton. Using neural nets to explore how this capacity is implemented in our brains would seem at first to be an impossible task because the kind of neural net that can process the temporal sequences of sounds that make up human speech, recurrent neural nets, has only the computational capacity of a finite state automaton. We will return to this important question at the end of this chapter.

Having defined the final state of the evolutionary process let's go back to its beginning: the emergence of reference. Having the ability to refer implies the creation of a conventional association between monolithic symbolic artifacts and real entities mediated by meanings. But what could "meanings" be in a world of pre-linguistic hunter-gatherers? In Chapter 6 it was argued that in both animals and early humans "meanings" are the prototypes that neural nets extract from sensory experience, nonlinguistic categories or generalizations stored as distributed patterns of activation. These distributed representations are associated to their referents directly because they are extracted from repeated encounters with many particular instances of a class of referents. In addition to giving us an account of the association between meanings and referents neural nets can also explain the association between meanings and sounds because the process of training that generates the distributed representations is often performed with the goal of producing a particular motor output. If we think of this motor output as involving the larynx as a source and the vocal cavity as a filter then the final product is a vocalization that is automatically associated with the distributed representation. Being in possession of an explanation for the link between meanings and referents and meanings and sounds all that is left to explain is the emergence of the link between *sounds and referents*. This is harder than it seems because pre-linguistic hunter-gatherers could not read minds, that is, they did not have access to each other's distributed representations. This implies that early humans had no choice but to use publicly available information to converge on a shared set of sound-referent associations.

To explore the emergence of this shared set we need to deploy a population of neural nets situated in a space containing simple referents and to give them a minimum of embodiment to ensure that the agents have no access to each other's minds. In fact, neural nets are not strictly necessary: we can use any other implementation of prototype-extraction, using video cameras and standard image processing software, for example, as is done in a simulation called *semiotic dynamics*.[4] In this simulation pairs of agents take turns playing the roles of speaker and listener. The agents inhabit a simple world of geometric figures (the potential referents) and possess three simple capacities: they can perceive and categorize the geometrical figures, they can point at a figure, and they can observe in what direction other agents are pointing. They are also able to produce arbitrary symbolic artifacts (random syllable combinations) to use as "words," artifacts that can either be invented or be already in use in the community. Thus, using semiotic dynamics to model the emergence of a shared set of sound-referent associations implies only the assumptions that pre-linguistic hunter-gatherers could use gestures to achieve shared attention and had the willingness to participate in ritualized tasks, such as taking turns to vocalize.

A semiotic dynamic simulation unfolds in the following way. Agents are paired at random to attempt to communicate. The agent whose turn it is to speak selects a geometric object as the topic of conversation, checks its memory to see what previous symbolic artifacts have been associated with it, and picks one; since at the beginning of the simulation no artifact is available it invents a new one. The agent playing the role of listener then checks its own memory to see if a previous association between that artifact and some referent has been made and uses that as its first guess. In the very first encounter it cannot find anything so it invents its own sound. Thus, the starting point for the simulation is a situation in which each agent has its own idiosyncratic vocabulary and the listeners always fail to guess the speakers referential intentions. But speakers can also help listeners by pointing to the intended referent and this can sometimes result in a correct guess after several trials. This random guessing cannot by itself converge to a single shared vocabulary for all the potential referents but convergence can be achieved if we give agents the capacity to keep score of what pairs of symbolic artifacts and referents have led to communicative success in the past.[5] When a speaker searches its memory for a previous artifact associated with its intended referent, for example, it may discover that there are several choices with different scores. The history of the different alternative associations, some of which have led in the past to more correct guessings, is reflected in those scores so all the speaker has to do is pick the one with the highest score. The listener too searches among competing associations for the least ambiguous one (the one with a single referent) and if there are several it picks the one with the highest score as its first guess. Iterating a process in which agents are attempting to guess each other's referential intentions and helping each other repair breakdowns in communication eventually leads to a stable repertoire of shared sound-referent associations.[6]

The outcome of this simulation is valuable but limited: the symbolic artifacts represent only one class of linguistic entities, labels or proper names, while the set of meanings is restricted to objects that have actually been experienced, not to meanings that can be defined compositionally by other words. Nevertheless, within its limited goals the simulation is a success because it shows how the process of linguistic evolution could have got started. To simulate the next step, the concatenation of labels into simple monolithic sentences, the agents must be situated in a world that demands from them engaging in causal reasoning. In the previous chapter we saw that pre-linguistic hunter-gatherers were capable of mastering complex sequences of manual operations as part of the production of stone tools. This task presented them with the opportunity to learn about linear causal relations by the direct observation of the constant conjunction of a cause and its effect. Expressing this constant conjunction symbolically would demand no more than concatenating the labels for the actions or events acting as cause and effect. The resulting symbolic artifact would not be a real sentence, since its meaning would not result from the composition of the meanings of the component labels, but it would nevertheless be capable of being true or false. On the other hand, if shared personal observations were sufficient to learn about causal relations what would have been the motivation for expressing them symbolically?

To answer this question the next simulation poses the following challenge: what if there were causal regularities that could not be easily observed by persons but only by entire communities? Would the production of artifacts expressing guesses about co-occurrences of events improve the chances that over several generations all members of the community would make the correct association? The situation confronting the simulated agents was inspired by a real example from contemporary hunter-gatherers. When the ocean tide is low a gradient of concentrated protein (shellfish) forms at the beach. If the agents lived near the beach they could directly observe low tides and know when to collect the shellfish. But if they lived far away they would have to use another observable event that correlated with a low tide, such as the phase of the moon. As it happens when the moon is new or full the tide reaches both its highest and its lowest points, maximizing the chances of finding shellfish. So a community could benefit if collective observations of the conjunction of tide states and moon phases could be encapsulated into a monolithic sentence.[7] The members of this community would not have to possess any knowledge of real mechanisms, that is, they need not know that when the moon is new or full its gravitational force is in phase with that of the sun and its effect on the state of the tide is greatest. On the other hand, the results of Chapter 7 allow us to assume that pre-linguistic hunter-gatherers could perform perceptual analyses of situations using script-like structures, assign interacting objects to the roles of causal agent and causal patient, and remember those experiences using episodic memory.

While the symbolic artifacts must have the capacity to be true or false, a capacity that propositions have, they need not necessarily have a propositional form: since the simulated agents have to solve a single causal problem in their lives a simple numerical vocabulary specialized to refer to tide states and moon phases will suffice. Nevertheless, it will be useful for us to imagine the symbolic artifacts as monolithic sentences like this:

FullMoonCausesLowTide

In this precursor of a real sentence the absence of spaces between words indicates that the labels for "full moon" and "low tide" cannot be used compositionally to generate other sentences, while the verb "causes" simply marks the fact that the co-occurrence of the two labels stands for the co-occurrence of the events playing the roles of cause and effect. At any rate, because in this simulation the agents are entirely disembodied and are not situated in a space in which the relevant events could take place, the terms "label" and "event" refer to activation patterns in neural nets supplied to the agents by the experimenter. Each agent consists of three neural nets, two used to handle the association between labels and the events to which they refer, and one used to create an association between the events themselves. The design of the two neural nets that handle the linguistic part of the task can be very simple because the emergence of a lexicon to refer to events has already been explained by simulations like semiotic dynamics. More specifically, the neural nets that handle labels and their referents do not need to have hidden layers capable of extracting prototypes. All they need to do is produce a label as an output if given an event as an input and vice versa, produce an event if given a label. The third neural net is a regular multilayer perceptron that takes events as its input and produces a causal association as its output. At any one time in this simulation a community of 20 agents exists, each spending its life learning about the link between moon phases and tide states from "direct experience" and from the monolithic sentences produced by prior generations. At the end of its life an agent dies leaving behind a monolithic sentence expressing its best guess about the causal link and a new untrained agent to replace it.[8]

Because the agents in this simulation are disembodied the responsibility for recreating the desired situation falls on the training process itself: if the multilayer perceptron was trained using only information about events then culture would not matter, and vice versa, if the only training examples were past symbolic artifacts then the events and their objective causal connections would not make a difference. So the set of training examples needs to find a good balance between the two. On one hand, it must make it hard for any agent to learn the association between events from direct experience, mimicking the effects of cloudy weather, distance, and other interferences that in real life would preclude personal observations of the constant conjunction between full or new moon and extreme tide variation. On the other hand, it must reflect the accumulated knowledge of past generations so that a bias toward true artifacts must be added to the training, a bias capturing the fact that in a real community the relative success of agents from previous generations would influence the choice of guesses used as a starting point by a new generation. With this bias acting as a selection pressure cultural evolution arrives at a situation in which the entire community can reliably learn about the relation between moon phases and tide states.[9]

The outcomes of this and the previous simulation suggest that monolithic symbolic artifacts could have emerged in a community of hunter-gatherers to perform simple referential functions and capture simple causal relations. This is not in itself surprising because as we argued in Chapter 7 chimpanzees possess the ability to associate labels (colored shapes) and their referents and to chain several labels together to express simple causal relations, although they need to be trained by humans to develop this ability and have never been observed exercising it in their natural habitat. But as was already pointed out this constitutes the part of the problem that is relatively easy to solve. The hard part is to simulate a process that can break down a set of monolithic sentences into recursively recombinable components, a process referred to as *grammaticalization*. Before discussing a simulation that tackles this problem it will be useful to describe the traditional account. Instead of explaining the human capacity to use and understand recursion by postulating an evolutionary process based on replicating acoustic matter, as we are doing here, the traditional explanation assumes that this capacity was produced by biological evolution.

This account starts by creating a formal model that can produce sentences through a recursive process. The model is based on rewriting rules, operators that take as their input strings of inscriptions, rewrite them, and produce a new string as their output. The strings are not random chains of sounds (or letters) but sequences already assigned to grammatical categories, like noun, verb, sentence, and so on. Both the rewriting rules and the grammatical categories are assumed to be innate constituting a universal grammar common to all languages.[10] The innate hypothesis is defended on the grounds that when children learn a language they acquire a capacity to produce an infinite number of sentences even though they are only exposed to the very small number of sentences actually produced by their parents. In other words, the poverty of stimulation characterizing the learning situation is taken to be evidence that children do not learn a grammar by making step-by-step inferences from adult sentences but rather that the latter act as mere triggers for rules and categories inherited biologically. To put this differently, if as automata theory shows the space of possible languages is infinite in size how can children learn a language given the poverty of the stimulation they receive from their parents? It would seem that we would need to postulate a way of constraining this space to make language acquisition not just possible but highly probable. A universal grammar is precisely such a constraint: it eliminates from the space of possibilities that the child must confront all except the humanly learnable languages.[11]

The traditional explanation runs into difficulties when trying to specify the evolutionary process that led to the development of innate rules and grammatical categories. This is not just a question of explaining the survival value of recursion given that linguistic communication can be achieved without it. It is also the problem of showing that genetic variation for the neural substrate of categories like "noun" and "verb" existed. The alternative account, on the other hand, must not only explain how language evolved externally driven by its capacity to encode propositional information about cause and effect relations, but in addition it must explain how it was later internalized.[12] The second requirement is necessary because we need to account for the existence of brain organs specialized for language, organs that can act as inheritable constraints on the space of possible languages. The two aspects of this alternative account have been successfully investigated using computer simulations: grammaticalization has been shown to emerge through cultural evolution in groups of interacting agents in which one generation plays the role of teacher and the other one of student; and the mechanism of internalization, the so-called *Baldwin effect*, has been shown to be viable in simulations of evolving neural nets. The first simulation does not have to produce the complex type of recursion that characterizes context-sensitive languages but only the simpler type of context-free languages. We can imagine that once such a simple recursive language emerged in ancient hunter-gatherer communities the Baldwin effect began to operate and that the remainder of the journey through the space of possible languages took place by evolutionary search based on both genetic and linguistic replicators.

The agents used in the simulation of grammaticalization are even more disembodied than those of the simulation just discussed. In particular, the agents have access to the intended meanings of monolithic artifacts. Since agents are supposed to learn from observing each other's behavior not by reading each other's minds this is a major limitation. In addition, the simulation does not use neural nets but stays within the world of automata, pushdown automata in the case of context-free languages, and the notation they understand. Thus the meaning of a monolithic sentence like:

FullMoonCausesLowTide

is a proposition that is expressed in automaton notation as:

Causes (Full Moon, Low Tide)

This choice is justified on the basis that using symbolic representations facilitates tracking the progressive evolution of compositionality and recursion: checking that a new syntactical feature has emerged is simply a matter of looking at the current repertoire of propositions in the population of agents.[13] A crucial component of the process through which compositionality emerges is the ability of the agents to generalize from experience. In a simulation using neural nets this would be implemented by the extraction of prototypes from sensory stimulation. In the present case, on the other hand, it is easier to implement this capacity through an inductive algorithm specialized to operate in the world of pushdown automata. Finally, the agents involved must be able to interact playing the role of teacher or student, an interaction that in the case of pre-linguistic hunter-gatherers would have taken place between parents and offspring, or between adults belonging to an extended family group and kindred children. During this interaction the students have direct access to the meaning of declarative sentences, that is, the teacher presents them with pairs of propositions and their monolithic symbolic expressions. To justify the use of mind reading we would have to assume that in another version of this simulation, a version in which agents would be embodied and situated in a space containing the referents of the labels, the propositions would be reconstructions of intended meanings that the agents would arrive at as they observed each other's interactions with those referents. We will return to the question of how to eliminate mind reading below.

The world in which the agents live is fixed and simple. In a typical run, for example, the simulation includes as referents for the labels five objects and five actions. Given that each proposition has two arguments, such as "full moon" and "low tide," and that these must be different from each other, this yields 100 possible propositions. Agents spend half their life as students of teachers belonging to the previous generation, the other half as teachers to a new generation. To include the effect of the poverty of stimulation each agent teaches only half of the possible propositions in its lifetime.[14] When the simulation starts all symbolic artifacts are monolithic and teaching involves making the student memorize a long list of associations. From the fact that these associations are taught as customary, however, students can infer the simple rule that a proposition like:

Causes (Full Moon, Low Tide)

belongs to the category "sentence" and that it has to be expressed as:

FullMoonCausesLowTide.

This rule can be expressed in a notation that a pushdown automaton would understand as:

S/Causes (Full Moon, Low Tide) → FullMoonCausesLowTide

In which "S/" means "belongs to the sentence category" and the arrow means "must be expressed as." At this point the symbolic artifacts used for teaching the previous sentence as well as the different sentence:

FullMoonCausesHighTide

are treated as if the fact that they both include the label "FullMoon" does not matter. Each monolithic sentence has to be learned independently and each has to be associated as a whole with its own proposition.

But then the generalizing abilities of the students come into action: the common part of these two sentences is detected and the two propositions are replaced by a more general one:

Causes (Full Moon, X)

together with an assignment of the category "noun" to possible values of the variable X. When the student that made the generalization becomes a teacher it does not teach the two original associations but the new one:

S/Causes (Full Moon, N/X) $\rightarrow$ FullMoonCausesX

At this point the poverty of stimulation characterizing the learning situation starts to work in favor of the more general forms because symbolic artifacts that are used more frequently tend to be overrepresented in the impoverished sample used for teaching. In other words, a sentence like "FullMoonCausesX" is used twice as often as the two symbolic artifacts it replaces since it can express the meaning of both, so the probability that it will be selected as a teaching example is twice as high. Ironically, the same poverty of the stimulus invoked as a justification for a universal grammar works here to eliminate the need for innate rules by acting as a bottleneck favoring the transmission of more general forms to future generations.[15] But it also leads to the start of the segmentation of the monolithic artifacts since the more general forms are also the ones that display compositionality. In other words, the bottleneck acts as a sorting device, favoring some replicators at the expense of others, while also creating the conditions for the further segmentation of monolithic sentences. In fact, all the simulations discussed in this chapter, as well as other related ones, operate by using a bottleneck as a selection mechanism.[16] In semiotic dynamics, for example, the original plurality of idiosyncratic vocabularies is slowly narrowed down to a single shared lexicon by the tendency of agents to choose symbolic artifacts according to how referentially successful they have been in the past. And similarly for the simulation of label concatenation as a means to express causality: every generation has a tendency to start with those monolithic sentences that were more predictive of the real link between moon phase and tide state, and this acts a bottleneck facilitating the passage of some but not other artifacts to the next generation.

As an example of how the grammaticalization bottleneck could lead to further segmentation let's imagine that the same process just described was applied to the monolithic sentences:

FullMoonCausesLowTide
NewMoonCausesLowTide

and that the resulting more general proposition, Causes (Y, Low Tide), was compared by a student with the previous one:

Causes (Full Moon, X)
Causes (Y, Low Tide)

The student may then realize that the label in the first proposition is a possible value for the variable in the second one and vice versa, and produce by generalization the abstract proposition:

Causes (Y, X)

At this point, a monolithic symbolic artifact has been effectively broken down into pieces that are now ready to enter into part-to-whole relations to compose other sentences. Not only have the labels for events been assigned to the category "noun" but the previously implicit predicate "Causes" has been isolated and can be assigned to the category "verb." In other words, compositionality has been achieved and grammatical categories have emerged in a purely cultural evolutionary process. But what about the other required component of a grammar, rewriting rules that can be used recursively? A simple form of recursion could emerge if to the primitive predicate "Causes" that takes events as its inputs we add a predicate like "Says" taking propositions themselves as inputs.[17] The new predicate can generate propositions like these:

Says(Tradition, Causes(Full Moon, Low Tide))
Says(My Teacher, Causes(Full Moon, Low Tide))

Or in English, "Tradition says that full moon causes low tide" or "My teacher says that full moon causes low tide." These are the kind of propositions that would arise spontaneously in a teaching situation whenever the content of what is being taught must be justified by ascribing it to a tradition or to the now dead teacher of the current teacher.

The type of recursion involved is, of course, very simple, but that is all we needed in the present context. Once an external language had acquired this minimal complexity it could start coevolving with its biological substratum through the Baldwin effect.

The Baldwin effect is not a general mechanism for the transformation of learned capacities into inheritable ones. Such a general mechanism does not exist. Rather, it is a means to give genetic adaptations that have little survival value in themselves a chance to increase in value by getting partial credit for their contribution to the fitness of a given generation. A learned capacity can become inherited only in very special circumstances: it must already have a genetic basis but one that does not fully determine it; it must directly increase reproductive success to help its associated genes propagate; and this propagation must be such that without the actual exercise of the learned capacity the genes would be eliminated by natural selection. One way in which the exercise of a capacity can affect biological evolution is if it is culturally transmitted from one generation to another giving it the necessary temporal stability to have relevant effects.[18] The capacity in question must also preexist the emergence of linguistic communication and be co-opted for this purpose. The perfect candidate would be the ability to exploit sequential dependencies in the operations involved in stone tool manufacture. This ability did have a partial genetic basis, it was transmitted across generations, and it had to be actually exercised to impinge on reproductive success. Its extension to sequences of sounds, on the other hand, must have been at first a learned capacity. How this extension took place is suggested by the operation of recurrent neural nets. These can be used to extract temporal dependencies in sequences of manual operations as well as in series of vocalizations. In fact, a simple recurrent neural net, one with the same computational capacity as the simplest automaton, can learn how to predict the next word in a sentence even if the sentence has embedded clauses. This does not contradict the idea that finite state automata cannot handle recursion because unlike a pushdown automaton the neural net does not have to be able to tell whether or not a sequence belongs to a context-free language. All it has to do is detect statistical patterns in a sample of sequences and extract the probability that a given word is a likely continuation of a particular sequence.[19]

The interaction of learning and inheritance involved in the Baldwin effect can be understood through the joint use of genetic algorithms and neural nets. There are two extreme cases of this combined use: a genetic algorithm can be used to find the final weights of a neural net's connections, in which case there is no room for learning, or used to specify only certain properties of the neural net (like its connectivity or the initial values of the weights) allowing the final setting of the weights to be done by training.[20] A simulation of the Baldwin effect must start with the second case, in which a learned ability is only partly genetically determined, and end with the first case, a fully genetically specified neural net. In one simulation extremely simple neural nets were used, much too simple to be useful in language processing, but the problem that had to be solved through the combined use of learning and genetics had only one solution. This means that the structure of the search space had the form of a "needle in a haystack," with the only good solution represented by a high fitness peak surrounded by low fitness points. Without the availability to learn from experience the fitness peak corresponding to the solution was so steep that it was basically impossible to climb. Introducing learning, on the other hand, changed the shape of the search space surrounding the peak with a gentle slope that facilitated evolutionary climbing.[21]

In our case, the needle in a haystack would be the problem of generating a full language, together with specialized brain organs for producing and parsing its sentences, using as a starting point an externally evolved language possessing only a minimum of compositionality and recursion. Before discussing how this process could have unfolded we need to address a limitation of the previous simulation: the assumption of direct access to propositional content. That is, we need to replace the capacity to read minds with the inference of communicative intentions from the observation of behavior. We argued in previous chapters that pre-linguistic humans shared with birds and other mammals the ability to analyze sensory experience in terms of complex scenes in which objects with enduring identities play roles of agents and patients, and that they shared with other primates the ability to detect tendencies to cooperate or cheat in social interactions. Understanding behavioral roles and detecting behavioral tendencies is not, of course, the same thing as guessing intentions but the abilities involved could have been further developed in that direction once simple reference and causal predication emerged.

The ability to achieve shared attention by the use of a common set of sound-referent associations could have led to the ability to infer intentions if the objects referred to had a capacity to affect and be affected by the agents, if the referent was a predator affording them danger or a prey affording them nutrition, for example. In other words, the intention to warn others of potential opportunities and risks would be easy to guess from the production of a sound if the latter took place in a situation to which all agents attributed significance. And similarly for the symbolic artifacts denoting the conjunction of causes and effects. If the production of the sound for "FullMoon-CausesLowTide" had acquired the status of an urgent call to go to the beach to forage for shell fish, agents would come to infer the customary intention behind the production of that sound. These abilities, primitive as they are, could have sufficed to replace the explicit presentation of propositional content in a learning situation if the teaching of linguistic associations had taken place as part of the performance of nonlinguistic tasks, such as hunting, gathering, or working stone. On the other hand, once monolithic artifacts began to be broken down a new type of observable behavior became available: *word-choice behavior*. In particular, words like "full moon" and "low tide" that tended to occur together more often than in the company of other words would have created patterns in the frequency of co-occurrence that were detectable in the choices of words made by agents.[22] These are exactly the kind of statistical patterns that can be extracted from a population of sentences by even the simplest recurrent neural nets.

From then on the history of language can be imagined to have proceeded on two levels at the same time: biological evolution continued to operate through the Baldwin effect helping to propagate the genes underlying the capacity to detect patterns of word co-occurrence, while cultural evolution began to transform customary patterns into obligatory constraints on word-choice behavior. While early on in the cultural evolutionary process the teacher–student interaction may have involved only the transmission of patterns that had become habitual, later on the patterns could have been transmitted as if they constituted an enforceable social obligation. That is, a word that used to require another one simply because the two tended to co-occur very often now obliged its user to provide the second word. This way cultural evolution could have provided a mechanism for the emergence of linguistic rules, that is, a mechanism to institutionalize habitual usage into an obligatory convention. The basis for such a mechanism would have already been available if, as was argued in Chapter 8, the habit of punishing those that do not punish departures from cooperative behavior (metanorms) had previously emerged. Once metanorms had become part of the cultural content that was transmitted from one generation to the next their use could have been extended to patterns of behavior that distinguished one community from another. In other words, metanorms could have become a mechanism not only for the emergence of solidarity and a sense of communal identity but also for the enforcement of behavioral patterns that were unique to a community and consolidated that identity.

A mechanism to transform habit into convention is an important component of theories of non-biological linguistic evolution at the level of both syntax and semantics. The way syntax could have been affected by institutionalization can be shown by going back to the previous example of the proposition "Causes (Y, X)." Once such an abstract proposition had emerged and the customary co-occurrence of a predicate and its arguments had become a conventional constraint, the pattern itself could have been used as a template (the operator-argument template) for many other expressions. In other words, the pattern could have been used by analogy to constrain the creation of new patterns the result being indistinguishable from sentences produced by the application of grammatical rules.[23] The effect of institutionalization on semantics, in turn, is related to the fact that when two words tend to co-occur with very high frequency, so that a listener can already tell what the second word will be once the first one is heard, the second word can be omitted from a sentence. That is, very high frequency of co-occurrence could have made some words redundant for a speaker since they could be supplied by the listener. In some cases this could have allowed entire phrases or even sentences to be compacted into a single word while preserving the meaning of the phrase or sentence. When the product of packing the composite meaning of series of words was made obligatory a powerful mechanism for the extension of vocabulary, and even for the production of new categories of words, would have come into existence.[24]

If this scenario is correct we can conclude that the possibility space that was searched through evolution, both biological and cultural, was isomorphic with but not identical to the space studied by automata theory. Automata theory charts the space of possible languages and of the computational capacities needed to master them in an entirely mechanism-independent way involving no commitment to any particular implementation of the automata themselves. This point is often overlooked by those who think our brains must embody a genetically coded linear-bounded automaton using an explicit context-sensitive "language of thought." When it comes to the design of future simulations of linguistic evolution keeping the distinction between mechanisms and mechanism-independent structure firmly in mind can have important consequences. In particular, useful as the just discussed simulation of grammaticalization is to study the decomposition of monolithic symbolic artifacts, performing it in a format that automata can understand reduces the degree to which the patterns that result can be considered to be truly emergent. More precisely, while compositionality did indeed emerge in that simulation the grammatical rules and categories did not emerge: they were partially built in by the choice of symbol sequences and inference algorithm.[25] What we need are simulations that can yield rules and categories as an emergent product by using recurrent neural nets to extract patterns of co-occurrence among words and by situating the agents in a social space in which the transformation of habitual practices into obligatory conventions can take place.

It is time now to return to a subject that was left unfinished at the end of the previous chapter. There we saw that detailed archeological simulations of mesolithic and neolithic communities failed at times to match the available evidence and that a possible explanation for this is that once complex meanings could be formed by the combination of words, and once the referents of those words ceased to be directly observable objects and actions, magical beliefs having a powerful effect on behavior could have emerged. In the next chapter we will tackle this kind of beliefs but without separating the imaginary worlds they give rise to from the material world of resource gradients.

To keep these two worlds together magical beliefs will be discussed as a means to generate a new kind of social gradient, a gradient of legitimacy, that government organizations can use to manipulate physical gradients to an extent that early humans would have found mystifying. In particular, the construction of huge funerary monuments, like the pyramids of Egypt, will be shown to have depended on the coupling of magical and practical beliefs, the pyramids themselves constituting a powerful mechanism for the production and maintenance of legitimate authority.

CHAPTER ELEVEN
Multiagents and Archaic States

Neolithic communities, like their hunter-gatherer predecessors, were relatively egalitarian. Certain personal qualities such as charisma, oratory prowess, or the ability to lead may have created differences among their members but these tended to be transient and had little impact in the long run. For this reason these communities had access to only one social gradient, a gradient of solidarity. But when differences in prestige were not dissipated quickly and were allowed to accumulate they began to form another gradient, a *gradient of status*, marking the beginning of the process of social stratification. Government organizations with a well-defined authority structure, on the other hand, needed more that status differences to emerge. Authority can always be enforced in a material way through physical punishment or confinement but it is much less costly and more stable if it is believed to be legitimate. And this implies that a *gradient of legitimacy* has been created, a concentration of the capacity to command justified by a religious tradition linking elite members to supernatural forces or, in some cases, justified by the successful practical reasoning of specialized bureaucracies.[1] The historical process that gave rise to these two new exploitable resources used to be conceptualized as a simple linear evolution: egalitarian agricultural tribes were superseded by chiefdoms organized around status differences which were, in turn, replaced by archaic states and their centralized authority. But archeologists have modified this simple model in several ways.

First, it has become clear that there is more than one transitional entity between rural and urban forms of social organization. At the very least we must make a distinction between simple and complex chiefdoms, the latter already displaying rigid social stratification but not centralized decision-making. Second, the focus of research has shifted from looking for similarities to exploring the wide range of variation of each of these social forms. And finally, the idea that these social forms followed each other in time has been replaced by the study of their coexistence in space: an archaic state may have formed the core of a large region dominating a few complex chiefdoms, with simple chiefdoms and agricultural villages forming an exploited periphery.[2] The concept of a linear evolution usually leads to models in which a single entity, "society as a whole," develops from one "stage of development" to another. But once we replace that conception with one involving the coexistence and complex interaction of agricultural communities, chiefly lineages, and institutional organizations, we need several models. In some cases we can take for granted the emergent properties of these larger individual entities—solidarity, status, or legitimacy—and model the entities themselves as agents. Individual organizations, for example, can be modeled as agents because they have their own goals (of which most of their staff may be unaware); are capable of affecting and being affected by their environment (as when an environmental crisis affects an entire organization); possess institutional knowledge and memory (written records, routines); have their own legal standing, rights, and obligations; and are capable of coordinating the activity of many workers and managers in the performance of complex tasks.[3]

Multiagent simulations in which the behavior of agents is entirely determined by formal rules are adequate to deal with this case, as we saw in Chapter 9 where individual communities were modeled as single agents. But if we want to explain how properties like the status of a lineage or the legitimacy of an organization emerge we must simulate the interactions between persons explicitly and model their behavior as determined by beliefs and desires: the belief that a sacred text justifies the authority of a supreme leader, for example, or the desire to be part of the mission of an organization. The agents we have discussed so far do not meet this requirement: the rules that guide their behavior may mimic the effect of having beliefs or desires but the latter are not explicitly modeled and cannot interact to produce emergent effects. The simplest way of modeling beliefs and

desires are as attitudes or stances taken by persons toward propositions, that is, as propositional attitudes. Using propositions as the
objects of mental attitudes disregards the fact that pre-linguistic
humans already possessed beliefs and desires relative to the content of
their episodic memories: the belief that something happened because
one witnessed it happening, for instance, or the desire for a flavor,
aroma, sound, or sight that one has previously experienced. But the
belief on supernatural forces or the desire not to offend those forces
cannot exist without language. To tackle more complex cases of personal agency recent approaches to the design of simulated agents have
replaced rigid rules with more flexible propositional attitudes. This is
the strategy followed in the so-called Belief-Desire-Intention (BDI)
approach.[4]

BDI agents are not, in fact, designed to deal with religious or
ideological beliefs but to reason about practical matters. As in the case
of other agent designs this involves mapping sensory inputs into
appropriate behavioral outputs but instead of using rules to mediate
between perception and action a more elaborate process is employed:
information about the world, about a certain distribution of resources,
for example, is first used to update an agent's beliefs; these are then
used to generate a set of options concerning the available opportunities and risks; the options are then checked for how desirable and
achievable they are; options that are desired and can be achieved
become goals and these, combined with a commitment to a course of
action, become the intentions driving the behavior of the agent.[5]
Using BDI agents for the simulation of supernatural beliefs would
involve two simple modifications. First we would have to give agents
the capacity to ascribe propositional attitudes to other agents in order
to make sense of their actions, a capacity referred to as taking "the
intentional stance" toward the explanation of behavior.[6] Second,
agents should be able *to treat resources as agents*.[7] Together these two
modifications would give BDI agents the capacity to adopt the intentional stance toward material gradients, attributing beliefs and desires
to entities like the sun, the rain, the soil, and so on. To transform a
few magical beliefs into an ideology one more ingredient would be
necessary: debates among agents aimed at persuasion. In the account
of the emergence of language given in the previous chapter it was
important to assume that agents did not have access to the contents

of each other's minds and that they could only form intentions about changing each other's behavior. But once language emerged and could express the content of propositional attitudes humans became able to form intentions in which the goal was to modify the very content of those beliefs and desires. If the subject matter of such persuasion attempts involved explanations of resource scarcity in intentional terms, like "The soil has become barren because the fertility goddess is angry," then from the ensuing discussions a coherent set of supernatural beliefs could emerge. Protocols for negotiation through which BDI agents can establish their positions on an issue, make concessions, and reach agreements are currently being developed.[8]

The BDI approach to agent design is in its infancy and the kind of application to archeological simulations just suggested does not yet exist. But simpler approaches using rules to generate behavior that mimics the effect of propositional attitudes are already yielding interesting results. One of them, called "Emergence of Society" (EOS), explores the first step in the evolution of organizational authority: the rise among egalitarian communities of *enduring leadership*. In a typical EOS simulation agents propose plans about specific ways of harvesting resources: what resource to target, how many other agents are needed, how to allocate their labor. If other agents believe that this plan is better than their own they adopt it. When an agent has participated in another agent's plan on several occasions it becomes a follower while those whose plans are followed become leaders. When a group has formed around a leader certain tendencies become manifest that strengthen the bonds holding the group together: its members tend to communicate with each other more often about the location and concentration of resources and tend to take each other into account in the formation of future plans.[9] Once this dynamic of group formation has been established the agents can be confronted with environmental crises to check what effects these have on the structure of the groups. In other words, what this simulation explores is the relation between enduring leadership and a space of possible resource distributions. This space may be pictured as consisting of two dimensions, one relating to relative abundances and scarcities, the other to relative concentrations and dispersions. Abundance weakens leadership since most agents can meet their metabolic needs by working alone while scarcity acts an incentive to work together.

Dispersion of resources, in turn, makes creating successful plans harder since it increases the difficulty of coordinating the actions of a group while concentration facilitates planning. The outcome of EOS simulations has increased the plausibility of an existing archeological hypothesis: that the historical emergence of enduring leadership was triggered by environmental changes leading to both scarcity and concentration of resources.[10]

This simulation captures the material aspect of the transition from a strict egalitarian community to one in which an accumulation of prestige around a leader is not rapidly dissipated. The maintenance of such a gradient over longer time scales, however, is problematic because in hunter-gatherer and agricultural communities departures from an egalitarian organization are actively prevented by internal devices. Leaders are demanded, for example, to be generous and redistribute in ceremonial feasts whatever food surpluses have accumulated in their hands, or else to ritually burn them. Customs like this may act as an unconscious mechanism to guard against the crystallization of formal authority.[11] Moreover, war heroes, prophets, or promoters of agricultural productivity may find their leadership compromised if any misfortune (a defeat in war, the failure of a plan, a natural disaster) is believed by their followers to be a supernatural sign that the leaders do not in fact possess the admired charismatic virtue. Magical beliefs, on the other hand, can in special circumstances stabilize rather than dissipate a status gradient. The catalyst for such a change can be a succession crisis ensuing after the death of a cherished leader. These crises can lead to the transformation of charisma from a personal characteristic into one that can be transmitted along a blood line, a transformation typically justified by the invocation of supernatural beliefs.[12] And once leadership can be inherited it can play a crucial role in the generation of enduring concentrations of prestige around particular kinship groups. Simulating this critical transition would involve augmenting simulations like the one just described with BDI agents capable of having magical beliefs and of engaging in debates about the sources and potential transmissibility of charismatic powers.

Once status becomes a property that can accumulate it opens the way for the differentiation of communities, or of groups within communities, into social strata. Archeological evidence for stratification comes from a variety of sources. Since complex chiefdoms organize entire geographical regions the remains of settlements in a region may be ranked by size, the number of ranks counted, and the distribution of settlement sizes per rank studied. This regional hierarchy can then be used as an indication of the number of hierarchical levels of decision-making that existed in those communities. At a smaller scale burial sites offer another window into social strata. Systematic burial was already practiced by humans in the middle paleolithic and by the upper paleolithic it had become ceremonial: the dead were buried clothed and wearing personal adornments.[13] The burial sites of chiefs contain in addition to personal information valuable indications about the *steepness* of status gradients: the size of a tomb, its demarcation from other graves, and more importantly, the richness of its contents. Of particular significance are the presence of adornments made from exotic materials ranging from obsidian, limestone, and basalt, to copper, lapis lazuli, turquoise, and alabaster. These rare objects are significant because they constituted a different form of wealth than agricultural products: they could be used not only to express status differences but also as a kind of political currency to confer status to others, as when the leader of a complex chiefdom distributed them to those of simple chiefdoms to cement alliances and define local rankings.[14] This movement of objects of status from a place of high concentration to one of low concentration confirms that prestige can form a gradient. Keeping it from dissipating involved the strict control of the long-distance trade of rare raw materials and of the specialized crafts needed to produce elite adornments. Indeed, burying these rare objects together with their former owners may have been a way to prevent "inflationary pressures" from developing by permanently taking them out of circulation.

The existence of an enduring gradient of status can lead to the creation of rank differences that are fluid and continuous as in simple chiefdoms or fixed and sharply discontinuous as in complex chiefdoms. To explore how these different outcomes may be produced we do not need simulations in which personal agency is modeled in detail but rather ones that capture the interaction between larger scale social entities taking place at longer temporal scales. One example is a simulation (called TongaSim) inspired by a contemporary case: the Tonga chiefdom in Polynesia. This chiefdom is organized into kinship groups called "lineages," each with its own chief or chiefs, that are ranked in terms of status. These rankings can change depending on the relations between lineages. Specifically, marriages among the offspring of titled chiefs can increase or decrease the rank of a lineage: if the titled heir marries someone from a higher status lineage his or her own lineage will gain in status and vice versa, heirs marrying down in status bring down their own lineage. Significant changes in the ranking of lineages can take up to four to five generations so only a series of bad marriage decisions can have this effect. Each lineage is involved in economic activity, its agricultural wealth determined by number of kin, the land available to it, and the personal ability of its chief to motivate both kin and commoners to work harder. This agricultural wealth, in turn, flows within lineages in the form of redistribution to commoners, and between lineages from wife-receiving to wife-giving ones. Agricultural wealth also flows in the form of tribute paid to lineages of higher rank.[15]

Thus in chiefdoms material and status gradients are intertwined, their interaction pivoting on marriage decisions as well as on decisions affecting the selection of titled heirs. The question that the simulation set out to answer is how the rigid social stratification observed in complex chiefdoms could emerge from the dynamics of these interacting gradients. One possible answer is the relaxation of prohibitions to marry close relatives. Incest taboos come in different strengths: they may prohibit the marrying of brothers or sisters; the marrying of first cousins; or the marrying of any relative however distant. The stronger the prohibitions the more likely it is that an heir belonging to a high status lineage will be forced to marry someone with lower status. It is therefore in the interest of those with the highest status to lower the strength of the taboo. Historically this could have been achieved through political strategies by chiefs but with simple simulated agents this level of scale cannot be captured. The relaxation of taboos, on the other hand, can be performed exogenously to check whether it has the postulated effect on degree of stratification. In the simulation ten chiefly lineages started the process. As population increased and some lineages ran out of agricultural land they split into two increasing the overall number. (The simulation could handle up to 50 lineages.) The simulation went through a series of cycles as each lineage ranked potential spouses and selected heirs, hundreds of simulated marriages took place, agricultural wealth flowed among lineages, and status was transmitted. Once this basic dynamic was established experiments on the effect of taboos of different strengths could be conducted. Measures of stratification included the steepness of the status gradient (how large the differences in status between lineages were) and the mobility of the lineages (how often changes in the ranking occurred). The outcome of the simulation confirmed the basic logic behind marriage strategies: the lower the strength of incest prohibitions the higher the degree of stratification.[16]

If the burial sites of titled chiefs can be said to be our window into social stratification then architectural monuments like pyramids, temples, and palaces are our main source of evidence for the existence of centralized decision-making in archaic states. The central decisions leading to the erection of monumental structures were based on both technical and magical beliefs and informed both material and ceremonial practices. Let's take the example of the famous pyramid of Giza in Egypt. On one hand, this funerary monument was clearly intended to have magical effects since it was supposed to function like a resurrection machine. Needless to say, the pyramid's internal mechanism did not allow it to actually transmute a king into a god but it nevertheless functioned like a machine for the production of legitimacy, both by its powerful effect on the religious beliefs of those who contemplated it and by serving as a ritual center for the continuous performance of traditional ceremonies associated with the cult of a dead king. On the other hand, the design of the monument involved highly technical knowledge such as the astronomical knowledge needed for its proper orientation toward the heavens—it is very precisely oriented true north—and the applied mathematical knowledge involved in calculating its shape. Its construction, in turn, demanded well-organized material practices. The pyramid is made of more than two million blocks of stone each weighing over two tons on average. These blocks were originally covered by polished white limestone that, unlike the core stone, was an exotic material transported from far away. Building such a structure in just over two decades is evidence of the relative efficiency of the bureaucratic organizations involved, the legitimacy of which derived from their pragmatic ability to overcome the cognitive, physical, temporal, and institutional limitations of personal agency. In short, the pyramids were both ceremonial and material entities, the first aspect related to their capacity to express in their solid permanence the validity and continuity of authority and the second to the fact that they constituted a frozen indication of the total amount of energy that a given elite was able to harness.[17]

Before the great pyramid of Giza there was only a century of construction experience starting with the very first Egyptian monument built entirely out of stone, the Step pyramid at Saqqara. In between these two there were a few experiments in the building of smooth-sided pyramids one of which seems to show that the architects were still learning since they changed the slope of the monument as it grew taller (the Bent pyramid at Dashur). On the other hand, prior to this relatively short burst of creative activity there was nearly a millennium of experience in the construction of tombs and other funerary monuments going back to the late pre-dynastic era when chieftain's tombs built out of brick with some stone elements seemed already intended to last for an eternity.[18] These two different time scales call for different explanations. Modeling a learning process lasting many centuries should use as agents the organizations themselves: royal workshops and the parts of the rising central government on which the workshops depended. Modeling a process involving two or three generations, on the other hand, a period of time in which projects grew so large so fast that bureaucrats had to learn to solve novel logistical problems during their lifetimes, should use simulated personal agents. One way to approach the simulation of organizational learning taking place at millennial time scales is to model it as an evolutionary process. Organizations can be modeled as entities capable of evolution if their daily routines and procedures, and their division of labor and coordination mechanisms, are passed from one generation to the next, or even from one organization to another within the same generation.[19]

We can imagine the activity of tomb building early on in Egyptian history as divided into separate tasks each performed by a separate artisan in which organizational learning involved the elimination of inefficiencies through further subdivision into subtasks. More specifically, if there were subtasks that had to be executed as part of several tasks then a certain degree of overlap existed among the activities. If a single artisan were assigned not one but two overlapping tasks then the shared subtasks would have had to be performed only once reducing the overall amount of effort involved. On the other hand, the effort of coordinating the different activities by overseers would have increased. Thus, there was a trade-off between the advantages of clustering overlapping tasks and the coordination costs incurred by such clustering. To simulate organizational evolution using genetic algorithms the routine task assignments must be coded into a chromosome in which the ones and zeroes stand for agents and subtasks, while the fitness function measures the overall amount of effort taken to complete the task. Simulations like these have been carried out and have shown that clustering of tasks does occur but not in a way that takes full advantage of functional complementarities among subtasks.[20] One way of improving organizational learning would be to model it not as a blind evolutionary search but rather as a hybrid of genetic algorithms and reinforcement learning. These hybrids are called *classifier systems*.[21] In a classifier system what evolves are rules that guide the performance of tasks, rules that specify that if a condition arises then a certain action must be taken. Fitness is evaluated not by the amount of effort spent performing a task but by the ability to get a reward from a performance. Moreover, fitness is assigned not to individual rules but to groups of related rules, a shared credit assignment that tends to produce coadapted sets of rules rather than a single fittest rule.[22] In the present case the condition-action rules would represent either customary activities in which behavioral responses to specific conditions have become rule-like or written regulations specifying the connection between a condition and an action. Royal workshops would be the evolving entities while the source of rewards would be other organizations on which the workshops depended for legitimacy and financing.

In addition to the slow organizational learning behind the practice of tomb building there is the much faster one leading to pyramid building. To get an idea of the challenge this task posed to architects, officials, and bureaucrats we need to model the construction process itself, a process involving a mix of the technical and the ceremonial. On one hand, the workforce was motivated by the intense religious feelings generated by its involvement in a divine project. Although in the past this workforce was assumed to be composed of unskilled slaves blindly following commands from above it is now clear that most of the operations involved in pyramid building demanded high skill and motivation. Recently excavated cemeteries in the town that used to house officials, overseers, artists, and artisans show that even the workers were buried respectfully, strong evidence that they were not slaves.[23] On the other hand, both the religiously motivated workforce and the religiously legitimated organizational structure above them had to take into account the capacity of the material world to be affected by human activity as well as the capacity of humans to affect the world at that scale. More specifically, to understand the material challenge posed by the activity of pyramid building we need to define both the objective nature of the task environment as well as the kinds of coordinating mechanisms needed to organize a large workforce to meet that challenge. In what follows we will concentrate on the technical component of the construction process but it should be kept in mind that without the ceremonial component the explanation would remain incomplete.

The way the Egyptians dealt with the construction problem was through a recursive decomposition approach, grouping together related tasks and assembling them as parts of a larger whole. The overall task of pyramid building was divided into at least three main task groups: quarrying the stone; transporting it to the construction site; and erecting it. Quarrying, in turn, was subdivided into several tasks: carving deep channels into a limestone bed nearby; carving narrow channels to subdivide it into blocks; and using wooden levers to detach them from the bed. Transporting the blocks was subdivided into the building of tracks and ramps on top of which they could be moved; loading them into wooden sledges; and pulling or rolling the sledges over cylindrical beams. Finally, erecting the stones involved setting them using wooden levers; carving marks on the stones to control the slope; and trimming the stones to their final shape.[24] The efforts of experimental archeologists in the past few decades have given us a sense of the size of the workforce and the amount of time taken to execute each task. In one experiment a team of 12 quarryman was able to produce eight stone blocks a day; 20 men could haul the blocks from the quarry to the building site at a rate of ten blocks a day; and a team of four men, two to push and adjust and two masons to perform the trimming, was needed to erect each block. To this we must add a variety of support workers, from carpenters and blacksmiths to create wooden sledges and metal tools, to potters, bakers, and brewers to produce containers, food, and drink. Overall this experiment showed that a force of 25,000 workers could have finished the task in the 23 years that the building of the pyramid originally took.[25]

In addition to these physical experiments to duplicate some of the original tasks multiagent simulations can be used to explore the part-to-whole relations between tasks and subtasks. While simple projects can be subdivided in such a way that they are no more than a sum of their parts, if there are interdependencies between component tasks then the components cannot simply be added but must be carefully articulated. The objective space of possibilities of different task environments can be explored using a formal language called "Task Analysis, Environment Modeling, and Simulation" (or Taems). Taems can be used to model the relation between the main task and its subtasks and to capture the interdependencies between individual tasks: performance of one task, for example, may enable the performance of another one so it must take temporal precedence; or it may merely facilitate its performance so the first task need not be fully completed before the second one can start; one task may replenish the resource needed by another task so the two may proceed simultaneously; or the two tasks may consume the same resource in which case there can be conflicts between them.[26] These relations—enables, facilitates, replenishes, and consumes—allow Taems to capture the structure of a task environment in the form of a hierarchical graph the terminal ends of which are directly executable operations.

When used as a tool to explore the objective possibility space of task environments these directly executable operations must be left unspecified and the definition of what they produce must be made very abstract capturing only the contribution of an operation to the solution of a problem. Using Taems this way is facilitated by the fact that its formalism was designed to be entirely domain-independent: a graph representing a given task decomposition may capture the structure of a task environment that is common to many domains (a factory, a hospital, an airport, a bureaucratic agency) explaining why human agents in those domains face similar organizational challenges. The dimensions of the possibility space are typically probabilistic because the properties of large graphs can only be given statistically: the average number of subtasks into which tasks are decomposed; the average duration of operations and tasks; the statistical distribution of hard interdependencies (like "enables") and soft interdependencies (like "facilitates"). On the other hand, the graph produced by Taems can be coupled to a multiagent system to investigate a specific task environment, in which case the operations as well as their products and durations must be fully specified. In the case of pyramid building the directly executable operations would be activities like measuring, aligning, chiseling, levering, cutting, polishing. These operations can be assigned the average time they take to be performed and the potential value of their product using the results from experimental archeology. This discipline can also provide insight into the subdivision of tasks and subtasks to be incorporated into a Taems graph. But in addition we would need another graph specifying the authority structure of the relevant parts of the Egyptian government. This can be reconstructed using existing textual evidence related to the building of the actual pyramids.

Control of the overall task was in the hands of the Vizier in his role of Overseer of Royal Works. Evidence for this comes from a text inscribed in hieroglyphs on the walls of several tombs known as "The Duties of the Vizier." From this text it is clear that authority roles had not yet differentiated into the plurality of functions with which we are familiar today. In particular, the Vizier played several roles: head of the civil administration with judicial and administrative responsibilities; managing director of the royal palace getting daily reports about security and logistic matters; and deputy to the king, personally hearing his commands and ensuring their enactment.[27] The Vizier controlled the conglomerate of central departments constituting the Egyptian bureaucracy as well as the local authorities of the different urban centers and their rural areas. The text also reveals that the different departments were relatively autonomous: although detailed written procedures existed to regulate their activities the Vizier does not seem to have initiated any of the departments' actions by direct command but only to have supervised the results after the fact.[28] This suggests a hierarchical coordinating mechanism but one in which only strategic goals were given as explicit orders while their tactical implementation was left to the personnel within the departments. Other texts give us the part-to-whole relations at the bottom end of the hierarchy: the workforce consisted of several crews, each composed of two gangs of 1,000 men divided into five groups of 200, each further subdivided into ten teams of 20 men called "divisions."[29] The overall hierarchical structure may be modeled by a graph in which nodes represent institutional roles, edges represent relationships between those roles, and arrows represent asymmetrical relations, such as those that exist between superiors and subordinates. The unity of command under the Vizier implies a graph with a single node at the top, while an unambiguous chain of command implies a graph in which all nodes but the top one have a single arrow pointing to them, representing the fact that every subordinate had a single direct boss.[30]

These two graphs, one describing the command hierarchy the other defining the specification and decomposition of the overall task, give us an objective view of the organization and the problem it must solve. But to animate them with agents the graphs must be supplemented by a plurality of partial views. The subjective view of the problem varies from agent to agent and it is determined in large part by the way in which the workforce is organized. If this organization is achieved in a rigid hierarchical way in which commands flow downwards while reports flow upwards, the agent occupying the top position must be modeled as having access to the objective task structure while subordinate agents should have only a fragmentary view, the more limited the lower their rank. If the organization included teams and if their members were allowed to communicate with one another, then agents may form in addition to their local views a non-local view through the information provided by their peers. This distinction also determines how interdependencies between tasks are handled by agents: in a rigid hierarchy schedules and deadlines for every subtask are centrally decided and implemented by command, while within teams agents must be able to negotiate deadlines and make commitments to one another.[31] In the case of pyramid building teams are needed to model what happens inside each of the hierarchical levels. The Vizier's office, for example, consisted of several people working together: the Vizier himself, his council, an official of internal affairs, and several scribes. Teams also existed inside each relatively autonomous government department and at the level of worker divisions where most physical operations were performed. This complexity calls for agents that are not just boundedly rational (as in most multiagent simulations) but also task oriented and socially situated.[32]

Finally, populating the graphs with agents and setting them into motion demands simulating a range of coordinating mechanisms. The simplest and better explored of these are prohibitions, that is, *simulated social laws* that generate commitments to avoid certain actions without incurring the costs of communication. An example of prohibitions are traffic laws. In a simulation of the building of a pyramid the need to regulate the traffic of agents would immediately become evident if the agents were situated in a two-dimensional space: different gangs would have to be assigned to different sides of the pyramid and within each side agents bringing stones, mortar, tools, food and drink would have to avoid collisions and create relatively efficient circulation paths. Moreover, if we added a third dimension to this space then as the pyramid grew taller and the room to maneuver decreased spatial assignments allowing the simultaneous performance of tasks would become even more important. Circulation patterns could be rigidly specified by a central controller but traffic laws can be a less expensive coordination mechanism if they are crafted to take advantage of the fact that agents can perceive one another within certain distance and can therefore contribute to the solution of circulation problems by making some local decisions themselves. Ideally, a social law should give agents enough freedom of action to construct a plan of action—find an optimal path from one point to another, for example—but not so much that they can interfere with the actions of others.[33]

The dynamics between different levels of the hierarchy can be captured by augmenting the interactions between agents with speech acts. These are actions in which the very utterance of a sentence carries binding social implications with different degrees of force: to promise, to request, to demand, and most importantly in the present case, to command.[34] Using the graph that captures the authority structure the binding force of these commands can be made to flow from their point of utterance to those that must ultimately execute them. The dynamics within teams, in turn, can be explored using an approach called "General Partial Global Planning" (or GPGP). In this approach agents use their partial beliefs about a task to form intentions to act and to sequence those actions to create a local schedule. Because the content of an agent's beliefs does not include information about other agents' tasks its local schedule may enter into conflict with their schedules. Thus, the first coordinating mechanism in GPGP is used to create non-local viewpoints. This mechanism allows an agent to get information about other agents' beliefs and to detect coordination problems between its tasks and those of others. A second mechanism allows agents to communicate the results of their operations to others but only those that are relevant since communication itself is costly. Other mechanisms are then used to aid agents in the solution of problems like avoiding redundancies and handling interdependencies. The end result is that agents can modulate their local scheduling to include commitments to others: a commitment to meet a deadline; to stop an action in order to free a resource; or to start an action at the earliest possible time after another agent's action is finished.[35]

Armed with these different coordinating mechanisms (traffic laws, central commands, negotiated commitments) it should be possible to use a Taems graph and a GPGP multiagent system to simulate the complex process of building giant funerary monuments: each set of coordinating mechanisms together with a proposed decomposition of the overall task into subtasks would constitute an archeological hypothesis about what really went on during the construction of the great Giza pyramid. Such a simulation would capture only a brief episode in the history of ancient Egypt and would include only a segment of Egyptian society: the Vizier as Overseer of Royal Works, the relevant department under him, and the crews of workers under the command of that department. This means that much of what made the workings of this social segment possible would be included only implicitly. The provinces that supplied food and labor to the central government, for example, would be included only as resource inputs. But as we have argued repeatedly in previous chapters there is nothing wrong with unexplained presuppositions as long as a simulation explains something else, such as the emergent capacity of an organization to plan and build large architectural structures, and as long as there are other models that account for the emergence of what is being presupposed.

Finally, there is the question of how to simulate the organizational learning process that led to a specific set of coordinating mechanisms. The century of pyramid building experience before Giza is too short for an evolutionary process to have yielded any significant results even if augmented by reinforcement learning. This means that we have no choice but to use personal agents capable of monitoring the execution of their own tasks and to detect problems like the performance of redundant subtasks, mistakes in the sequencing of operations, misallocated resources, or broken commitments. More importantly, once a problem is detected agents must be able to diagnose its cause and propose a solution. To have this capacity agents must use the portion of the Taems graph to which they have access to locate the detected problem in its proper context—to determine, for example, if interdependencies among subtasks were one of the causes—as well as use traces of past activity recording not only the series of decisions they took about what operation to execute and when to execute it, but also the reasons why those decisions were made.[36] In this scheme an agent has direct access only to its own memory traces but in the presence of task interdependencies it may have to request information about the traces of other agents to be able to reconstruct the process that led to the problem, and these requests can be costly. To keep communication costs low relative to the gains in efficiency agents should attempt to diagnose only situation-specific problems. In other words, agents should try to gather non-local information but only to the extent that it can be exploited locally.[37]

Through a process like this an organization can learn to improve coordinating mechanisms but only at the level of its teams. That is, once a correct diagnosis is made modifications to coordination rules will be applied only locally. This approach, on the other hand, can be extended to the entire hierarchy by applying it to all the different ranks. Historically, one of the first organizational roles to differentiate between a chief and his followers must have been that of overseer. Early on into Egyptian dynastic history several ranks of overseers already existed. But what is an overseer if not an agent that specializes in monitoring and detecting problems occurring at the rank just below and creating reports explaining problems addressed to those in the rank just above? In other words, the same diagnosing capabilities that team members have in this scheme could yield an agent playing the role of overseer. The difference between the two cases is that the higher the rank of an overseer the larger the portion of a Taems graph it would have access to. This means that an overseer of sufficiently high rank would not learn to improve the sequencing of operations like stone cutting or polishing, but the scheduling of entire task groups like quarrying, hauling, and erecting. The modifications to coordination mechanisms would be still be local and oriented to specific tasks but the higher the rank the more general in scope these local solutions would be.

Like genetic algorithms and neural nets, multiagent systems have a variety of industrial uses that have nothing to do with modeling social reality. These range from creating user interfaces for new software applications that can learn about the habits of human users, to increasing the efficiency of the allocation of resources in the internet by allowing autonomous agents to engage in decentralized trade.[38] These and other uses of multiagent systems will continue to drive their development regardless of the rate at which social scientists adopt this technology for modeling purposes. But it has been the underlying message of this chapter that social simulations as enacted thought experiments can greatly contribute to develop insight into the workings of the most complex emergent wholes on this planet. Whether its rate of adoption accelerates or not will depend on the imaginative use that social scientists make of these new resources as well as on their willingness to abandon the idea of "society as a whole" and replace it with a set of more concrete entities (communities, organizations, cities) that lend themselves to partial modeling in a way that vague totalities do not. In short, the future of multiagent simulations as models of social reality will depend on how social scientists can affect this technology by deploying it creatively and on how they can be affected by it through the possession of the right social ontology.

APPENDIX
Links to Assemblage Theory

The variety of mechanisms of emergence discussed in this book shows that the fears of the early emergentists, that clockwork mechanisms could not possibly account for the irreducible properties of a whole, were misplaced. There is nothing in the notion of a holistic property that emerges from the interactions between components that limits the potential complexity of those interactions. On the other hand, the concept of emergent property does place limits on the kinds of wholes that can be legitimately accepted. In particular, it militates against the idea of a totality the parts of which are so inextricably related that their very identity is constituted by their relations within the whole. In a seamless totality the properties of components derive from the role they play in the whole so detaching them from it would automatically deprive them from their defining characteristics. But none of the wholes we have discussed here, from thunderstorms to institutional organizations, are seamless totalities. The fact that the properties of a whole depend on the actual exercise of the capacities of its parts implies that removing one of them may indeed destroy the whole's identity, but the part itself need not lose its own identity: pulling a live animal's heart out will surely kill it but the heart itself can be implanted into another animal and resume its regular function. Thus, what we need is a concept that allows us to retain both irreducibility and decomposability, a concept that makes the explanation of synthesis and the possibility of analysis intelligible. We could, of course, simply build this requirement into the definition of the term "emergent whole" but since this concept has a history, and since in this history the restriction against totalities has not always been enforced, it will be useful to introduce a new word for wholes that are irreducible and decomposable. We will refer to these wholes as *assemblages*.[1]

The advantage of a new term is not limited to the fact that it is unblemished by past philosophical mistakes or that it is devoid of undesirable connotations. It also signals a fresh start and acts as an incentive to get things right this time around. So let's carefully define what else should be included in the content of this new concept. First of all, the identity of an assemblage should always be conceived as the product of a historical process, the process that brought its components together for the first time as well as the process that maintains its integrity through a regular interaction among its parts. This implies that the identity of an assemblage is always contingent and it is not guaranteed by the existence of a necessary set of properties constituting an unchanging essence. Or to put this differently, assemblages are not particular members of a general category but unique and singular individuals. Even if two assemblages resemble each other so much that no one can tell them apart, each will still be unique due to the different details of its individual history. In the last few chapters it was argued that despite the fact that the word "individual" has become synonymous with "person" it can legitimately be applied to individual communities, individual organizations, or individual cities. And this argument can be extended to the emergent entities of all other chapters: individual atoms and molecules, individual cells and organisms, individual species, and ecosystems. All these different assemblages are born at a particular time, live a life, and then die. It follows that knowledge about an assemblage does not derive from a "botanical" classification that takes properties for granted but from an account of the origin and endurance of those properties. Given the importance of the ontological status of assemblages we will need a technical term to refer to it: every actual assemblage is an *individual singularity*.

A second ontological commitment must be built into the definition of the term "assemblage" because these emergent wholes are defined not only by their properties but also by their tendencies and capacities. Tendencies can make the properties of a whole vary, sometimes even changing its identity, as when an ice sculpture characterized by its solidity and its shape manifests its tendency to melt at a certain temperature, losing those properties and much of its identity. Capacities, in turn, make wholes exhibit aspects of their identity that were previously hidden, as when an innocent looking plant turns out to be poisonous or, on the contrary, to possess unexpected healing powers. While tendencies make a list of essential properties look falsely permanent capacities explode it since for a given whole it would be impossible to list all the different ways in which it can affect and be affected by innumerable other wholes. And even if we could list all actually manifested tendencies and actually exercised capacities that would still not be enough since neither one has to be actual. To tackle this problem we used the notion of the structure of a possibility space, a structure that explains how tendencies and capacities can be real even when they are not actual. Although we saw how varied this structure can be and acknowledged many gaps in our conception of it, it is safe to say that it is characterized by special or remarkable traits the ontological status of which is that of *universal singularities*. The term "universal" is used for two related reasons: first, the events in which tendencies are manifested and capacities exercised may be entirely different in detail and yet be shaped by the same singularities; and second, two series of events each constituting a different mechanism may nevertheless possess overlapping possibility spaces and display common features that are mechanism-independent.[2]

In addition to these ontological commitments another requirement must be built into the definition of the term "assemblage." Although each assemblage is a unique historical entity it always belongs to a population of more or less similar assemblages. In other words, despite the individual singularity of each assemblage the process of assembly behind it tends to be recurrent so what is synthesized is never a single individual but many of them. The recurrence itself is explained by the fact that the assembly process is governed by universal singularities but the actualization of the latter is always subject to contingent events so what is generated is a population in which variants are distributed in a certain way. The fact that shared properties vary, and that the variation in a population displays a certain statistical distribution, is another reason why the identity of an assemblage should not be conceived in terms of a fixed list of properties. To facilitate "population thinking" we need a means to specify not only the possible ways in which the members of a population can change but also the state of their identity at any particular point in their history. This can be achieved by *parametrizing* the concept of assemblage, that is, by providing it with "knobs" with modifiable settings the values of which determine the condition of the identity of an emergent whole at any given time. This will make it easier to picture in our minds an entire population of assemblages each possessing a slightly different identity depending on the settings of the parameters. And it will also facilitate thinking of the population as an entity that can undergo an intense shock from the outside that drastically changes those settings producing variants that go beyond the normal range of variation. In short, a parametrized concept can populate our minds in a way that brings variation and the history of that variation with it.

One parameter must specify the relative homogeneity or heterogeneity of the components of an assemblage: if in a given population all assemblages use the exact same components they will share a better defined identity than if there is large degree of variation in those components. This parameter must also specify the state of the boundaries of an assemblage: sharp and fixed or, on the contrary, fuzzy and fluctuating. The term "boundary" refers to very different things depending on the assemblage: the outer shell of electrons in an atom; the membrane of a bacterium; the outer skin of a plant or animal; the geographical frontiers of an ecosystem; the reproductive barriers of a species. The parameter needs a name and since it partly determines defining boundaries we can call it *territorialization*.[3] The more homogeneous the internal composition of an assemblage and the better defined its outer boundaries the more territorialized its identity may be said to be. In addition, given that tendencies and capacities also determine identity we must include behavioral factors in these parameter. For example, one factor affecting the range of capacities actually exercised by an assemblage is mobility, since a mobile assemblage is more likely to encounter novel situations than an immobile one. In this sense we may say that an animal that can move around and that can affect and be affected by a wider range of other entities is more deterritorialized than a plant that is tied to the soil.

For some assemblages we may need more than one parameter since new ways of determining identity have emerged historically. One novel means of fixing identity is the genetic code, or more precisely, the complex machinery through which genetic information is expressed.

Genes can exercise tight control over the mechanisms of emergence behind organic wholes, as when they coordinate the gradients and emergent forms of a developing embryo. An obvious name for this new parameter would be *coding*. An organism, for example, may be said to be highly coded if every detail of its anatomy is rigidly determined by its genes and relatively decoded if the environment also contributes to its anatomical definition. And similarly for behavior: if the behavior of an organism is entirely inherited the coding parameter will have a high value and vice versa, if genes define only the connectivity of its neurons allowing much of its behavior to be determined by learning during its lifetime the parameter will have a low value. Entities other than genes can affect this parameter. Much as the territorialization parameter can apply to all sorts of boundaries so the coding parameter can be applied to other sources of information-based constraints, such as those provided by language. We can imagine a community of paleolithic hunter-gatherers, for example, using its newly acquired power of speech to rigidly categorize all the entities that are important for its continued existence: food could be coded as raw or cooked; sacred, taboo, or ordinary. And similarly for dress, behavior, and other cultural expressions of its identity. Another good example would be the institutional organizations belonging to an archaic state that code in written form all the material flows they control. Both of these assemblages may be said to be highly coded. Conversely, there may exist a few commercial organizations in the periphery of an archaic state that coordinate material flows using prices instead of official categories and central commands, so as assemblages these organizations may be said to be relatively decoded.[4]

Let's summarize what has been said about the term "assemblage" and then review the content of previous chapters in the light of this new concept. First of all, the term must refer to concrete wholes that are irreducible and decomposable, that is, it must accommodate the epistemological demands of both synthesis and analysis. These wholes must be assigned a clear ontological status. Every assemblage must be treated as a unique historical entity characterized both by a set of actual emergent properties (making it an individual singularity) as well as by the structure of possibility spaces defining its tendencies and capacities (a structure defined by universal singularities). This structure may be termed the *diagram* of the assemblage. The historically contingent identity of assemblages must be allowed to change so the concept must be supplied with one or more parameters defining those changes. And finally, assemblages must always be thought as parts of populations in which their identities can change within limits producing a certain statistical distribution of variation. The potential range and possible lines of variation are determined by the diagram shared by all population members but their actual degree of similarity is determined by the values of the parameters at any given time: the more territorialized or coded the members of the population are the more they will tend to resemble one another. This way the similarities that tempt us to classify the population's members under a general category, and then to reify that category, can be given a concrete historical explanation.

In Chapter 1 we examined the simplest way of creating an assemblage: placing two separate molecular populations (two bodies of air or water) at different temperature or pressure in contact with each other. This, of course, creates a gradient with the tendency to dissipate and the capacity to act as fuel for other processes. Because the two populations are identical in composition the only heterogeneity involved is the intensive difference itself. The territorialization parameter reduces in this simplest of all assemblages to the *distance from thermodynamic equilibrium*, that is, to the degree of intensity of the gradient. The diagram of this assemblage can be studied with the help of mathematical tools like state space, its trajectories, and singularities. The dimensions of the possibility space are the relevant ways of changing for an assemblage, that is, its degrees of freedom. If there are interactions between these degrees of freedom the diagram is nonlinear, possessing multiple singularities of different types, whereas if there are no interactions the diagram is linear, structured by a single singularity of the steady-state type. Finally, some of the members of these molecular populations may be recruited to form the component parts of larger assemblages the identity of which will be determined in part by the linear or nonlinear nature of the diagram and in part by their own territorialization parameter. Emergent wholes that form by dissipating a local gradient and reaching a low-intensity equilibrium, such as a minimum of bonding energy in the case of ice crystals or a minimum of surface tension in the case of air bubbles, may be said to be highly territorialized. Those that, on the contrary, emerge when a local gradient is intense enough and it is not allowed to dissipate, like the pattern of flow defining a convection cell, may be said to be more deterritorialized.

In Chapter 3 we generated the next layer of complexity by introducing chemical interactions and the synthesis of novel molecules, greatly increasing the heterogeneity of the molecular populations, as well as catalysts to manipulate the rapidity or slowness with which such syntheses take place. In some cases the outcome of chemical interactions is an equilibrium concentration of the products, a territorialized distribution of substances with a stable identity. In others the catalytic control of reaction rates is performed in a loop—one substance accelerating the production of another substance that, in turn, accelerates the rate of production of the first—driving the molecular populations away from equilibrium and leading to the emergence of more or less deterritorialized wholes: chemical clocks or more complex autocatalytic loops. Although the identity of an autocatalytic loop is stabilized by its components it is also subject to change as new components are added that catalyze and are catalyzed by existing ones. The diagram of these assemblages can still be studied using state space but now the number of dimensions of the space and the differential relations that define the distribution of singularities must be allowed to change to reflect the fact that entirely new substances can be produced and new chemical reactions made possible. To keep track of the changing dimensions of the possibility space we need a graph in which the nodes represent substances and the edges chemical reactions. An important singularity in the graph itself is a percolation threshold, a critical degree of connectivity at which the number of possible reactions changes from finite to infinite. After this threshold is reached the identity of the products of chemical interactions can vary in an infinite number of possible ways, or what amounts to the same thing, the diagram becomes filled with potential lines of deterritorialization.

Chapter 4 added one more layer of complexity by introducing the capacity for self-replication into molecular populations. A population of replicators, such as molecules of naked RNA, can follow a path of continuous change and adaptation as long as copying errors and other mutations modify the identity of its members. The disembodied replicators tend to form emergent entities called "quasi-species," clouds of mutants that evolve as a whole. Too much accuracy in the replication process leads to a high value for the territorialization parameter and a lower capacity to form quasi-species. But there is also a deterritorialization threshold constituted by too high a mutation rate that dissolves the identity of the mutant cloud. The diagram of these assemblages must capture the combinatorial possibilities of the replicators as well as the possible differences in replicative success that would result if the population confronted limited resources. All possible RNA sequences can be arranged so that they have as neighbors other sequences differing only by one mutation. In such a space a series of one-mutant neighbors defines a possible pathway for identity to change, a possible line of deterritorialization that can take a molecule of RNA and transform it step by step into an entirely different one. But whether such pathways can actually be followed depends on the distribution of fitness values. These form a topography of valleys and hills superimposed on the combinatorial space, a topography that determines the likelihood that a given path will be pursued. In particular, scarcity of resources will favor the climbing of hills pinning down a population once its top has been reached, homogenizing its composition, and territorializing its identity. Escaping from a fitness peak can be done by genetic drift, that is, by a series of changes that are neutral in fitness and invisible to selection pressures. Such an escape would constitute a relative deterritorialization.

In populations of disembodied replicators there is only one parameter affecting the identity of assemblages. But with the emergence of the genetic code and the acquisition of a minimum of embodiment through encapsulation within a membrane, identity could now be defined in two different ways. As we saw in Chapter 5 the behavior of all ancient organisms was rigidly determined by their genes, that is, they could only learn as a species over many generations, so the coding parameter had a fixed high value for several billion years. But the territorialization parameter could change and lead to different types of behavior. Early bacteria lacked the ability to move and tended to form colonies that accumulated as layers at the interface between water and bottom sediments. To a casual observer these bacteria would have looked just like another sedimentary layer, motionless and unchanging in its anatomy, that is, very territorialized. But enormous changes were taking place within their membranes as the machinery to tap into external gradients slowly evolved. Starting with the chemical machinery behind fermentation these creatures learned how to tap into the solar gradient using photosynthesis and how to greatly increase the energy that could be produced from earlier methods using oxygen. These evolutionary achievements were veritable metabolic deterritorializations. The first mobile predators emerged and were able to break away from a behaviorally territorialized life thanks to the fact that they did not have to develop their own capacity to drive metabolic processes away from equilibrium: they simply absorbed bacteria as a whole developing a symbiotic relationship with them.

Because we are dealing now with populations of organisms that are coupled to external gradients the diagrams of these biological assemblages must take this coupling into account. An important singularity in these possibility spaces is the carrying capacity, the critical density of a population that can be at long-term equilibrium with the available resources. Different reproductive strategies are available to unicellular organisms to couple their population density to gradients: a population can periodically overshoot the carrying capacity leading to a crash in its density followed by a slow recovery, or on the contrary, it can adjust its density to gently converge on the singularity. Unicellular predators tend to follow the latter strategy while their prey follow the former. In addition, the diagram of these assemblages must include the combinatorial spaces for the genotypes (and the associated spaces for their phenotypes) and these also exhibit coupling but of a different type. When the genotype of a prey population changes in a way that the resulting phenotypes are better able to prevent predation this causes changes in the fitness distributions of the predators, making some old genotypes less fit and acting as an evolutionary incentive to change. And vice versa, any genotypic change that increases predatory capacity changes the fitness distributions in the combinatorial space of the prey acting as a selection pressure on their populations. These "arms races" between predators and prey constitute a line of deterritorialization that sets their identity as species in continuous variation.

With the advent of multicellular organisms and differentiated cell types the coding parameter began to change as neurons slowly wrested control of behavior from the genes. As discussed in Chapter 6, simple neuronal assemblages acquired the capacity to modulate the intensity of inherited behavior through habituation or sensitization. These simple learning mechanisms are important not only because they coexist with more complex ones even in human beings, but also because they constitute the first form taken by subjective gradients: a simple organism may be surprised or startled by a novel stimulus, energetically responding to it until it gets used to it and ceases to react. But the first true departure from a rigid genetic determination of behavioral identity was classical conditioning, a form of associative learning in which an inherited reflex is used to anchor a learned response. Classical conditioning implies the existence of novel entities that emerge from the interactions between neurons, the stable patterns of neuronal activity we referred to as "distributed representations." These stable activity patterns are representational because their content is a prototype extracted from a sample of a population of similar entities that is sensed by an organism. That is, their content is based on the objective statistical properties of a population, properties that an assemblage of neurons can transform into a subjective but nonlinguistic category. Because these categories have the capacity to affect how the organism behaves toward entities resembling those in the learning sample, they effectively decode its behavior.

The extracted prototypes themselves, in turn, are highly deterritorialized entities. They cannot be reduced to neurons or their physical connections because they are not stored as such: all that is stored is a configuration of connection strengths in a neuronal assemblage that, given the right stimulation, can recreate the original pattern of activity. In other words, what is stored is a set of properties that give an assemblage of neurons the capacity to produce the prototype. When the neuronal assemblage is not actually stimulated a distributed representation exists only as the potential product of an unexercised capacity. The diagram of these assemblages is constituted by the structure of the possibility space for neuronal patterns of activity. As explained in Chapter 7, as a neuronal assemblage learns from exposure to a sample of a population it maps relations of similarity into relations of proximity in this space of possibilities: stimuli that resemble each other end up in the same region of the possibility space. Given that the relations of similarity in what is perceived are determined in part by the diagram associated with the population of entities producing the sensory stimulation, mapping external similarity relations into internal proximity relations may be seen as an *internalization of the external diagram*. In addition, because the extraction of prototypes from sensory experience often takes place in the context of motor behavior that must be adequate to that experience, the different regions of the possibility space are associated with assessments of significance. Ascribing behavioral significance to nonlinguistic categories transforms the capacities to affect and be affected of what is perceived into a set of potential opportunities and risks, strengthening the idea of the animal mind as an infolding of external diagrams.

In the case of insects assessments of significance are made by the species as it learns over many generations but in animals like birds or mammals the assessments are performed in part during the lifetime of individual organisms. Unlike insects, birds and mammals already possess a more or less rich subjective life, a subjectivity that may be thought of as an assemblage that emerges within populations of distributed representations and their associated subjective gradients (pain, anger, hunger, thirst). The stability of their subjective identity may be explained as an effect of habitual behavior: habits territorialize behavior, making certain patterns relatively uniform and repetitive, and under their influence a relatively deterritorialized field of extracted prototypes could become consolidated into a more or less coherent animal subject. The acquisition of habits, in turn, depends on a greater degree of decoding, that is, on the fact that birds and mammals can change their behavior through a type of associative learning that does not depend on inherited reflexes: instrumental conditioning. This kind of learning can elicit novel behavioral patterns by piecing together behaviors that occur spontaneously at low frequencies increasing their rate of occurrence through some form of reinforcement. The diagram of avian and mammalian minds can be studied with the help of structured representations like scripts that capture the action possibilities of routine situations. Scripts can help us understand how an animal's mind can have the capacity to make sense of scenes in which the objects perceived have an enduring identity and play roles like that of agent or patient.

Large animals can exercise their capacity for scene analysis not only to understand how their environment can affect and be affected by them but also to make sense of the opportunities and risks with which their conspecifics supply them. In particular, monkeys and apes can not only recognize one another as individual organisms and remember the outcome of past interactions but also relate to others in a strategic way that depends on their position in a social hierarchy. The question we explored in Chapter 8 was whether sets of mutually stabilizing interaction strategies could emerge in primate communities, strategies like the reciprocation of food sharing or grooming. Early studies seemed to indicate that reciprocal altruism could indeed become dominant in an entire community, that is, that a territorialized assemblage of strategies with a well-defined identity could establish itself after several generations. But because the fate of any strategy tends to be related to the proportion of animals using it the outcome may be more deterritorialized: as soon as one strategy starts to dominate its very high frequency of occurrence creates the conditions for another strategy to spread which, in turn, may favor the eventual propagation of yet another strategy, the entire assemblage changing identity as its internal composition varies continuously. This result was obtained in simulations in which the strategies were fully inherited, that is, the case we explored was the one with a high value for the coding parameter. But we saw no reason to expect that habits learned through reinforcement would lead to a more territorialized outcome. The diagram of these assemblages was studied using a payoff matrix to capture the opportunities to cooperate and the risks of being cheated, as well as singularities like Nash equilibria defining stable sets of strategies.

A similar approach was used to tackle to transition from the primate communities that were the last common ancestors of humans and chimpanzees to the communities of hunter-gatherers that characterized humanity for much of its history. The transition was modeled as involving a change from sets of strategies used in dyadic interactions to strategies involving a relation between a person and an entire community. A stable set of strategies in this case is one that results in a solidary community in which cooperative behavior toward other members defines the boundaries of the group. Such a territorialized assemblage is always threatened by free riders, community members who refuse to participate in collective hunting and gathering but enjoy the spoils when these are redistributed. Unlike the case of dyadic strategies in which punishing those who cheat is simply a matter of retaliating against them, in the multi-person case punishment is hard to focus and can have collective unintended consequences, like waves of retaliation that endanger solidarity and shared resources. Punishment is also costly so there are incentives to let others do the punishing. This means that an entirely new habit had to be added to the assemblage to stabilize its identity: metanorms, the habit of punishing those that do not punish cheaters. Although metanorms in pre-linguistic hunter-gatherer communities do not yet constitute a new type of coding, being simply a new territorializing device, they do prepare the ground for the eventual rise of linguistic categories transmitted from one generation to the next by enforced social obligation. The diagram of these more complex assemblages of strategies can also be studied using payoff matrices and Nash equilibria but as we saw applying these ideas to the multi-person case is more complicated and less well understood.

Once stable human communities emerged they became capable of interacting with other communities and form larger scale assemblages. Some of these were relatively stable and enduring, like the larger wholes constituted by many communities assembled into an urban center. Others were relatively ephemeral but if they were recurrent they could have interesting emergent properties of their own. In Chapter 9 we explored a particular recurrent inter-community interaction, trading interactions, the emergent property of which was prices. These were not, of course, prices defined in monetary terms but in customary amounts of one object in terms of another object. The reason we needed to analyze trade was to explain the long distances traveled by high-quality raw materials for the production stone tools. Once small urban centers specializing in long-distance trade had come into existence they can explain this phenomenon but evidence for the high mobility of materials like flint predates the emergence of towns. Either way, in the absence of a powerful trade partner that can set prices or of a powerful government organization that can replace them with central commands, an assemblage of trading communities and the flow of goods between them is relatively decoded. The diagram for two trading communities was studied with the help of indifference maps capturing the collective preferences of the communities. These maps were combined into an Edgeworth box to display the region of the space of possible combinations of traded objects containing the potential gains from trade. In this region a singularity defines the optimal outcome for the trading interaction, a singularity referred to as "competitive equilibrium." If actual trade always took place at the singularity, as economists sometimes assume, an assemblage of trading communities would be relatively territorialized, but as we saw this assumption is not necessary: actual trading interactions can take place away from equilibrium and still realize some of the gains from trade.

In that chapter it was suggested that trade may have preceded the emergence of language but that temporal precedence is not strictly necessary: language and trade may have coevolved not only with each other but with other practices like the ceremonial burial of the dead. As noted above, the effect of language on human behavior (as well as on the emergent behavior of communities and organizations) is so unique that it must be assigned its own parameter in an assemblage: words and sentences just like genes have the capacity to code identity. But languages and genomes are themselves assemblages that can be studied independently of the role they play as a coding parameter. Contemporary languages, for example, can form a deterritorialized continuum of dialects or a territorialized set of standard languages the boundaries of which are carefully fixed through the use of official dictionaries, grammars, and rules of pronunciation.[5] In Chapter 10 we approached the emergence of language as a process that began with monolithic symbolic artifacts that were slowly transformed into the kinds of entities that could form the parts of an assemblage: a finite set of words that could be syntactically combined into an infinite number of possible sentences. Going from a set of monolithic artifacts with a rigidly defined identity to a set of recombinable components the identity and meaning of which depends on what other words they co-occur with, is itself a process of deterritorialization. The diagram of these assemblages was studied taking advantage of the fact that the space of all possible languages, as defined by their syntax, is closely linked to the space of possible automata that can master that syntax. The automata can be considered singularities in the space of computational capacities, some exemplifying a minimum others a maximum of computational capacity.

Our final theme was organizational assemblages possessing an authority structure. It was argued that the rise of such assemblages was difficult to explain because of the active means that hunter-gatherer and agricultural communities had (and some still have) to prevent the crystallization of authority: dissipating gradients of status or prestige to prevent leadership from becoming permanent, or dissipating gradients of energy (surplus agricultural products) by burning them or redistributing them to prevent the creation of a stock. But if these mechanisms of prevention were necessary it was because the diagram of these communal assemblages, their social topology, already contained central authority as a possibility.[6] Communal assemblages were territorialized to different degrees: more if they had settled to practice agriculture and less if they remained mobile and ranged over a wider territory. By neolithic times both possessed language and this gave them the means to code their own identity. When the mechanisms of prevention failed and chiefdoms and archaic states emerged these simpler communities were not left behind as a primitive stage of development but coexisted with the more complex ones as part of an exploited periphery. As such they were subjected to an *overcoding* as state organizations superimposed their own codes of conduct on them without replacing the native ones.[7] In other words, communal assemblages became a component part of larger assemblages retaining some of their own identity but being forced to exercise capacities in the service of the production and maintenance of the identity of a larger whole.

The subject of centralized authority is complex because it involves several levels of the part-to-whole relation. There is the largest assemblage in which a central state occupies a core surrounded by large chiefdoms and a periphery of small chiefdoms and agricultural communities. Then there is the assemblage of the capital city itself, made up of a variety of communities and organizations (temples, monuments, workshops, residences, and the royal palace itself) as well as the physical infrastructure linking all these together. Finally, there is the individual organizations acting as institutional agents with their own goals and the resources to achieve those goals. The territorialization parameter can have different values for each level of the part-to-whole relation but in general the rise of a central state can be conceived as the product of a powerful deterritorialization. At the largest scale it involved a change in the way the identity of a social whole is related to its physical territory: communal assemblages occupy a territory and the piece of land on which they are settled or around which they roam is part of what makes them who they are; state organizations controlling a vast territory, on the other hand, detach themselves from the land to be able to make objective comparisons about its agricultural productivity, assigning different value to different plots for administrative purposes.[8] At the smallest scale an individual organization can be said to be deterritorialized if the resources it controls are linked to an office as opposed to the incumbent of that office. Traditional legitimacy, what made the authority of an Egyptian pharaoh flow down directly from the gods, left plenty of room for personal caprice so office and incumbent were not separate. But the legitimacy derived from the capacity of an organization to solve problems of security, logistics, monumental construction, and other activities in which the outcome depends on the successful matching of means to ends, was more impersonal. The coexistence of different sources of legitimacy implies that there were two poles defining organizational assemblages in archaic states, the magical and the legal-rational.[9] These two poles can be seen materialized in the Giza pyramid, a monument that was at once a resurrection machine and a feat of structural engineering.

In Chapter 11 we concentrated on the second pole at the smallest scale: the laws, chain of command, task definitions and assignments, and control of near and far resource gradients, through which government organizations solved the problem of pyramid building. We saw that the diagram of these organizational assemblages could be studied with the help of graphs of different types, some to capture the hierarchical relations in a chain of command others to display the division of labor within each of the ranks. The first graph reveals whether, for example, there are possible conflicts of authority in the case of a rank whose members must obey commands from more than one direct boss. The second graph displays the interdependencies among tasks that specialized workers must take into account as they carry out those commands, interdependencies that mark points of possible conflict in schedules or in the use of resources. These potential authority or performance conflicts are like singular events structuring the space of possibilities for the assembly process of giant funerary monuments and other large-scale government projects. They partly specify the problem that an organization must solve much as other diagrams define problems for other assemblages: the state space of coupled molecular populations defines a problem for a gradient, the problem of what flow pattern to generate to dissipate as much energy as possible; the coupled spaces for possible genotypes and phenotypes define problems for evolving organisms, problems solved by searching these spaces for solutions; the opportunities and risks afforded by the environment define problems for learning organisms the solutions of which involve the development of associations of stimuli, good habits, or even skills; and the social dilemmas generated by the choice to cooperate or cheat define problems for animals or humans involved in indefinitely repeated strategic interactions.

Our characterization of assemblage theory needs only one more feature to be complete. The identity of an assemblage is not only embodied in its materiality but also expressed by it. This distinction corresponds to that between matter-energy on one hand and information on the other, not the semantic information conveyed by the meaning of words or sentences, but raw physical pattern. A live gradient, for example, may contain the same amount of energy as one that has become dissipated but it contains more information because its composing molecules are ordered and have pattern. In addition to defining the degree of order in an assemblage physical information can express its identity. To use a simple example, atoms can express their chemical identity because one of their properties (a certain distribution of electrons) gives them the capacity to interact with radiation and leave a unique "fingerprint" in it: each electron shell absorbs some wavelengths of the radiation but not others creating an information pattern that can be used to identify the chemical species of the atom. Astrophysicist use these patterns (the patterns that the fingerprints leave in photographic plates) to identify the components of far away stars, but even if no one used this information the expressive patterns would still be there. It was because the world in which living creatures evolved was filled with information—from the nutrient gradients that a bacterium can climb; to the odors, colors, and shapes that a honeybee can use to find nectar; to the silhouette or gait pattern that a predator can use to identify its prey—that they were able to start forming internal models of their environment.

While the distinction between the material and the expressive, between matter-energy and information, is important to track the parallel histories of bodies and minds, it is also relevant here because the computer simulations discussed throughout this book are emergent wholes composed of information existing above the computer hardware that provides their material and energetic substratum. The technology that makes simulations possible had to undergo several transformations that can also be explained within the framework of assemblage theory. The most important deterritorialization was the transformation that converted a special-purpose Turing machine, rigidly defined by its internal states and the symbols it uses to write on its memory tape, into a universal Turing machine capable of simulating any special-purpose one. This simulating capacity derives from the correspondence between automata and languages, a correspondence that allows a special-purpose automaton to be given a symbolic expression and be placed on the memory tape of the universal automaton. Although these automata are conceptual entities they can be given a material form that clearly displays the deterritorialization involved: when a special-purpose Turing machine is materially embodied its identity is fixed by its specialized task but a universal Turing machine has an identity that is *programmable*, defined by whatever special-purpose machine it is currently simulating. Thus the first deterritorialization brings the metalevel (operations on data) into direct contact with the object level (data) creating the possibility of *assemblages made out of operators and data*. The components of a genetic algorithm, for example, can be divided into operators—mutation and crossover, fitness function, selection function—and data, the population of symbol strings constituting the simulated chromosomes. As with any assemblage these components must interact, the interaction reducing in this case to the application of an operator to the data serving as its input.

These interactions, on the other hand, must be choreographed since the order in which operators are applied or the number of times they are applied must be carefully specified. This involves an additional component for the assemblage: control structures like loops and branching instructions. All together, operators, control structures, and data allow an automaton with fixed identity to be coded in the memory tape of a universal automaton transforming it into a piece of software: an application like a word processor, a spread sheet, or a web browser. This implies the possibility that the identity of a coded automaton can undergo changes through decoding, a process that depends on the type of programming language used to express it symbolically. Old programming languages (like Fortan, Pascal, or C) control computational processes in a rigid hierarchical way: a master program, embodying the basic identity of an application, yields control whenever it calls a subroutine to perform a particular task but it recovers it the moment the subroutine finishes its task. The latter may in turn surrender control to an even more basic subprogram but eventually control of the process moves back up the hierarchy to the master program. In other programming languages, referred to as *object-oriented*, there are no master programs or subroutines. Control is always decentralized as software objects encapsulating a set of operators are called into action by patterns in the very data they operate on. This implies that the identity of an application is defined dynamically in interaction with the data: if the latter changes so will within limits the application's own identity. If deterritorialization transforms a piece of hardware into software, decoding eliminates a rigid master program in favor of a population of autonomous and flexible software objects. These two transformations provided the environment in which the simulations discussed in this book could be born and thrive.

On the other hand, while a deterritorialization may explain the existence of assemblages of operators and data it does not account for the fact that the behavior of those operators as they act on data can mimic the behavior of material processes. In Chapter 1 it was argued that an explanation of the isomorphism between a mathematical model and the process it models can be given if the objective existence of the diagrams of assemblages is accepted. The universal singularities structuring these diagrams are by definition real but not actual, although they can become actualized when tendencies are manifested or capacities exercised. The universality of the structure of possibility spaces means that two entirely different processes can share the same diagram, or that their diagrams can overlap so the processes share some of the same singularities. In these terms, the isomorphism between models and what they model can be explained as a *co-actualization* of the same diagram, or of different but overlapping diagrams.[10] In that chapter we went on to argue that the main danger of this account is making universal singularities into transcendent entities, entities existing entirely independently of the material world. But this potential pitfall can be avoided by always treating diagrams as immanent to matter, energy, and information: while the objective existence of diagrams may not depend on any particular material, energetic, or informational mechanism, it does depend on the actual existence of some mechanism or another. If this account turns out to be correct then it will point to an intimate link between ontology and epistemology. And the existence of such a link, in turn, will constitute a powerful argument for breaking with the ontology we inherited from the classical Greek philosophers, an ontology based on the general and the particular, and an incentive to develop a new one based on the individual singular and the universal singular.

Notes

Introduction

1 John Stuart Mill. *A System of Logic. Ratiocinative and Inductive.* (London: Longmans, Green, and Co., 1906). p. 243.
2 George Henry Lewes. *Problems of Life and Mind.* Vol. 2. (London: Trübner & Co., 1875). p. 415.
3 Samuel Alexander. *Space, Time, and Deity.* Vol. 2. (London: MacMillan, 1920). p. 46–47. See also: C. Lloyd Morgan. *Emergent Evolution.* (New York: Henry Holt, 1931). p. 8.

Chapter One

1 Peter W. Atkins. *The Second Law.* (New York: Scientific American Library, 1984). p. 73.
2 Peter W. Atkins. Ibid., p. 38.
3 Eric D. Schneider and Dorion Sagan. *Into the Cool. Energy Flows, Thermodynamics, and Life.* (Chicago: University of Chicago Press, 2005). p. 112–13.
4 Gregoire Nicolis and Ilya Prigogine. *Exploring Complexity.* (New York: W.H. Freeman, 1989). p. 12.
5 Joseph M. Moran and Michael D. Morgan. *Meteorology. The Atmosphere and the Science of Weather.* (New York: MacMillan Publishing Co., 1986). p. 287.
6 Joseph M. Moran and Michael D. Morgan. Ibid., p. 71.
7 Joseph M. Moran and Michael D. Morgan. Ibid., p. 301 and 315.
8 Gregoire Nicolis and Ilya Prigogine. *Exploring Complexity.* Op. Cit. p. 18–20.
9 Alan Garfinkel. *Forms of Explanation.* (New Haven: Yale University Press, 1981). p. 58–62.

[10] Peter Smith. *Explaining Chaos*. (Cambridge: Cambridge University Press, 1998). p. 72.

[11] William J. Kauffman III and Larry L. Smarr. *Supercomputing and the Transformation of Science*. (New York: Scientific American Library, 1993). p. 14–15. Credit for this landmark simulation is given to Robert Wilhelmson. It made its debut at SIGGRAPH '89, and was nominated for an Academy Award for animation. Details and graphics can be found in the website of the National Center for Supercomputing Applications.

[12] William J. Kauffman III and Larry L. Smarr. Ibid., p. 13.

[13] Eugene P. Wigner. *The Unreasonable Effectiveness of Mathematics in the Natural Sciences*. In Symmetries and Reflections. (Woodbridge: Ox Bow Press, 1979). p. 222–37.

[14] Morris Kline. *Mathematical Thought from Ancient to Modern Times*. Vol. 3. (New York: Oxford University Press, 1972). p. 882.

[15] Morris Kline. *Mathematical Thought from Ancient to Modern Times*. Vol. 2. Ibid., p. 732.

[16] June Barrow-Green. *Poincare and the Three Body Problem*. (Providence, RI: American Mathematical Society, 1997). p. 32–3.

[17] Ian Stewart. *Does God Play Dice: The Mathematics of Chaos*. (Oxford: Basil Blackwell, 1989). p. 107.

[18] Alexander Woodcock and Monte Davis. *Catastrophe Theory*. (New York: E.P. Dutton, 1978). p. 42.

Chapter Two

[1] William Poundstone. *The Recursive Universe*. (New York: William Morrow, 1985). p. 26–31.

[2] William Poundstone. Ibid., p. 82.

[3] William Poundstone. Ibid., p. 38–40.

[4] William Poundstone. Ibid., p. 105.

[5] William Poundstone. Ibid., p. 202.

[6] The implementation of this machine was performed in the year 2000 by Paul Rendell, and can be seen in operation at his website.

[7] Stephen Wolfram. Universality and Complexity in Cellular Automata. In *Cellular Automata and Complexity*. (Reading: Addison-Wesley, 1994). p. 140–55.

8 Stephen Wolfram. Two Dimensional Cellular Automata. In *Cellular Automata and Complexity*. Ibid., p. 213.

9 Christopher G. Langton. Life at the Edge of Chaos. In *Artificial Life II*. Edited by Christopher G. Langton, Charles Taylor, J. Doyne Farmer, and Steen Rasmussen. (Redwood City: Addison-Wesley, 1992). p. 44.

10 Christopher G. Langton. Ibid., p. 83.

11 Stephen Wolfram. *A New Kind of Science*. (Champagne: Wolfram Media, 2002). p. 845.

12 Brosl Hasslacher. Discrete Fluids. In *From Cardinals to Chaos: Reflections on the Life and Legacy of Stanislav Ulam*. Edited by Necia Grant Cooper. (New York: Cambridge University Press, 1989). p. 181.

13 Tomasso Toffoli and Norman H. Margolus. Invertible Cellular Automata: a Review. In *Cellular Automata. Theory and Experiment*. Edited by Howard Gutowitz. (Cambridge: MIT Press, 1991). p. 231.

14 Brosl Hasslacher. Discrete Fluids. Op. Cit. p. 188–9.

15 Stephen Wolfram. Thermodynamics and Hydrodyamics of Cellular Automata. In *Cellular Automata and Complexity. Collected Essays*. (Reading: Addison-Wesley, 1994). p. 260.

16 Tsumu Shimomura, Gary D. Doolen, Brosl Hasslacher, and Castor Fu. Calculations Using Lattice Gas Techniques. In *From Cardinals to Chaos*. Op. Cit. p. 202–10.

17 Tomasso Toffoli and Norman H. Margolus. *Cellular Automata Machines. A New Environment for Modeling*. (Cambridge: MIT Press, 1987). p. 153.

18 Tomasso Toffoli and Norman H. Margolus. Invertible Cellular Automata. Op. Cit. p. 244–5.

19 Peter Galison. Computer Simulations and the Trading Zone. In *The Disunity of Science*. Edited by Peter Galison and David J. Stump. (Standford: Standford University Press, 1996). p. 138–44.

Chapter Three

1 Ronald E. Fox. *Energy and the Evolution of Life*. (New York: W.H. Freeman, 1988). p. 58–9.

2 Stuart Kauffman. *The Origins of Order. Self-Organization and Selection in Evolution*. (New York: Oxford University Press, 1993). p. 290–6.

3 David Dressler and Huntington Potter. *Discovering Enzymes*. (New York: Scientific American Library, 1991). p. 168–72. And: N.C. Veitch and J.P. Williams. The Molecular Basis of Electron Transfer in Redox

Enzyme Systems. In *Frontiers of Biotransformation*. Vol. 7. (Berlin: Akademie Verlag, 1992). p. 283–90.

[4] Stuart Kauffman. The Origins of Order. Op. Cit. p. 302–3.

[5] Stuart Kauffman. Ibid., p. 309–10.

[6] Stuart Kauffman. Ibid., p. 320.

[7] Richard J. Bagley and J. Doyne Farmer. Spontaneous Emergence of a Metabolism. In *Artificial Life II*. Edited by Christopher G. Langton, Charles Taylor, Doyne Farmer, and Steen Rasmussen. (Redwood City: Addison-Wesley, 1992). p. 112.

[8] Richard J. Bagley and J. Doyne Farmer. Ibid., p. 118–26.

[9] Walter Fontana. Algorithmic Chemistry. In *Artificial Life II*. Op. Cit. p. 168.

[10] Walter Fontana. Ibid., p. 179.

[11] Walter Fontana. Ibid., p. 184.

Chapter Four

[1] Manfred Eigen. *Steps Towards Life*. (Oxford: Oxford University Press, 1992). p. 28.

[2] Manfred Eigen. Ibid., p. 65–7.

[3] Peter Schuster. How Do RNA Molecules and Viruses Explore Their Worlds? In *Complexity. Metaphors, Models, and Reality*. Edited by George A. Cowan, David Pines, David Meltzer. (Reading: Addisson-Wesley, 1994). p. 400.

[4] Manfred Eigen. *Steps Towards Life*. Op. Cit. p. 92–5.

[5] Stuart Kauffman. *The Origins of Order. Self-Organization and Selection in Evolution*. (New York: Oxford University Press, 1993). p. 34–5.

[6] Stuart Kauffman. Ibid., p. 45–62.

[7] Manfred Eigen. Steps Towards Life. Op. Cit. p. 28–9.

[8] Manfred Eigen. Ibid., p. 82–6.

[9] Melanie Mitchell and Stephanie Forrest. Genetic Algorithms and Artificial Life. In *Artificial Life*. Edited by Christopher Langton. (Cambridge: MIT Press, 1997). p. 272.

[10] David E. Goldberg. *The Design of Innovation: Lessons from and for Competent Genetic Algorithms*. (Boston: Kluwer Academic Publishers, 2002). p. 3.

[11] David E. Goldberg. *Genetic Algorithms in Search, Optimization, and Machine Learning*. (Reading: Addisson-Wesley, 1989). p. 125–30.

NOTES

[12] Peter Schuster. Complex Optimization in an Artificial RNA World. In *Artificial Life II*. Edited by Christopher G. Langton, Charles Taylor, Doyne Farmer, and Steen Rasmussen. (Redwood City: Addison-Wesley, 1992). p. 281–3.

[13] Peter Schuster. Ibid., p. 287.

[14] John R. Koza, Forrest H. Bennett, David Andre, Martin A. Keane. Genetic Programming: Biologically Inspired Computation that Exhibits Creativity in Producing Human-Competitive Results. In *Creative Evolutionary Systems*. Edited by Peter J. Bentley and David W. Corne. (San Diego: Academic Press, 2002). p. 283–90.

[15] John R. Koza. *Genetic Programming. On the Programming of Computers by Means of Natural Selection*. (Cambridge: MIT Press, 1992). p. 80–8.

[16] John R. Koza. Ibid., p. 329.

[17] John R. Koza, Forrest H. Bennett, David Andre, Martin A. Keane. Genetic Programming: Biologically Inspired Computation that Exhibits Creativity in Producing Human-Competitive Results. In Op. Cit. p. 284.

[18] John R. Koza, Martin A. Keane, Matthew J. Streeter, William Mydlowec, Jessen Yu, and Guido Lanza. *Genetic Programming IV. Routine Human-Competitive Machine Intelligence*. (New York: Springer, 2003). p. 229–30.

[19] John R. Koza et al. Ibid., p. 268–71.

[20] John R. Koza et al. Ibid., p. 237.

[21] Walter Fontana. The Topology of the Possible. *Journal of Theoretical Biology*, Vol. 213, No. 2. (New York: Academic Press, 2001). p. 241–74.

[22] Stuart Kauffman. *The Origins of Order*. Op. Cit. p. 115.

[23] John Holland. *Adaptation in Natural and Artificial Systems*. (Cambridge: MIT Press, 1992). p. 68.

[24] Colin R. Reeves and Jonathan E. Rowe. *Genetic Algorithms*. (Boston: Kluwer Academic Publishers, 2003). p. 65.

[25] David E. Goldberg. *The Design of Innovation*. Op. Cit. p. 122–5.

[26] Michael G. Rossmann. Introductory Comments on the Function of Domains in Protein Structure. In *Intervening Sequences in Evolution and Development*. Edited by Edwin M. Stone and Robert J. Schwartz. (New York: Oxford University Press, 1990). p. 5–7.

[27] S. K. Holland and C. C. F. Blake. Proteins, Exons, and Molecular Evolution. In Ibid. p. 11–13.

Chapter Five

[1] J. William Schopf, J.M. Hayes, and Malcolm R. Walter. Evolution of Earth's Earliest Ecosystem. In *Earth's Earliest Biosphere*. Edited by J. William Schopf. (Princenton: Princeton University Press, 1983). p. 375–81.

[2] Franklin M. Harrod. *The Vital Force. A Study of Bioenergetics*. (New York: W.H. Freeman, 1986). p. 187.

[3] George Wald. The Origin of Life. In *The Chemical Basis of Life*. (San Francisco: W.H. Freeman, 1973). p. 16–17.

[4] Jan Sapp. Living Together: Symbiosis and Cytoplasmic Inheritance. In *Symbiosis as a Source of Evolutionary Innovation*. Edited by Lynn Margulis and Rene Fester. (Cambridge: MIT Press, 1991). p. 16–17.

[5] John Maynard Smith. A Darwinian View of Symbiosis. In Ibid., p. 30–6.

[6] J. Van McArthur. *Microbial Ecology*. (Amsterdam: Elsevier, 2006). p. 134–47.

[7] Manfred Peschel and Werner Mende. *The Predator-Prey Model*. (Vienna: Springer-Verlag, 1986). p. 19–21.

[8] Stuart L. Pimm. *The Balance of Nature*. (Chicago: University of Chicago Press, 1991). p. 105.

[9] Stuart L. Pimm. Ibid., p. 115–31.

[10] Filippo Menczer and Richard K. Belew. Latent Energy Environments. In *Adaptive Individuals and Evolving Populations*. Edited by Richard K. Belew and Melanie Mitchell. (Reading: Westview Press, 1996). p. 194.

[11] Filippo Menczer and Richard K. Belew. Evolving Sensors in Environments of Controlled Complexity. In *Artificial Life IV*. Edited by Rodney A. Brooks and Pattie Maes. (Cambridge: MIT Press, 1996). p. 215.

[12] Filippo Menczer and Richard K. Belew. From Complex Environments to Complex Behaviors. In *Adaptive Behavior*. Vol. 4, No. 3/4. (Sage Journals Online, 1996). p. 317–63.

[13] Stuart Kauffman. *The Origins of Order. Self-Organization and Selection in Evolution*. (New York: Oxford University Press, 1993). p. 243.

[14] Stuart Kauffman. Ibid., p. 263.

[15] John H. Holland. Hidden Order. *How Adaptation Builds Complexity*. (Reading: Addison-Wesley, 1995). p. 104–7.

NOTES

16 John H. Holland. *Hidden Order. How Adaptation Builds Complexity*. (Reading, Addison-Wesley, 1995). p. 111–13.

17 Peter. T. Hraber, Terry Jones, and Stephanie Forrest. The Ecology of Echo. In *Artificial Life*, Vol. 3, No. 3. (Cambridge: MIT Press, 1997). p. 11–19.

18 Sorin Sonea. Bacterial Evolution Without Speciation. In *Symbiosis as a Source of Evolutionary Innovation*. Op. Cit. p. 100–2.

19 John H. Holland. Hidden Order. Op. Cit. p. 115–20.

20 John H. Holland. Ibid., p. 122–23.

21 Mark A. Bedau, Emile Snyder, Norman H. Packard. A Classification of Long-Term Evolutionary Dynamics. In *Artificial Life VI*. Edited by Christoph Adami, Richard K. Belew, Hiroaki Kitano, and Charles E, Taylor. (Cambridge: MIT Press, 1998). p. 231–2.

Chapter Six

1 John H. Holland. *Hidden Order. How Adaptation Builds Complexity*. (Reading: Addison-Wesley, 1995). p. 32.

2 Ronald J. MacGregor and Edwin R. Lewis. *Neural Modeling*. (New York: Plenum Press, 1977). p. 21–30.

3 John T. Bonner. *The Evolution of Culture in Animals*. (Princeton: Princeton University Press, 1980). p. 113.

4 James L. Gould. Ethological and Comparative Perspectives on Honey Bee Learning. In *Insect Learning*. Edited by Daniel R. Papaj and Alcinda C. Lewis. (New York: Chapman and Hall, 1993). p. 31.

5 James L. Gould. Ibid., p. 31–8.

6 Elizabeth A. Bernays. Aversion Learning and Feeding. In *Insect Learning*. Op. Cit. p. 10.

7 N. J. Mackintosh. *Conditioning and Associative Learning*. (Oxford: Clarendon Press, 1983). p. 189–92.

8 N. J. Mackintosh. Ibid., p. 52–5.

9 William Bechtel and Adele Abrahamsen. *Connectionism and the Mind. An Introduction to Parallel Distributed Processing in Networks*. (Cambridge: Basil Blackwell, 1991). p. 106–7.

10 Karl Sims. Evolving 3D Morphology and Behavior by Competition. In *Artificial Life IV*. Edited by Rodney A. Brooks and Pattie Maes. (Cambridge: MIT Press, 1994). p. 33.

[11] James J. Gibson. *The Ecological Approach to Visual Perception.* (Boston: Houghton Mifflin, 1979). p. 15–16.

[12] The animation, called "Evolved Virtual Creatures," may be watched at the author's website.

[13] David E. Rumelhart and James L. McClelland. PDP Models and General Issues in Cognitive Science. In *Parallel Distributed Processing. Explorations in the Microstructure of Cognition.* Vol. 1. Edited by David Rumelhart and James McClelland. (Cambridge: MIT Press, 1986).

[14] David E. Rumelhart, Geoffrey E. Hinton, and Ronald J. Williams. *Learning Internal Representations by Error Propagation.* In Ibid., p. 322.

[15] Neil Gershenfeld. *The Nature of Mathematical Modeling.* (Cambridge: University Press, Cambridge, UK, 1999). p. 157–9.

[16] William Bechtel and Adele Abrahamsen. *Connectionism and the Mind.* Op. Cit. p. 32.

[17] Paul F. M. J. Verschure and Anthony C. C. Coolen. Adaptive Fields: Distributed Representations of Classically Conditioned Associations. In *Network: Computation in Neural Systems.* Vol. 2, No. 2. (Informa Healthcare, Online Journal, 1991). p. 189–206.

[18] Geoffrey Hinton, James McClelland, and David E. Rumelhart. Distributed Representations. In *Parallel Distributed Processing.* Op. Cit. p. 86–7. And: Tim Van Gelder. Defining "Distributed Representation." In *Connection Science,* Vol. 4, No. 3. (Oxfordshire: Carfax, 1992). p. 176–87.

[19] William Bechtel and Adele Abrahamsen. *Connectionism and the Mind.* Op. Cit. p. 126–8.

[20] Filippo Menczer and Richard K. Belew. Latent Energy Environments. In *Adaptive Individuals and Evolving Populations.* Edited by Richard K. Belew and Melanie Mitchell. (Reading: Westview Press, 1996). p. 196.

[21] James L. Gould. Ethological and Comparative Perspectives on Honey Bee Learning. In *Insect Learning.* Op. Cit. p. 19.

Chapter Seven

[1] Daniel L. Schacter and Endel Tulving. What Are the Memory Systems in 1994? In *Memory Systems 1994.* Edited by Daniel L. Schacter and Endel Tulving. (Cambridge: MIT Press, 1994). p. 28.

[2] Daniel L. Schacter and Endel Tulving. Ibid., p. 9.

[3] Stephen Walker. *Animal Thought*. (London: Routledge and Kegan Paul, 1985). p. 243.

[4] Howard Eichenbaum. *The Hippocampal System and Declarative Memory in Humans and Animals. In Memory Systems*. 1994. Op. Cit. p. 152–5.

[5] Stephen Walker. *Animal Thought*. Op. Cit. p. 257–8.

[6] Paul M. Churchland. *The Engine of Reason, the Seat of the Soul*. (Cambridge: MIT Press, 1996). p. 40–5.

[7] Paul M. Churchland. Ibid., p. 47–51.

[8] Derek Blackman. *Operant Conditioning: An Experimental Analysis of Behavior*. (London: Methuen, 1974). p. 48.

[9] Derek Blackman. *Operant Conditioning*. Ibid., p. 35 and 97.

[10] David G. Mayers. *Exploring Psychology*. (New York: Worth Publishers, 2005). p. 345.

[11] A. Harry Klopf, James S. Morgan, and Scott E. Weaver. Modeling Nervous System Function with a Hierarchical Network of Control Systems that Learn. In *From Animals to Animats 2*. Edited by Jean-Arcady Meyer, Herbert L. Roitblat, and Stewart W. Wilson. (Cambridge: MIT Press, 1993). p. 255.

[12] Federico Cecconi and Domenico Parisi. Neural Networks with Motivational Units. In *From Animals to Animats 2*. Ibid., p. 346–7.

[13] Stephen Walker. *Animal Thought*. Op. Cit. p. 359–64.

[14] Roger C. Schank and Robert P. Abelson. *Scripts, Plans, Goals, and Understanding*. (Hillside: Lawrence Earlbaum, 1977). p. 18.

[15] Roger C. Schank and Robert P. Abelson. Ibid., p. 42.

[16] Risto Miikkulainen. *Subsymbolic Natural Language Processing: An Integrated Approach to Scripts, Lexicon, and Memory*. (Cambridge: MIT Press, 1993). p. 5–6.

[17] Jeffrey L. Elman. *Finding Structure in Time. Cognitive Science*, Vol. 14. (Norwood: Ablex Publishing, 1990). p. 179–211.

[18] Teuvo Kohonen. *Self-Organizing Maps*. (Berlin: Springer, 2001). p. 106–19.

[19] Bernd Fritzke. Growing Self-Organizing Networks. In *Kohonen Maps*. Edited by Erkki Oja and Samuel Kaski. (Amsterdam: Elsevier, 1999). p. 131–3.

[20] Risto Miikkulainen. *Subsymbolic Natural Language Processing*. Op. Cit. p. 19–29.

[21] Risto Miikkulainen. Ibid., p. 124–5.

²² Philip E. Agre. Computational Research on Interaction and Agency. In *Computational Theories of Interaction and Agency*. Edited by Philip A. Agre and Stanley J. Rosenschein. (Cambridge: MIT Press, 1996). p. 12.

²³ Yves Lesperance and Hector J. Levesgue. Indexical Knowledge and Robot Action. In *Computational Theories of Interaction and Agency*. Ibid., p. 443.

²⁴ Lokendra Shastri. Advances in Shruti. A Neurally Motivated Model of Relational Knowledge Representation and Rapid Inference Using Temporal Synchrony. In *Applied Intelligence*. Vol. 11, No. 1. (Amsterdam: Springer Netherlands, 1999). p. 79–108.

²⁵ Paola Baldasari, Paolo Puliti, Anna Montesanto, and Guido Tascini. Self-Organizing Maps Versus Growing Neural Gases in a Robotic Application. In *Computational Methods in Neural Modeling*. Vol. 2. Edited by Jose Mira and Jose Alvarez. (Berlin: Springer-Verlag, 2003). p. 201–3.

²⁶ Nelson Goodman. Seven Strictures on Similarity. In *Problem and Projects*. (Indianapolis: Bobbs-Merrill, 1972). p. 445.

Chaper Eight

¹ Frans B. M. De Waal. Social Syntax: The If-Then Structure of Social Problem Solving. In *Animal Social Complexity*. Edited by Frans B. M. De Waal and Peter L. Tyack. (Cambridge: Harvard University Press, 2003). p. 237–46.

² Duane Quiatt. Language and Evolution in the Middle Stone Age. In *Language Evolution*. Edited by Gabor Gyori. (Frankfurt: Peter Lang, 2001). p. 29–34.

³ Samuel S. Komorita and Craig D. Parks. *Social Dilemmas*. (Boulder: Westerview Press, 1996). p. 12–13.

⁴ Robert Axelrod. The Evolution of Cooperation. (New York: Basic Books, 1984). p. 59.

⁵ Robert Axelrod. Ibid., p. 42.

⁶ Susan E. Riechert. In *Game Theory and Animal Behavior*. Lee A. Dugatkin and Hudson K. Reeve. (Oxford: Oxford University Press, 1998). p. 77.

⁷ M. Keith Chen and Marc Hauser. Modeling Reciprocation and Cooperation in Primates: Evidence for a Punishing Strategy. In *Journal of Theoretical Biology*. Vol. 235. (Amsterdam: Elsevier, 2005). p. 6–7.

NOTES

8. Sarah F. Brosnan and Frans B. de Waal. A Proximate Perspective on Reciprocal Altruism. In *Human Nature*, Vol. 13, No. 1. (New York: Walter de Gruyter, 2002). p. 148.

9. Robert Axelrod. *The Complexity of Cooperation*. (Princeton: Princeton University Press, 1997). p. 17–21.

10. Robert Axelrod. The Evolution of Cooperation. Op. Cit. p. 54.

11. Martin A. Nowak. *Evolutionary Dynamics*. (Cambridge: Belknap Press, 2006). p. 86–90.

12. Ken Binmore. *Game Theory and the Social Contract*. (Cambridge: MIT Press, 1998). p. 314–21.

13. Joshua M. Epstein and Ross Hammond. In Joshua M. Epstein, *Generative Social Science*. (Princeton: Princeton University Press, 2006). Chapter 3.

14. Ken Binmore. *Game Theory and the Social Contract*. Op. Cit. p. 319.

15. Brian Skyrms. The Dynamics of Rational Deliberation. (Cambridge: Harvard University Press, 1990). Chapter 6.

16. Ken Binmore. *Game Theory and the Social Contract*. Op. Cit. p. 403.

17. David W. Stephens and Kevin C. Clements. Game Theory and Learning. In Game Theory and Animal Behavior. Op. Cit. p. 244.

18. Michael Macy. Natural Selection and Social Learning in Prisoner's Dilemma. In Sociological Methods and Research. Vol. 25, No. 1. (Sage Publications, On Line Journal, 1996). p. 122–4.

19. Martin A. Nowak. *Evolutionary Dynamics*. Op. Cit. p. 79.

20. Michael Macy. Natural Selection and Social Learning in Prisoner's Dilemma. Op. Cit. p. 125.

21. Ken Binmore. *Game Theory and the Social Contract*. Op. Cit. p. 294–6.

22. Martin A. Nowak. *Evolutionary Dynamics*. Op. Cit. p. 145–59.

23. John W. Pepper and Barbara B. Smuts. The Evolution of Cooperation in an Ecological Context: an Agent-Based Model. In *Dynamics in Human and Primate Societies*. Edited by Timothy A. Kohler and George J. Gumerman. (Oxford: Oxford University Press, 1998). p. 63–4.

24. Domenico Parisi, Federico Cecconi, and Antonio Cerini. Kin-Directed Altruism and Attachment Behavior in an Evolving Population of Neural Nets. In *Artificial Societies. The Computer Simulation of Social Life*. Edited by Nigel Gilbert and Rosaria Conte. (London: University College of London Press, 1995). p. 238–48.

[25] Christoph Hauert. Cooperation, Collectives Formation, and Specialization. In *Advances in Complex Systems*, Vol. 9, No. 4. (Singapore: World Scientific Publishing, 2006). p. 316.

[26] Thomas C. Schelling. *Micromotives and Macrobehavior*. (New York: W. W. Norton, 1978). p. 110–4.

[27] Robert Axelrod. *The Complexity of Cooperation*. Op. Cit. p. 52.

[28] Robert Axelrod. Ibid., p. 52–5.

[29] Tomohisa Yamashita, Kiyoshi Izumi, and Koichi Kurumatani. Effect of Mutual Choice Metanorm in Group Dynamics for Solving Social Dilemmas. In *Agent-Based Simulation. From Modeling Methodologies to Real World Applications*. Edited by Takao Terano, Hajime Kita, Toshijuki Kaneda, Kiyoshi Arai, and Hiroshi Deguchi. (Tokyo: Springer-Verlag, 2005). p. 38–46.

[30] Ken Binmore. *Game Theory and the Social Contract*. Op. Cit. p. 344–58.

Chaper Nine

[1] Mary D. Leakey. Cultural Patterns in the Olduvai Sequence. In *After the Australopithecines: Stratigraphy, Ecology, and Culture Change in the Middle Pleistocene*. Edited by Karl W. Butzer and Glynn Isaac. (The Hague: Mouton Publishers, 1975). p. 477.

[2] S.A. Semenov. *Prehistoric Technology*. (Totowa: Barnes and Noble Books, 1985). p. 39–55.

[3] Clive Gamble. Exchange, Foraging, and Local Hominid Networks. In *Trade and Exchange in Prehistoric Europe*. Edited by Chris Scarre and Francis Healy. (Oxford: Oxbow Books, 1993). p. 36.

[4] Chris Scarre. Introduction. In *Trade and Exchange in Prehistoric Europe*. Ibid., p. 1.

[5] Marshall Sahlins. *Stone Age Economics*. (Chicago: Aldine-Atherton, 1972). p. 277–80.

[6] Marshall Sahlins. Ibid., p. 10–12.

[7] Harold L. Dibble and Nicolas Rollard. On Assemblage Variability in the Middle Paleolithic of Western Europe. In *The Middle Paleolithic: Adaptation, Behavior, and Variability*. Edited by Harold L. Dibble and Paul Mellars. (Philadelphia: University Museum, University of Pennsylvania, 1992). p. 10–11.

NOTES

[8] Lawrence Guy Straus. Even the Notion of "Transitional Industry" Is a Suspect Typological Construct. In *New Approaches to the Study of Upper Paleolithic "Transitional Industries" in Western Eurasia*. Edited by Julien Riel-Salvatore and Geoffrey A. Clark. (Oxford: Bar, 2007). p. 11–15.

[9] Leonard Joy. One Economist's View of the Relation Between Economics and Anthropology. In *Themes in Economic Anthropology*. Edited by Raymond Firth. (London: Routledge, 1967). p. 34.

[10] Paul Wonnacott and Ronald Wonnacott. *Economics*. (New York: John Wiley & Sons, 1990). p. 393–8.

[11] Thomas M. Humphrey. The Early History of the Box Diagram. (*Federal Reserve Bank of Richmond Economic Quarterly*, Vol. 82/1, Winter 1996). p. 37–51.

[12] Leigh Tesfatsion. Agent-Based Computational Economics: A Constructive Approach to Economic Theory. In *Handbook of Computational Economics*, Vol. 2. (Amsterdam: Elsevier, 2006). p. 845–50.

[13] Dan K. Gode, Stephen E. Spear and Shyam Sunder. *Convergence of Double Auctions to Pareto Optimal Allocations in the Edgeworth Box*. (Yale School of Management, working paper, 2004).

[14] Jeffrey S. Dean, George J. Gumerman, Joshua M. Epstein, Robert L. Axtell, Alan C. Swedlund, Miles T. Parker, and Stephen McCarroll. Understanding Anasazi Culture Change Through Agent-Based Modeling. In Joshua M. Epstein. *Generative Social Science*. (Princeton: Princeton University Press, 2006). p. 99. Joshua M. Epstein and Robert Axtell. *Growing Artificial Societies*. (Cambridge: MIT Press, 1996). p. 23–6.

[15] Joshua M. Epstein and Robert Axtell. Ibid., p. 30–2.

[16] Joshua M. Epstein and Robert Axtell. Ibid., p. 104–6.

[17] Joshua M. Epstein and Robert Axtell. Ibid., p. 109–11.

[18] Joshua M. Epstein and Robert Axtell. Ibid., p. 120.

[19] Steven Mithen. Simulating Prehistoric Hunter-Gatherer Societies. In *Simulating Societies*. Edited by Nigel Gilbert and Jim Doran. (London: UCL Press, 1994). p. 181–3.

[20] Jeffrey S. Dean et al. Understanding Anasazi Culture Change Through Agent-Based Modeling. Op. Cit. p. 94–8.

[21] Steven Mithen. Simulating Prehistoric Hunter-Gatherer Societies. Op. Cit. p. 179.

[22] Steven Mithen. Ibid., p. 169–70.

[23] Mark Winter Lake. MAGICAL Computer Simulation of Mesolithic Foraging. In *Dynamics in Human and Primate Societies. Agent-Based Modeling of Social and Spatial Processes.* Edited by Timothy A. Kohler and George J. Gumerman. (Oxford: Oxford University Press, 2000). p. 115–6.

[24] Mark Winter Lake. Ibid., p. 118.

[25] Mark Winter Lake. Ibid., p. 130.

[26] Mark Winter Lake. Ibid., p. 137–8.

[27] Grahame Clark. *World Prehistory.* (Cambridge: Cambridge University Press, 1977). p. 64.

[28] Jeffrey S. Dean et al. Understanding Anasazi Culture Change Through Agent-Based Modeling. Op. Cit. p. 94–100.

[29] Jeffrey S. Dean et al. Ibid., p. 103.

[30] Jeffrey S. Dean et al. Ibid., p. 106–7.

Chapter Ten

[1] Mark D. Hauser and W. Tecumseh Fitch. *What Are the Uniquely Human Components of the Language Faculty?* In Language Evolution. Edited by Morten H. Christiansen and Simon Kirby. (Oxford: Oxford University Press, 2003). p. 161–8.

[2] Sonia Ragir. *Towards an Understanding of the Relationship between Bipedal Walking, Encephalization, and Language Origins.* In Language Evolution. Edited by Gabor Györy. (Frankfurt: Peter Lang, 2001). p. 84–5.

[3] Richard Y. Kain. *Automata Theory.* (New York: Mcgraw-Hill, 1972). p. 84–90 (Turing machines), 122–4 (linear-bounded automata), 142–4 (push-down automata).

[4] Luc Steels and Frederic Kaplan. Bootstrapping Grounded Word Semantics. In *Linguistic Evolution through Language Acquisition.* Edited by Ted Briscoe. (Cambridge: Cambridge University Press, 2002). p. 56–7.

[5] Luc Steels and Frederic Kaplan. Ibid., p. 59.

[6] Luc Steels and Frederic Kaplan. Ibid., p. 71.

[7] Edwin Hutchins and Brian Hazlehurst. *Learning in the Cultural Process.* In Artificial Life II. Edited by Christopher G. Langton, Charles Taylor, Doyne Farmer, and Steen Rasmussen. (Redwood City: Addison-Wesley, 1992). p. 693.

8   Edwin Hutchins and Brian Hazlehurst. Ibid., p. 697–8.

9   Edwin Hutchins and Brian Hazlehurst. Ibid., p. 702–4.

10 Noam Chomsky. *Aspects of the Theory of Syntax.* (Cambridge: MIT Press, 1965). p. 66–73.

11 Natalia L. Komarova and Martin Nowak. *Language, Learning, and Evolution.* In Language Evolution. Edited by Morten H. Christiansen and Simon Kirby. Op. Cit. p. 326–8.

12 Steven Pinker. *Language as an Adaptation to the Cognitive Niche.* In Ibid., p. 25–8.

13 Simon Kirby. Learning, Bottlenecks, and the Evolution of Recursive Syntax. In *Linguistic Evolution through Language Acquisition.* Op. Cit. p. 177–8.

14 Simon Kirby. Ibid., p. 184.

15 Simon Kirby. Ibid., p. 192.

16 James R. Hurford. *Expression/Induction Models of Language Evolution: Dimensions and Issues. In Linguistic Evolution through Language Acquisition.* Op. Cit. p. 306–11.

17 Simon Kirby. Learning, Bottlenecks, and the Evolution of Recursive Syntax. Op. Cit. p. 189.

18 J. Mark Baldwin. A New Factor in Evolution. In *Adaptive Individuals in Evolving Populations. Models and Algorithms.* Edited by Richard K. Belew and Melanie Mitchell. (Reading: Westview Press, 1996). p. 64.

19 Morten H. Christiansen and Nick Chatek. Finite Models of Infinite Language: A Connectionist Approach to Recursion. In *Connectionist Psycholinguistics.* Edited by Morten H. Christiansen and Nick Chatek. (Westport: Ablex Publishing, 2001). p. 147.

20 Richard K. Belew, John McInerney, and Nicol N. Schraudolph. Evolving Networks: Using the Genetic Algorithm with Connectionist Learning. In *Artificial Life II.* Op. Cit. p. 527–30.

21 Geoffrey E. Hinton and Steven J. Nowlan. How Learning Can Guide Evolution. In *Adaptive Individuals in Evolving Populations.* Op. Cit. p. 451.

22 Zellig Harris. *A Theory of Language and Information: A Mathematical Approach.* (Oxford: Clarendon Press, 1981). p. 367.

23 Zellig Harris. Ibid., p. 393–7.

24 Zellig Harris. Ibid., p. 339.

25 James R. Hurford. *Expression/Induction Models of Language Evolution.* Op. Cit. p. 320–1.

Chapter Eleven

[1] Max Weber. *The Theory of Social and Economic Organization*. (New York: Free Press, 1964). p. 124–32.

[2] Kristian Kristiansen. Chiefdoms, States, and Systems of Social Stratification. In *Chiefdoms: Power, Economy, and Ideology*. Edited by Timothy Earle. (New York: Cambridge University Press, 1991). p. 24.

[3] Kathleen M. Carley and Lee Gasser. *Computational Organization Theory*. In Multiagent Systems. Edited by Gerhard Weiss. (Cambridge: MIT Press, 2001). p. 300.

[4] Michael Wooldridge. Intelligent Agents. Ibid., p. 54–6.

[5] Michael Wooldridge. Intelligent Agents. Ibid., p. 58.

[6] Daniel C. Dennet. True Believers. In *The Intentional Stance*. (Cambridge: MIT Press, 1990). p. 15–22.

[7] Jim E. Doran. Trajectories to Complexity in Artificial Societies. In *Dynamics in Human and Primate Societies. Agent-Based Modeling of Social and Spatial Processes*. Edited by Timothy A. Kohler and George J. Gumerman. (Oxford: Oxford University Press, 2000). p. 94–5.

[8] Michael N. Huhns and Larry M. Stephens. *Multiagent Systems and Societies of Agents*. In Multiagent Systems. Op. Cit. p. 85–95.

[9] Jim E. Doran and Mike Palmer. The EOS Project: Integrating Two Models of Paleolithic Social Change. In *Artificial Societies. The Computer Simulation of Social Life*. Edited by Nigel Gilbert and Rosaria Conte. (London: University College of London Press, 1995). p. 106–11.

[10] Jim E. Doran and Mike Palmer. Ibid., p. 113–20.

[11] Pierre Clastres. *Society Against the State*. (New York: Zone Books, 1987). p. 30.

[12] Max Weber. *The Theory of Social and Economic Organization*. Op. Cit. p. 359–66.

[13] Grahame Clark. World Prehistory. (Cambridge: Cambridge University Press, 1977). p. 105.

[14] Elizabeth M. Brumfiel and Timothy K. Earle. Introduction. In *Specialization, Exchange, and Complex Societies*. Edited by Elizabeth M. Brumfield and Timothy K. Earle. (Cambridge: Cambridge University Press, 1987). p. 3–4.

[15] Cathy A. Small. The Political Impact of Marriage in a Virtual Polynesian Society. In *Dynamics in Human and Primate Societies*. Op. Cit. p. 228–31.

[16] Cathy A. Small. Ibid., p. 234–9.

[17] Barbara Price. Irrigation: Sociopolitical Dynamics and the Growth of Civilization. In *The Asiatic Mode of Production*. Edited by Anne M. Bailey and Josep R. Llobera. (London: Routledge & Kegan Paul, 1981). p. 218.

[18] Alexander Badawy. A History of Egyptian Architecture. Vol. 1. (Giza: Studio Misr, 1954). p. 49.

[19] Richard Nelson and Sidney Winter. *An Evolutionary Theory of Economic Change*. (Cambridge: Belknap, 1982). p. 98–100.

[20] Kevin Crowston. Evolving Novel Organizational Forms. In *Computational Organization Theory*. Edited by Kathleen M. Carley and Michael J. Prietula. (Hillsday: Lawrence Erlbaum, 1994). p. 27–9.

[21] Tim Kovacs. Two Views of Classifier Systems. In *Advances in Learning Classifier Systems*. Edited by Pier Luca Lanzi, Wolfgang Stolzmann, Stewart W. Wilson. (Berlin: Springer-Verlag, 2002). p. 77.

[22] Larry Bull and Tim Kovacs. Introduction. In *Foundations of Classifier Systems*. Edited by Larry Bull and Tim Kovacs. (Berlin: Springer-Verlag, 2005). p. 8.

[23] Zahi Hawass. *Mountains of the Pharaohs*. (New York: Doubleday, 2006). p. 7.

[24] Mark Lehner. *The Complete Pyramids*. (London: Thames and Hudson, 1997). p. 203–10.

[25] Mark Lehner. Ibid., p. 224–5.

[26] Keith S. Decker. Task Environment Centered Simulation. In *Simulating Organizations*. Edited by Michael J. Prietula, Kathleen M. Carley, and Les Gasser. (Cambridge: MIT Press, 1998). p. 108.

[27] G.P. F. Van Der Boorn. *The Duties of the Vizier*. (London: Kegan Paul, 1988). p. 310.

[28] G. P. F. Van Der Boorn. Ibid., p. 318–20.

[29] Zahi Hawass. *Mountains of the Pharaohs*. Op. Cit. p. 160.

[30] David Krackhardt. Graph Theoretical Dimensions of Informal Organizations. In *Computational Organization Theory*. Op. Cit. p. 91–5.

[31] Keith S. Decker and Victor Lesser. Designing a Family of Coordination Algorithms. In *Readings in Agents*. Edited by Michael N. Huhns and Munindar P. Singh. (San Francisco: Morgan Kaufmann, 1998). p. 453.

[32] Keith S. Decker. Task Environment Centered Simulation. Op. Cit. p. 107.

[33] Yoav Shoham and Moshe Tennenholtz. On Social Laws for Artificial Agent Societies: Off-Line Design. In *Computational Theories of Interaction and Agency*. Edited by Philip A. Agre and Stanley J. Rosenschein. (Cambridge: MIT Press, 1996). p. 598–603.

[34] Michael N. Huhns and Larry M. Stephens. Multiagent Systems and Societies of Agents. In *Multiagent Systems*. Op. Cit. p. 87.

[35] Keith S. Decker and Victor Lesser. Designing a Family of Coordination Algorithms. Op. Cit. p. 455.

[36] Toshiharu Sugawara and Victor Lesser. Learning to Improve Coordinated Actions in Cooperative Distributed Problem-Solving Environments. In *Machine Learning 33*. (Amsterdam: Kluwer Academic Publishers, 1998). p. 136.

[37] Toshiharu Sugawara and Victor Lesser. Ibid., p. 133.

[38] Pattie Maes and Robyn Kozierok. Learning Interface Agents. In Proceedings of AAAI '93 Conference. (Seattle: AAAI Press, 1993). p. 459–65. M.S. Miller and K.E. Drexler. Markets and Computation: Agoric Open Systems. In *The Ecology of Computation*. Edited by Bernardo Huberman. (Amsterdam: North-Holland, 1988). p. 150.

Appendix

[1] Manuel DeLanda. A New Philosophy of Society. Assemblage Theory and Social Complexity. (London: Continuum, 2007), p. 8–11.

[2] Manuel DeLanda. Ibid., p. 26–32.

[3] Manuel DeLanda. Ibid., p. 13, 50, 58, 74, 90, 98, 101–2.

[4] Manuel DeLanda. Ibid., p. 15, 59, 62, 75, 91.

[5] Manuel DeLanda. A Thousand Years of Nonlinear History (New York: Zone Books, 1997), Chapter 3.

[6] Gilles Deleuze and Felix Guattari. A Thousand Plateaus (Minneapolis: University of Minnesota Press, 1987), p. 431.w

[7] Gilles Deleuze and Felix Guattari. Ibid., p. 427–8 and 435.

[8] Gilles Deleuze and Felix Guattari. Ibid., p. 441.

[9] Gilles Deleuze and Felix Guattari. Ibid., p. 424–6.

[10] Manuel DeLanda. Intensive Science and Virtual Philosophy. (London: Continuum, 2007), p. 147–8.

Index